RESURRECTION

RESURRECTION

MICHAEL L. BROWN, PhD

CHARISMA
HOUSE

RESURRECTION by Michael L. Brown, PhD
Published by Charisma House
Charisma Media/Charisma House Book Group
600 Rinehart Road, Lake Mary, Florida 32746

Visit the author's website at https://askdrbrown.org/, BooksbyDrBrown.com

Library of Congress Cataloging-in-Publication Data:
An application to register this book for cataloging has been submitted to the Library of Congress.
International Standard Book Number: 978-1-62999-692-9
E-book ISBN: 978-1-62999-693-6

TABLE OF CONTENTS

PREFACE

WHEN I LIVED in Maryland from 1987 to 1996, I had a friend who was working toward a master's degree in Semitic languages, and I helped tutor him in biblical Hebrew during his studies. Although we shared the same faith as Jewish believers in Jesus, we had some doctrinal disagreements, and we would often have lively debates about our differences.

One day, before he came to my house to study with me, I prayed a very unusual prayer. I said to the Lord, "Father, if my friend is right about this one particular doctrinal point, have him ask me if we could study Palestinian Hebrew texts without vowels today." Yes, it was an unusual prayer!

Of course there is no way he would ever make this request. After all, we studied biblical texts when we got together, not texts written hundreds of years after the Hebrew Scriptures were completed. And we studied texts with vowels, not without vowels. Why in the world would he ask to study Palestinian Hebrew texts without vowels?

Well, you can guess what happened next. He came over that day and asked me, quite out of the blue, if we could study those very texts. I was silently shocked. And, as you would expect, I decided to look once again at that area of disagreement between us.

Fast-forward to August 2018. While deep in prayer one morning, I became gripped with the theme of this book, sensing God wanted to use it to reach many Jewish people with the gospel—especially religious Jews—and to open the eyes of many Christians. My heart burned with these themes, and the more I prayed, the more I felt a mandate from heaven to write.

That afternoon, I went to our studio to do my daily, live radio broadcast, and when the show was over, I saw there was a voice mail from my old friend from Maryland. We had talked perhaps three times in the last twenty-plus years, so I was surprised to see that he had called. But the surprise quickly turned to stunned amazement. He was asking me to recommend books to read *on the exact subject of this book*, saying he was thinking of writing a little book on it.

How absolutely unreal and what an amazing confirmation. The Lord certainly knows how to get a point across! With that I knew God was calling me to do the research and write the pages that follow. And now it is my joy to present this book to you, whether you are a fellow believer in Yeshua, whether you believe the Lubavitcher Rebbe is Moshiach, or whether you are an interested seeker. Whoever you are, I pray you will be enriched and blessed as you read the pages that follow.

My appreciation again to the great team at Charisma Media, especially to my editor Adrienne Gaines and to Christianne Squires, who worked closely on the project, carefully reviewing every word and checking every endnote. I'm also grateful to Mike Licona for sharing some of his valuable research on the resurrection of Jesus, and to Jonathan Mann and Erik Mattson, younger Messianic Jewish colleagues whose chat with me about the resurrection helped plant some seeds that led to writing this book. I would also like to thank the ultra-Orthodox rabbis who have dialogued with me over the years, challenging me at every point and forcing me to fine-tune my arguments. I pray that the Lord would reveal the real Messiah to them, just as they pray for me.

May the risen Messiah shine His light on you as you read! And if the book blesses you, especially if you are a Jewish person discovering the truth about Yeshua, please contact us at AskDrBrown.org.

—MICHAEL L. BROWN, PHD
NOVEMBER 2019

INTRODUCTION

FROM GALILEE TO BROOKLYN:
IN SEARCH OF THE
REAL MESSIAH

ACCORDING TO THE first followers of Jesus, all of them Jews, after their leader died a horrible death on the cross, He rose from the dead, never to die again. According to the followers of Rabbi Menachem Mendel Schneerson, all of them Jews, after dying at the age of ninety-two in 1994, he continues to live among them, guiding them with his presence.

The followers of Jesus claim it was He who was the promised Messiah. Many of Rabbi Schneerson's followers make the same claim: "Our Rebbe[1] is Moshiach (Messiah)!" Other Jews say, "Neither one can be the Messiah, since the real Messiah will not die before completing his mission."

But what if that Messianic candidate died and rose from the dead? Would that change things? What if there was powerful evidence that one of these revered Jewish leaders rose from the grave and continues to live to this day? Would that reinforce his Messianic credentials?

Unfortunately, there were no video cameras back in the year AD 30,[2] when Jesus, whose Hebrew name was Yeshua, reportedly rose from the dead. Of course, if you are a follower of Jesus, as I am, there is nothing simply "reported" about His resurrection. We *know* that He rose from the dead as surely as we know our own names. But others do not have that certainty—especially the vast majority of Jews, who do not believe that Jesus rose from the dead.

Thankfully, we now have a unique opportunity to revisit the question of Jesus' resurrection in light of the claims made about Rabbi Schneerson, otherwise known as the Lubavitcher Rebbe. Perhaps by comparing what happened to these two movements—the movement that proclaimed Yeshua as Messiah and the movement that proclaims the Rebbe as Messiah—after the deaths of their leaders, we can shed light on what really happened two thousand years ago.

Both of these Jewish leaders had and have devoted Jewish adherents. Both of these Jewish leaders were reportedly miracle workers and prophets. And both are allegedly alive today, in some kind of real, tangible sense. And for the Christian reader, the story of the Rebbe is a fascinating one, as he lived and died recently, in the twentieth century, and he was one of the leading religious figures of his generation. His followers are making claims about him similar to claims that the followers of Jesus make about their Lord.

Yet there are profound and telling differences between these two leaders and their movements, and by analyzing both the men and their followers, we will come to some startling conclusions. Are you ready for the investigative journey of a lifetime?

CHAPTER 1

COULD A RABBI FROM BROOKLYN BE THE MESSIAH?

JUNE 12, 1994. It is well past midnight, but the streets of Crown Heights, Brooklyn, are marked by a growing number of religious Jewish men, conspicuous with their full beards and black outfits. They have just received horrific news. Their beloved rabbi, Menachem Mendel Schneerson, known simply as "the Rebbe," has passed away at the age of ninety-two.

But they are not mourning. They are dancing. And their voices ring out, "The Rebbe is Moshiach [Messiah]. The Rebbe will rise!"[1]

Almost twenty-five years later, Yossi Newfield, who in 1994 was a devout follower of the Rebbe, takes us to these very streets. He was there, among these religious Jews. He was an eyewitness.

It was three in the morning, and the Rebbe's adoring disciples were passing by his corpse, which was laid out on the floor in accordance with Jewish tradition. The place was 770 Eastern Parkway, the nerve center of the Rebbe's movement.

Newfield recalls:

> Outside, I saw a small group of about twenty men holding cups of whiskey and dancing. [In these religious circles, whiskey was reserved for special celebrations.] One of the leaders of this group was a former camp counselor who I respected for his knowledge and piety. If he was dancing, I thought, it must be the right thing to do. So I joined the dance, chanting with the others: "Long live the Rebbe, King Messiah, forever and ever." We were convinced if we kept dancing, we could hold off the funeral. Surely the Rebbe would be resurrected and continue his leadership on earth, and not, heaven

1

> forbid, be buried in the ground. I continued dancing until 6 AM. With the first light of dawn I joined the morning service (*Shacharit*) getting underway inside the synagogue. Following the service, I walked home exhausted. I collapsed into bed at 9 am.[2]

After just a few hours of sleep, Newfield made his way back to the headquarters at 770 Eastern Parkway:

> Hundreds of men were inside the synagogue singing Hasidic melodies [the group's unique Jewish tunes]. They had no intention of joining the funeral procession which was scheduled for 4 pm. They felt that since the Rebbe was going to be the Messiah, attending the funeral would be wrong. He would come back to life. I wanted to stay with them, but I also wanted to follow my Rebbe. I waited and prayed and waited—but there was no resurrection. I slipped out and joined thousands of people gathered in front of the synagogue.[3]

When the realization finally hit that the Rebbe was not going to rise, the weeping began: "The moment the casket came out of the front door of the synagogue, a ray of sun broke through the darkened clouds. The hysterical shrieking from the women's side of the street was terrifying."[4] The celebration had turned to mourning.

The Rebbe had been very sick in the previous months, the result of two severe strokes suffered over the previous two years. But even though he had been totally incapacitated, unable to speak or communicate in any visible way, his followers were sure he was about to be fully restored, revealed to the world as the Messiah. They even wore beepers (this was before the days of ubiquitous cell phones), waiting for the news that he had been revealed in full glory. Sadly the news never came.

As the *Washington Post* reported on June 13, 1994, "Even as his pine coffin was placed in the hearse, a panicked crowd of [the Rebbe's] faithful chanted prayers for Schneerson to rise and reveal himself to be the Messiah for whom Jews have waited since antiquity."[5] But it was not to be, and so, "A sea of thousands of somber, black-hatted men and sobbing women and children filled the streets of Crown Heights and surged after the hearse. Women put away the tambourines they had brought to shake in ecstasy at the first glimpse of the Messiah."[6]

Others, however, refused to be daunted. They maintained, "The Rebbe is still alive! His death was just a test of our faith. It is a physical illusion. The Rebbe never left us!" Still others recognized his death was real but were sure it was not the end, saying, "The Rebbe will rise!"[7] Years later, many are still convinced: The Rebbe is alive. The Rebbe is the Messiah. The Rebbe is our Redeemer.

A website hosted by some of his followers still carried this announcement in 2019: "On the third of Tammuz 5754 [June 12, 1994, the day of his death]...the Rebbe's physical presence was concealed from our eyes."[8] As far as they are concerned, their leader never died. To this day, calendars designed by some of his followers do not mark the third of Tammuz as the anniversary of his death.[9] Why should they if he is not deceased?

In December 1994, six months after the Rebbe's passing, one of the top leaders in the "Rebbe is the Messiah" movement, Rabbi Shmuel Butman, proclaimed boldly that "it is not some of the people in the community, but all of the people in the community as well as Lubavitch [the Jewish sect led by the Rebbe] throughout the world, who believe...that the Rebbe will take us out of exile, and that the Rebbe will lead us to the great final redemption."[10] That is quite a proclamation.

Who exactly was this Rebbe? Why were his followers so sure he was the one? And how is it that these very traditional Jews could embrace what appeared to be a very Christian message—namely, that the Messiah would die before completing his mission and then rise from the dead?

When Rabbi Aaron Soloveichik, a highly respected Orthodox Jewish leader, was informed of Rabbi Butman's words, he responded, "I don't believe it. I don't believe it. It is incredible." Indeed, he stated, "there is no possibility whatsoever" that the Rebbe would rise from the dead and be the Messiah. "That could be possible in the Christian faith," he said, "but not Judaism." No, Rabbi Soloveichik said, despite his great respect for the Rebbe, he simply "can't be the Messiah—he is not living—a Messiah has to be living—a living Messiah, not a dead Messiah."[11]

This was confirmed by a statement made by the Rabbinical Council of America on June 1, 1996: "In light of disturbing developments which have recently arisen in the Jewish community, the Rabbinical Council of America in convention assembled declares that there is not and has never been a place in Judaism for the belief that Mashiach Ben David [Messiah son of David] will begin his Messianic Mission only to experience death, burial, and resurrection before completing it."[12]

But these rabbis were not speaking on their own authority. They relied on the teachings of previous great leaders, whose views had become codified and fixed. According to Moses Maimonides (1135–1204), the author of a definitive Jewish law code, if someone was identified as a potential Messiah but died before completing his mission, that person was not the Messiah. To illustrate his point, Maimonides pointed back to Jewish history, referring to the Jewish general Simeon Bar Kochba. This general led the Second Jewish Revolt against Rome (AD 132–135) before suffering a crushing defeat that led to tremendous Jewish suffering. (The name Bar Kochba is Aramaic for "son of the star," taken to have Messianic import based on Numbers 24:17.)

The greatest rabbi of the day, Rabbi Akiva, had believed that Bar Kochba was the Messiah, publicly proclaiming him as such. But after Bar Kochba was killed in battle, other rabbis changed his name to Bar Koziba, meaning "son of the lie."

Maimonides writes:

> Do not think that the Messianic King will have to perform signs and wonders and bring about novel things in the world, or resurrect the dead, and other such things. It is not so. This is seen from the fact that Rabbi Akiva was a great sage...and he was an armor-bearer of King Bar Koziba and said of him that he is the Messianic King: [R. Akiva] and all the wise men of his generation considered him to be the Messianic King until [Bar Koziba] was killed because of sins, and when he was killed they realized that he was not; but the sages had not asked him for any sign or wonder.[13]

Even before the Rebbe died, Rabbi Eliezer Schach (an ultra-Orthodox leader in Israel who passed away in 2001 at the age of 103 or older) categorically rejected any possibility that the Rebbe was Messiah. He called it "total heresy" and stated that those who make such a claim "will burn in hell."[14] He even referred to the Rebbe, who was a world-renowned leader, as "the madman who sits in New York and drives the whole world crazy."[15] Another prominent rabbi commented when the Rebbe died, "Now we have to wait for the real Messiah."[16]

Rabbi Chaim Keller, yet another respected Orthodox Jewish leader, scornfully summarized the progression of beliefs about the Rebbe among his followers:

The Rebbe progressed in the eyes of one faction within the movement from being a navi [prophet] to being the most probable candidate for Moshiach, to being "bechezkas" Moshiach [the presumptive Messiah], to being Melech HaMoshiach [King Messiah], to being a dead Moshiach who has not died, to being "omniscient," "omnipotent" and being "the Essence and Being [of G-d] enclothed in a body!"[17]

Yes, some of the Rebbe's followers proclaimed him to be God in the flesh—shades of Christian beliefs in Jesus!

Yet to this day, despite these strong objections, thousands of the Rebbe's followers proclaim that he is the Messiah, and they believe they have answers—meaning, traditional Jewish answers—for every objection raised by those who deny his Messiahship.

Who, then, was this Rebbe? Why was he so revered by his followers? And is there any possibility within traditional Jewish teaching that the Messiah could be one who dies and then rises from the dead? Could a deceased and then resurrected rabbi be the Messiah?

WHO WAS THE REBBE?

Before we can look at one person—namely, the Rebbe of Lubavitch—it's important that we understand the unique role of the Rebbe in Hasidic Judaism, which is a branch of ultra-Orthodox Judaism tracing its roots back to the early 1700s in Ukraine. A popular website explains:

> Hasidic Judaism is an Orthodox spiritual revivalist movement that emerged in Eastern Europe in the 18th century. Followers of Hasidic Judaism (known as *Hasidim*, or "pious ones") drew heavily on the Jewish mystical tradition in seeking a direct experience of God through ecstatic prayer and other rituals conducted under the spiritual direction of a Rebbe, a charismatic leader sometimes also known as a *tzaddik*, or righteous man. At the movement's height in the 19th century, it is estimated that roughly half of Eastern European Jews were Hasidic. The movement was decimated by the Holocaust, but dozens of Hasidic sects (or courts) exist today centered mainly in Israel and the New York metropolitan area.[18]

The various Hasidic groups, often named after the city where they were founded, each have their own Rebbe. As explained by professor Simon Dein:

> The tzaddik, meaning "righteous man," is the charismatic leader in Hasidism, also known as the Rebbe in order to distinguish him from the Rabbi in the conventional sense. This type of spiritual guide, renowned not for his learning but for his saintliness and ability as a religious mentor, is not entirely unknown in traditional Judaism.... But only in Hasidism, from the earliest days of the movement, did the figure of the tzaddik come to occupy a supreme role, with total submission to him being demanded of his followers.[19]

For an outsider, it is difficult to realize just how deeply a Hasid (meaning an individual Hasidic Jew) feels joined to his rebbe and just how much he reveres him, so it can sometimes be shocking to hear Hasidim tell stories about their rebbe. For example, in August 1973 I met with two Hasidic rabbis who were committed followers of the Lubavitcher Rebbe. They explained to me that telling stories about him was actually a valid way of worshipping God. This was part of their religious tradition.

A year or two later, while going to class on my college campus in Queens, New York, I met another follower of the Rebbe, a man in his twenties who shared with me that the only sin the Rebbe committed in his whole life was causing his mother pain in childbirth. But, this Hasidic Jew was quick to explain, by now, the Rebbe had "taken care of that" too. Seriously! Other followers of the Rebbe told me that he met with people from around the world and was able to speak all of their languages fluently. And of course, they all attested to an endless stream of miracles purportedly wrought by their revered leader.[20]

That's why a highly educated scientist like Herman Branover could write an adoring biography of the Rebbe titled *The Ultimate Jew*, unashamedly proclaiming him as Messiah.[21] What makes this all the more noteworthy is that Branover himself is a Russian-Israeli physicist, "known in the scientific community as a pioneer in the field of magnetohydrodynamics (MHD)."[22] Yet when he wrote about the Rebbe, he wrote as if he was speaking about someone who was on an entirely different plane, both intellectually and spiritually.[23] Even a staunch critic of the "Rebbe is Messiah" movement could say that "the Rebbe was an extraordinary individual of almost irresistible personal charisma, immense learning, exceptional leadership skills, and profound piety."[24]

Who, then, was this man? And how did such legends and accounts about him arise? Menachem Mendel Schneerson was the seventh—and last—Rebbe of the Chabad-Lubavitcher dynasty, named after the city of Lubavitch in Russia. The founder of this dynasty was Rabbi Schneur Zalman (1745–1812), most famous for his book called *Tanya*, which is still studied daily by his followers.

Zalman was succeeded by his son Dov Ber (1773–1827), who was the first to live in Lubavitch and who became the second Lubavitcher Rebbe; the third Rebbe was Menachem Mendel Schneersohn (1789–1866; with the same name as the seventh Rebbe)[25] and was Dov Ber's son-in-law; the fourth Rebbe was Shmuel Schneersohn (1834–1882), the seventh son of the previous Rebbe; the fifth was Sholom Dovber Schneersohn (1860–1920), the second son of the previous Rebbe; and the sixth was Yosef Yitzchak Schneersohn (1880–1950), also the son of the previous Rebbe.

It was Yosef Yitzchak who brought his followers to America, having escaped decades of Russian persecution and a season of imprisonment. And it was Yosef Yitzchak, the sixth Lubavitcher Rebbe, who increasingly emphasized the coming redemption, even suggesting that the Messiah would come during the time of the seventh Rebbe.[26] (Note that the Lubavitcher movement is also known as Chabad, a title that will also be used throughout this book.)[27]

But when Yosef Yitzchak died without a son of his own, it was his son-in-law, Menachem Mendel—also a descendant of Schneur Zalman, the first Lubavitcher Rebbe—who became the new leader. Consequently, by the time the seventh Lubavitcher Rebbe assumed his leadership role (with great reluctance, it should be noted, feeling quite unworthy of the task), there was a sense of expectancy in the air. The Messiah's coming was near!

The seventh Rebbe was born in 1902 in what is today Mykolaiv, Ukraine, but was then part of the Russian Empire. He was the descendant of a long line of devout rabbis and Jewish scholars, and he was recognized as a prodigy at a young age. He spent many hours a day immersed in rabbinic texts, mastering a vast array of Jewish literature by the time he was a young teenager. He also had a keen interest in secular studies, which was unusual for an ultra-Orthodox Jew, ultimately studying at famous secular universities in Berlin and France. Through the rest of his life he astonished a wide range of scholars from many fields by his intimate familiarity with their areas of learning, including a knowledge of the latest academic debates coupled with a detailed understanding of the most complex subjects.

According to one account, he shocked a leading Israeli mathematician by isolating a problem in one of his equations, a problem that took two years for this professor and his team to confirm using the best computers available. Yet the Rebbe recognized the problem as he made the calculation on the fly, in his head, as the great mathematician was sharing his research with him.[28]

The Rebbe was also famed for his reading speed, reportedly reading a letter of between ten and fifteen pages in twenty seconds (this, according to the man who brought him the letter!), then responding to it in careful detail. Reportedly, as he was dictating responses to letters to his team of secretaries, he was simultaneously reading the next letter (yes, allegedly, while in the very midst of dictation).[29]

He was said to understand Russian, Hebrew, Yiddish, German, French, Italian, English, and Latin,[30] and over a forty-year period he corresponded with tens of thousands of seekers and inquirers, with some of the exchanges amounting to several thousand pages. He also met face to face with many thousands more, including presidents, prime ministers, and other government leaders, along with artists and scholars, secular Jews and religious Jews, and a multitude of leading rabbis. Many a prominent Gentile visited with him as well, leaving his presence deeply moved, if not astonished. And his work ethic was legendary. As reported by one of his followers, "During his decades of leadership, the rebbe worked over 18 hours a day and never took a day of vacation."[31]

Rabbi Shmuley Boteach, today known as "America's most famous rabbi," had a close relationship with the Rebbe as a young man and wondered aloud about the Rebbe's greatness. Describing the Rebbe as a "world-renowned spiritual authority," Rabbi Shmuley asked who had ever heard of a leader of the Rebbe's stature who never took a single vacation, or a single day off, in the forty-odd years he headed the world's largest Jewish organization; who stood on his feet every Sunday to meet thousands of common-folk and give them a personal blessing; and died with almost no money to speak of. How was it possible that a man with that level of power and influence could have emerged without having changed in the slightest or benefited personally from his position?[32]

We are told:

> The Rebbe managed to combine exalted spirituality with the organizational skills of a Fortune 500 CEO. He achieved a complete mastery of Judaism's sacred texts, even as he pursued a secular education at the University of Berlin and the Sorbonne....
>
> As the head of the Lubavitcher movement, Rabbi Schneerson gave himself over entirely to a single cause: promoting religious observance among non-Orthodox Jews in the United States and, indeed, in the far reaches of the globe. Not surprisingly, these efforts aroused a strong sense of messianic expectation within the movement. This quickening of the messianic pulse was further strengthened by developments on the world stage, most especially the collapse of communism in the Soviet Union and the Gulf War. For the Lubavitchers, events in Russia had particular meaning, since the Communists were the sworn enemy of Chabad and had forcibly separated Joseph Isaac from his hasidim. From this vantage point, the death of communism had the stamp of the messiah written all over it; as [Menachem] Friedman notes, "the matter [had] been rectified and the circle...closed, with victory ultimately belonging to Chabad." As for the Gulf War, it was seen by the Lubavitchers as epitomizing the messianic era...a conflict "in which Israel did not participate and in which Jews were not harmed."[33]

In 1928, Menachem Mendel Schneerson had married Chaya Mousia, the daughter of the sixth Lubavitcher Rebbe, Yoseph Yitzchak Schneerson. (So, the two men had the same last name, even though they were not father and son.) But the Rebbe and his wife were unable to have children, and so when the Rebbe died in 1994 at the age of ninety-two, he had no successor. Yet his followers were not concerned, since by the time of his death, many (if not almost all) of them were convinced that he was the Messiah. Why would he need a successor?

As explained by professor Menachem Friedman:

> The fact that the Rebbe has no children and has never groomed a successor from among his more distant relatives during his decades of "presidency" renders the issue of continuity of the Chabad dynasty a threatening question. The messianic response is virtually the only one capable of allaying these fears.... To the Chabad hasidim, the

Rebbe's advanced age and the absence of an heir has become a somewhat paradoxical basis for messianic faith: if the Rebbe has no heir, then he must have no need for one, for he is soon to reveal himself as the messiah, whom death cannot conquer.[34]

THE REBBE IS MOSHIACH (MESSIAH)!

In 1995, Rabbi Shmuel Butman, who still leads the International Campaign to Bring Moshiach,[35] wrote a book titled *Countdown to Moshiach: Can the Rebbe Still Be Moshiach?* In this book Butman explained:

> There were seven leaders between Avraham [Abraham] and Moshe [Moses]. *Seven* and not *eight*! By the same token, says the Rebbe, there are *seven* Tzaddikim [righteous men] who, each in his generation, helps to bring the revelation of Moshiach into the world. Again, *seven* and not *eight*! And the Midrash states that "Every seventh is beloved."
>
> Each of the previous six Rebbes needed a successor who would bring the Gilluy (revelation) of Moshiach a step closer to this world: from the first Chabad leader...Rabbi Schneur Zalman, to the second leader...Reb DovBer, and so on. The Rebbe is the *seventh* Rebbe. The *last* Rebbe, who brings the actual revelation down into this world. There *is* no successor because *there is no need* for a successor. The Rebbe completes the task.
>
> In the words of the Rebbe himself [November 4, 1991]: "The work of Shlichus [Chabad's outreach program to Jews] has been completed. All we have to do is greet Moshiach."...In simple terms, there is no need for a successor—because the *Rebbe*, as *Moshiach*, will take us out of exile immediately.
>
> This is the Divine plan that the Rebbe revealed to us on 10 Shevat, 5711 (1951) and in his subsequent Maamorim and Sichos [Hasidic discourses and lectures] throughout the years.[36]

So, according to Butman, as soon as the seventh Rebbe took his position, all the way back in 1951, he began to share these Messianic insights. As the Rebbe taught in his inaugural talk, there was a special demand put on every Lubavitcher Hasid in this seventh generation, even though it was not their choice to be born at this time. Nonetheless, the Rebbe explained, "all sevenths are precious," and "we are now very near the approaching footsteps of Moshiach, indeed, we are at the conclusion of this period, and our spiritual task is to complete the process of drawing down the Shekhinah [the divine presence]...into our lowly world."[37]

As he added in 1952, "*Moshiach* is about to arrive....And not only the younger of the group but the eldest of the group—in his lifetime *Moshiach* will come."[38]

In the years that followed, the Rebbe continued to emphasize the theme of the imminence of the Messiah, in 1969 calling for the completion of a special Torah scroll that was to be given to the Messiah, and in the early 1980s launching the "We Want Moshiach" campaign.[39]

By 1991, with Messianic fervor in the movement increasing by the day, many were convinced that the time of redemption had come. And then, in November 1991, the Rebbe brought an important, urgent message. They had been waiting for the Messiah for too long! He said:

> How is it that ten Jews can gather together and, notwithstanding everything that has been done, we have not brought Mashiach? It's utterly incomprehensible.
>
> Then people offer their explanations, and ask yet another question. There is another *farbrengen* [talk by the Rebbe], which obviously is written down, and the assiduous students remember everything that is written; but then it just sits there. But the thought is deemed acceptable, G-d forbid, that Mashiach won't come tonight, or tomorrow, or the next day.
>
> You cry out for Mashiach, and you follow my instructions to do so, but if you really meant it sincerely there is no doubt that Mashiach would have come a long time ago, with the true and complete Redemption.
>
> What more I can do, I don't know. Because everything I've done until now has been futile and ineffective. Nothing has come of it. We have remained in exile, and what is worse, our worship suffers from an ingrained exile mentality, as I have stated on a number of occasions.
>
> The only thing I can do is to hand this over to each one of you: *Do everything you can to bring Mashiach!*[40]

As biographer Chaim Miller notes:

> The sense of frustration and resignation in the Rebbe's words, even in print, is palpable. From that evening, until the Rebbe's eventual

passing three years later, Chabad remained haunted by the sermon. The Rebbe doesn't know what to do? Everything has been futile and ineffective? He has resigned the matter into our hands? Such thoughts were unprecedented and absolutely shocking.[41]

Some of his followers, however, were convinced that the solution was right before their eyes. *It was the Rebbe who was the Messiah.* The key was to recognize *him.*[42] Everything else was in place, and the Rebbe had already established his credentials. He was the greatest Jewish leader of the generation, proving himself to be a prophet (for example, prophesying that the people of Israel would be safe during the Gulf War of 1991), increasing Jewish education around the world, bringing thousands of Jews back to Torah observance, and bringing worldwide awareness to the concept of Messiah.

In his humility, it was thought, he would not proclaim himself to be the Messiah, but it was only right for his followers to make this known. And so a movement began within Lubavitch—including a petition drive—announcing the belief that the seventh Lubavitcher Rebbe, Menachem Mendel Schneerson, was in fact the long-awaited Messiah. And while he sometimes rebuked such claims directly, his devotees were quick to point out that when a new song was sung to him stating, "We want Moshiach now," he expressed his approval. They claimed he knew it was about him![43]

Then, unexpectedly, the Rebbe had a stroke, followed by another, even more severe stroke. Now he could not speak or communicate. Surely this too was a sign. As written in Isaiah 53:7, the servant of the Lord would be silent, like a lamb being led to slaughter. The Rebbe was silent too!

His motionless body would be brought onto a balcony overlooking the main synagogue where he could look at his followers, who would then begin to sing to him with great passion and devotion, hailing him as Messiah. And if there was the slightest sign of him moving, the slightest change of expression, they would be worked into a frenzy. They said, "The Rebbe is acknowledging that he is Moshiach!"[44] And then he died, and the dream was over. Or was it?

In 2007, Bruce Warshal, a liberal rabbi, recounted what happened to him when, a few months earlier, he was walking in Times Square in New York City and met two Lubavitchers handing out literature proclaiming that the Rebbe, Menachem Schneerson, was the Messiah (Moshiach). They were in competition with a guy up the street with a sign proclaiming the end of the world and that Jesus will save us if we believe in him.

Being a curious person, or maybe just a contentious one, I approached the Chabad-Lubavitchers and asked how the Rebbe could be the Messiah since he died in 1994 and was buried in Queens? They responded that he really wasn't dead and that the person buried in the grave in Queens was his father-in-law. I walked away amused and a little irritated that these jokers were there in the name of Judaism.[45]

So, more than a dozen years after the Rebbe's death, his followers were still declaring that he was somehow alive (yet hidden) and that he certainly was the Messiah.

The next year, 2008, Eli Soble wrote an op-ed for the *Jerusalem Post* titled, "Our Rebbe Is the Messiah." Like Butman, he pointed back to the Rebbe's talk in 1951, noting that throughout the entire history of the Chabad movement (dating back more than two hundred years), one of its fundamental principles was "to bring the messiah and the revelations of redemption to all of mankind."[46] This was emphasized in the Rebbe's discourse in 1951, his first as the leader of the movement, where he explained that the present generation was the seventh since the founding of Chabad. And just as Moses, who was the leader of the seventh generation after Abraham, was appointed by God to bring "the divine presence into the world," the Rebbe was now tasked with bringing "the divine presence into the world permanently, with the full redemption."[47]

Quite strikingly, "almost every week in 1991 and 1992, the Rebbe reiterated, verbally and in writing, that this generation is the last of exile and the first of geula, or salvation."[48] Indeed this meant that "this redemption will soon materialize, and the Rebbe is the messiah," and it was the task of his followers "to provoke the full revelation, in order to see the Rebbe's transition from presumed to confirmed Moshiach."[49] This, without a doubt, was what the Rebbe was saying. His disciples needed to believe his every word and work tirelessly to see the Rebbe revealed.

To this day all over Israel you will find giant billboards with the Rebbe's picture, proclaiming him as King Messiah, but the Lubavitch movement worldwide is divided, with many openly proclaiming the Rebbe as Messiah, many others openly denying it, and still others believing it but not saying it. (As one Lubavitch rabbi said to me, "If you ask us if the Messiah, when he comes, will look like the Rebbe, we would say yes.") To this day, in the main headquarters on 770 Eastern Parkway, Brooklyn, some of his followers sing to his empty chair (claiming he is literally there with them, only invisibly),[50] others pray to him, and others proclaim him as God incarnate.[51] And all Lubavitchers on all sides of the debate would be quick to point out that rather than their movement dissipating after their beloved Rebbe left the scene, it has instead grown exponentially. Doesn't this buttress the claims of those who believe he was—and is—the Messiah?

Let's continue our investigation, which will become more and more fascinating with each chapter. Can a deceased rabbi be raised from the dead, proving himself to be the long-awaited Messiah?

CHAPTER 2

THE MESSIAH CONCEALED
AND THEN REVEALED

A S I WRITE this chapter, a beautiful, coffee-table-type book sits on my desk. It is titled *And He Will Redeem Us: Moshiach in Our Time*, and it features a large color picture of the Lubavitcher Rebbe on the front cover. Along the bottom of the cover run these Hebrew words (but written in English, as here): *Yechi Adoneinu Moreinu v'Rabbeinu Melech HaMoshiach L'Olam Va'Ed*, meaning, "May our Master and Teacher and Rabbi, King Messiah, Live Forever!"

This prayer is prayed until this day by some of the Rebbe's most devoted followers as they proclaim, "May he live forever!"—even though he died in 1994. In fact, *And He Will Redeem Us* was published in 1994, shortly after the Rebbe's death, yet on page after page the book boldly proclaims the Rebbe as the Messiah.

Other rabbis, as we saw in chapter 1, fervently reject this notion (even though they respected the Rebbe), noting that Judaism does not teach that the Messiah will die before completing his mission. How, then, do the Rebbe's followers respond to this objection?

Interestingly, one of the highly respected Orthodox rabbis who reacted so strongly against the idea that the Rebbe was the Messiah, Rabbi Aaron Soloveichik, subsequently said this (although there is some dispute about the contents of his letter):[1]

> Before the passing of the Rebbe, I included myself among those who believe that the Rebbe was worthy of being Moshiach. And I strongly believe that had we, particularly the Orthodox community, been united, we would have merited to see the complete Redemption.

Insofar as the belief held by many in Lubavitch—based in part on similar statements made by the Rebbe himself concerning his predecessor, the Previous Rebbe, including prominent *rabbanim* and *roshei yeshiva* [meaning prominent rabbis and heads of schools of rabbinic study]—that the Rebbe can still be Moshiach in light of the Gemara in Sanhedrin, the Zohar, Abarbanel, *Kisvei Arizal, S'dei Chemed* [referring to highly respected rabbinic writings and authorities], and other sources, it cannot be dismissed as a belief that is outside the pale of Orthodoxy. Any cynical attempt at utilizing a legitimate disagreement of interpretation concerning this matter in order to besmirch and to damage the Lubavitch movement that was, and continues to be, at the forefront of those who are battling the missionaries, assimilation, and indifference, can only contribute to the regrettable discord that already plagues the Jewish community, and particularly the Torah community.[2]

In Rabbi Soloveichik's view, while it was completely foolish to believe in a resurrected Messiah, it was not outside the pale of Judaism to countenance such a view. Could it be, then, that a case can be made for a prominent Jewish leader to be the Messiah even if he died before completing his mission—that is, as long as he was resurrected and continued his Messianic mission after death?

As noted by Christian scholar Jim Melnick:

Without question, [David] Berger's book and comments [which challenged the orthodoxy of those who believed that the Rebbe could still be Messiah after his death] created a firestorm and a major counter-response among many Lubavitchers and their defenders, including a book by Rabbi Chaim Dalfin called *Attack on Lubavitch: A Response*.[3] Dalfin cited the opinion of Professor Aviezer Ravitzky, chairman of the department of Jewish philosophy at Hebrew University concerning the view of some Lubavitchers that Schneerson might be resurrected as the Messiah: "...those inside Lubavitch who wait for their rebbe to return from the dead and redeem the world may be foolish, but by no means is this expectation heretical or antithetical to Judaism." Another rabbi, who is critical of some within the Lubavitch movement for pushing the doctrine of Schneerson's messiahship ("a vocal faction" he says), nevertheless wrote the following: "Does this mean to say that I agree with Berger, in principle, that the notion of a resurrected Messiah, is in reality a definite error....? Absolutely not!"[4]

So, we repeat our question: Could it be that a case can be made for a prominent Jewish leader to be the Messiah even if he died before completing his mission—that is, as long as he was resurrected and continued his Messianic mission after death? A Lubavitch website in New Jersey cites a traditional Jewish source that states, "Rabbi Berachia, in the name of Rabbi Levi said: Just like the first redeemer, Moses, revealed himself to the Jews and then concealed himself...similarly, the final redeemer will reveal himself, then conceal himself...and then return and reveal himself again."[5] This sounds almost Christian!

Let's recall that, at the age of forty, Moses stood up for his fellow Israelites when he was a prince in Egypt, but his people were not ready for him. He was then "hidden" for forty years in the wilderness before God sent him back to deliver the entire nation out of Egyptian slavery. Could it be the same thing with the Messiah? Could it be that the first time, he was not recognized by his generation, leading to an extended period of "concealment," after which he will "return" and then be recognized? (Others point to Moses being "concealed" on Mount Sinai, hidden away with the Lord, before he came back to his people, as further discussed below.)

The same Lubavitch website also cites Rabbi Isaac Luria, who was one of the most influential teachers of Kabbalah. He taught that "Moshiach will first redeem himself once and then ascend on high, body and soul, and only afterwards 'he will be recognized and all the Jews will gather towards him.'"[6] This sounds even more Christian!

Similarly, professor Herman Branover writes:

> Our sacred texts speak of a period in which Moshiach will be hidden following his initial revelation. (Some texts compare this to the disappearance of Moshe [Moses] following his message to the Jewish people that the Exodus was imminent.) This would allow for some to challenge faith in Moshiach's promise of imminent redemption and to assert that the presumed Moshiach is gone and is not the long awaited redeemer.[7]

So, according to this view, the Messiah's death and concealment would produce a trial of faith, with many saying, "I guess he wasn't the Messiah after all. If he really was the Messiah, he wouldn't have died. Or if he died, he would have been resurrected and finished his mission. The fact that he hasn't done this so far proves he was not the 'long awaited redeemer.'" But for Branover, this is just a test of our faith. We must hold fast and continue to affirm that the Rebbe, indeed, is the Messiah and Redeemer, despite his prolonged "concealment," now more than twenty-five years long.

Could it be, then, that Jewish tradition allows for a scenario in which a Jewish leader could be recognized as the Messiah, only to suffer death, causing his followers to go through a serious test of faith when he is "concealed," only for him to be revealed later on? More importantly, does the Bible allow for this kind of scenario? We'll return to the question of what the Bible says about a dying and rising Messiah in chapter 7, but for now let's look more into what the Rebbe's followers have written. Do they have a case?

One website flatly says no, analyzing the argument that the Rebbe is only "concealed"[8] and claiming that rabbinic sources (such as Midrash Rabbah to Numbers 11:3) say that the Messiah will come, then disappear, then at some time later return. This would be similar to what happened to Moses, who revealed himself to Israel, only to be hidden before returning to his people again. And this in turn would appear to be very similar to Christian belief in the second coming of Jesus. Christians have been waiting millennia for the Lord's return; Lubavitchers have been waiting decades for their leader's return.

The website continues:

> In reality, when ancient Jewish sources speak of Mashiach's concealment and return, they do not mean that Mashiach will disappear for millennia, or even decades. The Midrash cited above itself says that Moses was hidden from the Israelites for three months, and Mashiach would be hidden for only 45 days. Though there are other opinions, the lengthiest is three years (based on Isaac disappearing from the Torah narrative for three years following the Akedah). And so, the potential for the Rebbe being Mashiach appears to have long expired.[9]

This same website notes that "the Rebbe constantly made clear that he is not Mashiach. In his monumental biography of the Rebbe, Joseph Telushkin devotes a chapter to this question," citing him at length.[10] As Telushkin noted, speaking of events in 1991:

> In an urgent audience to which the Rebbe summoned Chabad activist Rabbi Tuvia Peles, the Rebbe rebuked those who were making Messianic claims about him, saying, "They are taking a knife to my heart" and "they are tearing off parts of me."...
>
> Some months later, and shortly before the Rebbe's stroke, the Alaska-based *shliach* [emissary], Rabbi Yosef Greenberg (author of *Y'mei Bereishit*), brought a letter to be given to the Rebbe in which he referred to him as "King Messiah." Later that same day, Rabbi Groner told Greenberg that the Rebbe had looked at the letter, thrown it down in frustration, and then wrote on it, "Tell him that when the Moshiach comes, he should give him the letter."
>
> An even more definitive statement of the Rebbe on this same issue occurred at around the same time. An Israeli journalist, Sarah Davidowitz of the *Kol Ha'ir* newspaper, approached the Rebbe and said, "We appreciate you very much, we want to see you in Israel; you said soon you will be in Israel, so when will you come?" The Rebbe responded: "That depends on the Moshiach, not on me." The journalist persisted, "You are the Moshiach!," to which the Rebbe responded: "I am not."[11]

But didn't the Rebbe respond in similar ways when he was urged to succeed his father-in-law decades earlier? Didn't he demur, saying this was not his calling and he was not worthy? Perhaps these denials were more of the same. That's certainly what many of his followers would say. After all, when presented with a letter recognizing him as the new leader of the Lubavitch Hasidim after his father-in-law's death, he burst into tears, saying, "Please leave. This has no relevance to me."[12]

In fact, Shloma Majeski, a Lubavitcher rabbi, made this very argument in 2017, stating that just as Menachem Mendel Schneerson initially refused to become the seventh Lubavitcher Rebbe, he initially refused to be recognized as the Messiah.[13] Rabbi Majeski also mentions that the fifth Lubavitcher Rebbe, known as the Rebbe Rashab, adamantly refused to accept the position for ten years. As Rabbi Majeski said, "Things change," just as at one time of the year it's right to wear summer clothes, but at another time of the year it's right to wear winter clothes.

A MOVEMENT DIVIDED

What is striking is that there remains a deep division that cuts to the center of the Lubavitch movement, a division between those who openly proclaim the Rebbe as Moshiach and those who believe it is unwise and even dangerous to do so. In her 2003 book, *The Rebbe's Army*, Sue Fishkoff wrote, "That same wound ripped through the streets of Crown Heights after Schneerson's death, setting family against family in the most serious division ever to have hit the Chabad movement."[14]

At one point, in 1993, before the Rebbe's death but when he was unable to communicate, Rabbi Shmuel Butman, whom we noted was one of the leaders proclaiming the Rebbe as Messiah, was sending out faxes from the official Lubavitch headquarters at 770 Eastern Parkway in Brooklyn, spreading his Messianic message. Yet from elsewhere in the same building, on another floor, other Lubavitch leaders were sending out counter-faxes, urging others not to listen to any communication from that address that did not come from them.[15] Talk about division and confusion.

> Already in 2003 Fishkoff could write that the belief that the Rebbe is the Messiah has done more harm to Chabad outreach—and to the movement itself—than any other single factor. While the numbers of Lubavitchers who promulgate this belief dwindle with each passing year, messianist strongholds still exist, to the chagrin of the movement's leadership and to the consternation of many in the outside Jewish world who remember the billboards and bumper stickers that proliferated in the early 1990s showing the message "Welcome King Moshiach" below the Rebbe's smiling face.[16]

And yet more than fifteen years after *The Rebbe's Army* was published, the belief in his Messiahship appears to be holding steady rather than dwindling, even if there is great division in the movement over this. The belief might even be growing.

As noted in a 2017 article in the Jewish *Forward*:

> For decades, many within the movement believed that their beloved rebbe, Menachem Mendel Schneerson, was the Messiah. When he died in 1994 without having revealed himself as such, his closest advisers—the highest levels of Chabad's leadership—tried to put an end to the overt messianic fervor. But the belief persisted, and

has now morphed into both a power struggle and something of a public relations problem for the organization, whose "mitzvah campaigns" and "Chabad houses" reach millions of Jews each year. Even as Chabad's leadership is still trying to purge its movement—and its headquarters—of members who would call Schneerson "Messiah," they are loath to admit that such people exist.[17]

Other respected Orthodox Jewish leaders, like Dr. Norman Lamm, also found these beliefs deeply troubling, saying, "What a waste. They're doing so much good, why in heaven's name do they have to get latched onto this dreadful messianic business? There's an element of idolatry there that scares me very much. Imagine if they didn't have this messianic fixation, how much they could have achieved."[18]

And yet the Lubavitchers who believe the Rebbe is Messiah have an answer: This is all part of the plan. The Messiah's present concealment is in accordance with Jewish tradition. Soon he will be revealed. As explained by Rabbi Zalman Shmotkin, "The single most underappreciated thing in all this is that there are credible, traditional sources that allow the possibility for a *tzaddik* [righteous man] to be resurrected and become Moshiach. We can't come out and say the Rebbe or Moses or King David will not be the Messiah because we are simply not God. Only He can know."[19]

Again, others have dismissed such views with scorn. As noted by Melech Jaffe, the Lubavitcher Rebbe taught that it was theoretically possible for a resurrected dead man to be the Messiah, citing traditional sources to back this position.[20] Yet the Rebbe knew full well these same sources indicated that there was an order to God's plan: first, the Messiah brings the era of redemption, then the resurrection of the dead would take place.

In other words, Judaism teaches that redemption will come to Israel and the nations, bringing in the Messianic age, and then the final resurrection will come. So, it is redemption first, then resurrection, whereas the idea that the Rebbe will rise from the dead in order to bring redemption is backwards. In Jaffe's words, "As the Rebbe taught, as is clear from the tradition, and as is clear in Jewish law, life does not return to the dead until after the redemption process is already commenced by Moshiach, a living Moshiach who could not have died."[21]

As for the Rebbe being alive today, Jaffe mocks the idea, writing, "Of course the Rebbe is not alive. Everyone knows this. I once read somewhere that the Internet is 'the world's junkyard of useless information,' but this debate about whether the Rebbe is alive makes the rest of the Internet look like the Library of Alexandria."[22]

A REBBE WHO COMES BACK?

But what if the Rebbe rose from the dead ahead of time in order to bring redemption, similar to what the New Covenant Writings say about Yeshua, namely, that He was the first to rise from the dead?[23] Why couldn't this be true?

According to the Lubavitch leader Rabbi Sholom Ber Kalmanson, this is in accordance with Jewish tradition (not, of course, what I have said about Jesus, but the idea that there can be individual resurrections before the final resurrection following the redemption): "*T'chias ha'meisim* [the resurrection of the dead] has taken place throughout the ages."[24]

According to Rabbi Majeski, "The Midrash says that when [the Messiah] will be hidden, it will be a very difficult time. There will be people who will stop believing in him because of that, and that ultimately he will come."[25] Rabbi Majeski said this some years ago, but he still holds to these views, professing the Rebbe as Moshiach and stating in 2017 that the delay will only serve to strengthen our faith and hasten the redemption.[26]

In keeping with his convictions, in 2018 Rabbi Majeski released a video responding to the question, "Why identify one person as Moshiach instead of waiting to see who He is when He comes?"[27] Then, in 2019 he released a video that answered the question, "What are we waiting for if we are told that Moshiach is already here?"[28] Yes, in his view, on some level, "Moshiach is already here." So, he is "here" in a certain spiritual sense now, after being "here" in a physical body, but in the future he will be "here" once more, this time in a physical body. To quote Rabbi Majeski once more, "After [Moshiach] will be here, and not everyone will accept him, he will disappear, then come back, take the *Yidden* [Jews] out of *Galus* [exile], and then everyone *will* accept him."[29]

Similarly, Rabbi Heschel Greenberg argues, "The fact that somebody is considered to be Moshiach and he passes on physically, or it appears he passes on—he's in a state of concealment—that doesn't disprove anything, because what he has done to make himself worthy of being Moshiach continues to exist."[30]

Not surprisingly, given the exalted status of the Rebbe in the eyes of his followers, professor Elliot Wolfson explains how many of the Rebbe's followers believe that he still continues to function as their Rebbe, noting that in Hasidic thought, a righteous man is even more alive after physical death than during earthly life, and so death is understood "as an apparent withdrawal rather than an actual termination." This concept, Wolfson adds, is then enhanced technologically, in particular by audio and video messages of the Rebbe through which he continues to be a living presence among his followers.[31]

So, the Rebbe didn't *really* die. He simply withdrew. Indeed, as Professor Wolfson explained, when the sixth Rebbe died, he was freed from the limitations of a physical body and accomplished even greater, miraculous feats, "including returning to the world to lead the Jewish people to welcome the Messiah." As for the reality of his physical demise, that was merely a test of faith for his Hasidim, empowering them to rise above earthly realities, which were merely "birth pangs" that preceded the coming of the Messianic redeemer, thereby revealing God's higher, spiritual truths.[32]

To quote Wolfson once more:

> It is no exaggeration to say that the vast majority of Lubavitchers presently believe that what Schneerson said about the sixth Rebbe pertains to him, that is, he continues to affect the physical and spiritual matters of people's lives, particularly with respect to the activity of bringing the redemption, and some even believe that he will rise from the grave to lead the Jewish people into the messianic era.[33]

And, Wolfson notes, while this sounds blasphemous to our ears, all this is merely the "hyperliteral reading" of the rabbinic concept that the wicked are called "dead" even while they are physically alive, while the righteous are called "living" even when they are physically dead.[34]

But are there other traditional Jewish sources that allow for the Messiah to be one who comes back from the dead? The Law of Messiah website sums up the standard arguments raised by Messianist Lubavitchers, arguing:

> Many have said unequivocally the Messiah cannot come from the dead. This is a perfect example of people having preconceived ideas without looking and studying what it says in Torah. When this question comes up—"Is this according to Judaism?"—the answer is that

the definition of Judaism is that which is written in Torah. Torah defines Judaism. We must search and see if the Messiah can be someone from among the dead. There is a number of sources for this belief.[35]

What are these alleged sources? The first comes from the Talmud, b. Sanhedrin 98b, which says that if Messiah is among those who are living, then it's Rabbeinu HaKodesh (Rabbi Judah the Prince, who compiled the Mishnah), and if he's among those who passed on, then it's Daniel. Another citation offered is also from the Talmud y. Berachot 2:4, which teaches that if Messiah is among the living, then his name is David, and if he's from among those who passed on, then it's David the King himself. (See also Midrash Rabbah to Lamentations 1:51.)

The Law of Messiah site reinforces this position with a citation from Rabbi Don Isaac Abarbanel (fifteenth century), who wrote, "There should not be a question in your mind whether Messiah could be someone who will come after passing, because it says this in the Gemara [Talmud]. The Gemara says there is that possibility: if he's among those who passed on, then it's Daniel Ish Chamudos [a man highly favored]."[36]

The argument, then, is simple: According to the Talmud, the Messiah could be a righteous person from a previous generation, someone who died centuries ago. The fact that he died doesn't rule him out as a potential future Messiah.

Then, after citing other respected rabbinic leaders in support of their thesis, the website claims, "The Zohar says that the Messiah is one who will be here, pass on, and then he'll come back and take the Yidden [Jews] out of exile. So it is indeed very possible for the Messiah to be one from among the dead."[37]

To be sure, an entire book has been written in response to these arguments, claiming that they are completely misinterpreting these traditional sources.[38] For example, we are told that when the texts say that the Messiah could be someone who previously died, like Daniel, what they mean is that if the Messiah was like someone from a past generation, it would be someone like Daniel. That's it. Nothing at all about Daniel rising from the dead and becoming the Messiah. As to biblical texts that speak of the Messiah being named David, there are those who believe that David himself will be raised from the dead to be Messiah. But, the rebuttal would be, that applies to David alone, not to another potential Messiah.

The Messianists would respond by saying:

> The definition of Jewish belief is that which is written in Torah. That defines Jewish belief. This possibility—that Moshiach comes, and after his coming and revelation there's an interruption, and then he completes the process—this is found in a number of places in Torah. Let me just mention a few. One is *Midrash Rabba Shir HaShirim* 2:22, on the *pasuk "Domeh dodi l'tzvi."* And the Midrash says, just like a deer is revealed, and hidden, and again hidden. I guess it means that when it runs, it runs between the trees—you see it and then you don't see it. That's what happened with Moshe Rabbeinu in Egypt. He came, and then he was concealed for a few months—there are different opinions how many months—and then he was revealed again and took the Jews out of Mitzrayim [Egypt]. The Midrash concludes the same thing will be with Moshiach: He will be revealed, then he will be hidden, and then he will be revealed again. In fact, the Midrash says that when he will be hidden, it will be a very difficult time. There will be people who will stop believing in him because of that, and that ultimately he will come.[39]

Naturally, many Messianic Jews have drawn attention to these concepts, arguing, "That's what we have been telling you all along about Yeshua! In fact, looking back at the Torah, this is what happened to Jacob's son Joseph too!" As I wrote in 2003:

> We see that the life of Joseph also points to several unique aspects of the ministry of Jesus. (Remember that events and people that foreshadow the Messiah are not meant to be specific in every detail but rather illustrative in broad, sweeping ways. The parallels in the lives of Jesus and Joseph, however, are really quite striking.) Joseph was rejected by his own brothers (Genesis 37), suffered because of false accusations and slander even though he himself was righteous (Genesis 39), but was then exalted to become the savior of Egypt and the world (Genesis 41). And during the entire time that he was respected and revered by these Gentiles, he was unknown to his own brothers, considered as good as dead. In fact, the first time they saw him in his exalted position in Egypt, they did not recognize him

(Gen. 42:7–8). It was only the *second time* that he revealed himself to them: "So there was no one with Joseph when he made himself known to his brothers" (Gen. 45:1). Ironically, it was his brothers' betrayal of him when he was only a teenager that caused Joseph to go to Egypt, resulting in the saving of the lives of many Gentiles and then, ultimately, of his own flesh-and-blood family: "God sent me ahead of you to preserve for you a remnant on earth and to save your lives by a great deliverance" (Gen. 45:7).

So also, Yeshua was betrayed by his own people, slandered and falsely accused (though he was perfectly righteous), delivered over to death, and then exalted to be the Savior of the Gentile world—precisely because his own nation rejected him. In the end, in what is commonly called his *second coming*, he will make himself known to his brothers, and the weeping will be great (Zech. 12:10–14; note also Gen. 45:2). Even traditional Jewish scholars have noted the pattern of a rejected, then hidden, then revealed, Messiah. It is certainly apt![40]

Interestingly, an interviewer in Israel asked religious Jews if the Rebbe could be the Messiah, even though he died. To those who responded positively (and quite a few did), he asked, "Then what about Jesus?" The answer for them was simple: The Rebbe was a great Torah leader, whereas Jesus led Israel away from Torah.[41]

But did He? Is this an accurate belief? Is it possible that Jesus—known in His day as Rabbi Yeshua ben Yoseph—has been concealed within the church and hidden within Christian beliefs? Is it possible that He, not the Rebbe, will one day be revealed as Messiah of the Jewish people? Could it be that the outward clothes that have been put on Him—the "clothes" of Christianity—have obscured His real identity, just as Joseph was obscured by the garments of Egypt?

As we continue on our investigative journey, let me leave you here with a verse from Micah (chapter 4, verse 8), as paraphrased in Targum Jonathan, a foundational Jewish source. The Targum states, "And you, O anointed One [Messiah] of Israel, who have been hidden away because of the sins of the congregation of Zion, the kingdom shall come to you, and the former dominion shall be restored to the kingdom of the congregation of Jerusalem."[42]

The Messiah hidden away because of Israel's sins? Could it be true?

I mentioned at the beginning of this chapter the book titled *And He Will*

Redeem Us. It includes this fervent prayer: "May we merit to see and be together with the Rebbe, down here in a physical body and within our reach, *and he will redeem us.*"[43]

Will the Rebbe reveal himself in the future, here in our midst, in a physical body, to finish the work of redemption? Or is there another candidate who has been hidden from Jewish sight for almost two thousand years?

CHAPTER 3

THE GILGUL, REINCARNATION, AND A POTENTIAL MESSIAH IN EACH GENERATION

THERE IS A fascinating rabbinic tradition that claims the Messiah was born the day the second temple was destroyed.[1] Yet that event happened almost two thousand years ago, in the year AD 70. Does that mean that the Messiah is nearly two thousand years old?[2]

There are other rabbinic traditions that teach that one of the seven things God created in the beginning was the name of the Messiah, which means that the concept of the Messiah was in God's mind from the very beginning of time.[3] But that's different than saying the Messiah was actually born in the year 70 of this era. What are we to make of this?

Another rabbinic tradition claims the Messiah was alive more than 1,700 years ago, afflicted with leprosy and sitting at the gates of Rome. (His leprous condition was tied to Isaiah 53:4, which speaks of the Messiah being "smitten," here taken to mean smitten with leprosy.)[4] This is the account as recorded in the Talmud, depicting a conversation between Rabbi Yehoshua ben Levi, who lived in the first half of the third century, and Elijah the prophet, who appears from time to time in rabbinic stories:

> Rabbi Yehoshua ben Levi *said to* Elijah: *When* will the *Messiah come?* Elijah *said to him: Go ask him.* Rabbi Yehoshua ben Levi asked: *And where is he sitting?* Elijah said to him: *At the entrance of* the city of *Rome.* Rabbi Yehoshua ben Levi asked him: *And what is his* identifying *sign* by means of which I can recognize him? Elijah answered: *He sits among the poor who suffer from illnesses.*

And all of them untie their bandages *and tie* them all *at once*, but the Messiah *unties one* bandage *and ties one* at a time. *He says: Perhaps I will be needed* to serve to bring about the redemption. Therefore, I will never tie more than one bandage, so *that I will not be delayed.*[5]

What a moving picture. The Messiah sits among the poor and the sick, changing his bandages one at a time, in contrast with the other sufferers, who change their bandages all at once. "Perhaps I will be needed," he says, which explains why he changes one bandage at a time. This way, should he be summoned on Israel's behalf, he will be able to come at once.

The story continues:

Rabbi Yehoshua ben Levi *went to* the Messiah. *He said to* the Messiah: *Greetings to you, my rabbi and my teacher.* The Messiah *said to him: Greetings to you, bar Leva'i.* Rabbi Yehoshua ben Levi *said to him: When will the Master come?* The Messiah *said to him: Today.* Sometime later, Rabbi Yehoshua ben Levi *came to Elijah.* Elijah *said to him: What did* the Messiah *say to you? He said to* Elijah that the Messiah said: *Greetings [shalom] to you, bar Leva'i.* Elijah *said to him:* He thereby *guaranteed* that *you and your father* will enter *the World-to-Come,* as he greeted you with *shalom.* Rabbi Yehoshua ben Levi *said to* Elijah: The Messiah *lied to me, as he said to me: I am coming today, and he did not come.* Elijah *said to him* that *this* is what *he said to you:* He said that he will come *"today, if you will listen to his voice"* (Psalms 95:7).[6]

So, according to this Talmudic account, the Messiah was here on earth, ready to be revealed during the lifetime of Rabbi Yehoshua ben Levi, who died more than 1,700 years ago. Does this mean he has been here on earth all this time, waiting for the moment of redemption when he can be revealed? If so, does he live without aging? Or was he here, then caught up to heaven, waiting for the time when he will return to earth again? And what of the rabbinic texts that speak of the Messiah being in heaven the whole time, suffering for Israel's sins, waiting for the day when he can be revealed?[7]

A GENERATIONAL HOPE

According to one rabbinic concept, there is a *potential Messiah* in each generation, meaning that in every generation there will be a specially gifted, uniquely holy, Jewish leader, and if the generation is worthy, he will be revealed as the Messiah. If not, he will simply be remembered as a great rabbinic leader, and no one will know for sure that he could have been the redeemer.

As explained in the book *And He Will Redeem Us* (written, you'll recall, about the Lubavitcher Rebbe shortly after his death):

> A fundamental corollary of the belief in Moshiach states that in every generation there is one born of Davidic descent who is worthy of redeeming the community of Israel. When the time is ripe for Redemption, G-d will charge this individual with the responsibility of actualizing his potential. The first step in exercising his mandate will entail establishing himself as the indisputable spiritual authority of his generation. The simple meaning of the word Moshiach, the "anointed one," implies the relevance of this title to any figure who inspires the reverence and allegiance of his people. Consequently, one must look to the recognized leader of one's time for signs of his more exalted potential....
>
> As the Rebbe increasingly began to emphasize the need to acknowledge the covert yet palpable presence of Moshiach in our time [meaning that he, himself, was the Messiah], it became obvious to his followers that only one individual could possibly possess the necessary qualifications for meriting such presumed status.[8]

As expressed by other followers of the Rebbe:

> In every generation there is a "tzadik"—righteous man, able to assume the role of the Redeemer of the Jewish people. This righteous man—the leader of generation and Moshiach of the generation. This is the Lubavitcher Rebbe...the head of our generation and the prophet, who lives in 770 Eastern Parkway in New York.[9]

Another follower of the Rebbe, Yossi Schneerson from Kiryat Malachi, Israel, said this when the Rebbe suffered a stroke in early March 1992: "I feel he is the man. Moses also had physical problems, he could not speak properly. The Rebbe is only flesh and blood. His soul is that of the Messiah."[10]

But doesn't the Talmud refer to *the Messiah* in the text we just read from the Talmud? Wouldn't that, then, argue against the concept of a potential Messiah in each generation? After all, according to this Talmudic text, Elijah was not talking about a potential Messiah. He was talking about *the* Messiah, here in the flesh and ready to be revealed if Israel would repent. How do we make sense of this?

Before we try to answer these questions, let's look at one more Talmudic text, which states: "*The Holy One, Blessed be He, sought to designate* King *Hezekiah* as the *Messiah and* to designate *Sennacherib* and Assyria, respectively, as *Gog and Magog*."[11] Yes, the Talmud claims that "God wanted to make Hezekiah the Messiah. Had he fulfilled his Messianic potential, history as we know it—including the destruction of the temple—would not have happened."[12]

The Jewish History website, which makes available the teachings of the widely respected Orthodox Rabbi Berel Wein, shares the story in more detail, expanding on 2 Kings 19:35, which recounts how God's angel killed 185,000 members of the Assyrian army before they could destroy Jerusalem. According to Jewish tradition, this happened on the night of Passover, which means that the Jewish people went to sleep that night in fear of being devastated by a powerful enemy:

> There was a constant propaganda barrage against them in their native tongue. They had doubters from within. They went to sleep Passover night with no realistic hope.
>
> However, they woke up the morning of Passover and the threat was suddenly gone. Someone had smitten the outstretched arm of the enemy with the sword it had raised against them.
>
> At that moment, the Talmud remarks, Hezekiah had the chance to become the Messiah. All he had to do was sing the praises of God. Moses and the people had done so after the Egyptians were drowned in the sea. Had Hezekiah done the same he would have been the Messiah and history as we know it would have proceeded differently.
>
> However, he did not sing. That is why he was not worthy to be the Messiah. The opportunity was lost.[13]

As explained by professor Gershom Scholem, with reference to the teaching of Jewish mystics and with a direct quote from a follower of Shabbetai Zevi, the "mystical Messiah" whom we'll discuss in the next chapter:

> The Talmudic statement that God had intended to make King Hezekiah the messiah indicated to the kabbalists that God sent a spark of the messiah-soul into this world in every generation. Its function is "to redeem [Israel] if they repent, or to preserve the world in evil times, as in the generation of the great [Hadrianic] persecution, or else to enlighten the world in the period of exile through His Torah."[14]

Is that, then, the way we should read these texts, that these leaders were all *potential* Messiahs, men in whom "a spark of the messiah-soul" lived? And could it be that in every generation, this spark indwells one key leader? If so, does that mean Judaism believes in some kind of reincarnation? Before we turn to *that* subject, namely, the subject of reincarnation, called *gilgul* in Hebrew, let's look at one more fascinating Talmudic discussion about Hezekiah being a potential Messiah:

> *Rabbi Hillel says: There is no Messiah coming for the Jewish people, as they already ate* from *him,* as all the prophecies relating to the Messiah were already fulfilled, *during the days of Hezekiah. Rav Yosef says: May the Master forgive Rabbi Hillel* for stating matters with no basis. With regard to *Hezekiah, when was* his reign? It was *during the First Temple* period. *Whereas Zechariah* ben Berechiah, the prophet, *prophesied during the Second Temple* period *and said:* "*Rejoice greatly, daughter of Zion; shout, daughter of Jerusalem; behold, your king will come to you; he is just and victorious; lowly and riding upon a donkey and upon a colt, the foal of a donkey*" (Zechariah 9:9). In the generations after Hezekiah, there are prophecies about both redemption and the coming of the Messiah.[15]

This is making more sense now. A rabbi named Hillel (not the famous Rabbi Hillel who died near the beginning of the first century) alleged that Israel would not have a Messiah, because they missed their chance in the days of Hezekiah. The Messianic prophecies were lining up in his day, and he was supposed to be the Messiah, but the opportunity was not seized, so that's that.

He was rebuked by another rabbi who rightly pointed out there were clear Messianic prophecies, such as Zechariah 9:9, yet these prophecies were spoken more than 150 years after the death of Hezekiah. This means that yes, absolutely, Israel can still expect a Messiah. But that does not answer the question of whether Hezekiah was a *potential* Messiah, nor does it address the question of the soul of the Messiah being reincarnated in every generation until one of those generations proves itself worthy.

IS JEWISH REINCARNATION REAL?

Ovadia Yosef (1920–2013) was one of the leading rabbis in Israel, serving as the chief rabbi of the Sephardic community from 1973–1983. (Sephardic Jews were those who lived in the Iberian Peninsula prior to 1492 but live mainly in Israel today.) While highly respected for his great learning and for the inspirational leadership he provided for his community, he was also known to make extremely controversial statements, including this one, made during a Saturday night sermon in August 2000: "The six million Holocaust victims were reincarnations of the souls of sinners, people who transgressed and did all sorts of things which should not be done. They had been reincarnated in order to atone."[16]

What? The Holocaust victims were Jewish sinners from previous generations? They were reincarnated to make atonement for their sins? You can understand why this was such a controversial statement!

You're probably also wondering, "Does Judaism teach reincarnation?" The answer is that yes, in a certain way, some streams of Judaism do teach a form of reincarnation, although not exactly like the Hindu religion. Still, this concept of reincarnation (called "transmigration" or "metempsychosis," or just *gilgul* in Hebrew) ties in with the idea that in every generation there is a potential Messiah. So, what does Judaism teach about the transmigration of souls?

Growing up in a fairly nominal, Jewish home, I had no idea that there was such a concept in my faith. I had no idea that before going to sleep at night, some religious Jews recite a series of prayers called the "Bedtime Shema" (the Shema is a foundational prayer in Judaism, based on

Deuteronomy 6:4–9), and that one of the prayers, composed by Rabbi Isaac Luria, contains these interesting words, highlighted here:

> Master of the universe! I hereby forgive anyone who has angered or vexed me, or sinned against me, either physically or financially, against my honor or anything else that is mine, whether accidentally or intentionally, inadvertently or deliberately, by speech or by deed, *in this incarnation or in any other*—any Israelite; may no man be punished on my account.[17]

Did you catch that? Every night before bedtime some religious Jews forgive anyone who has hurt them, either "in this incarnation [Hebrew *gilgul*] or in previous ones." What an unusual concept, especially for Christian readers, for whom the concept of reincarnation is totally foreign. But should it be foreign? Does the Bible itself teach reincarnation (or transmigration of souls)?

In 1992 a book was published arguing that there were people alive at that time who were reincarnated souls from the Holocaust. It was written by a Jewish rabbi and titled *Beyond the Ashes: Cases of Reincarnation From the Holocaust.* In it the author, Rabbi Yonassan Gershom, claims to present "compelling evidence" that there are people living today (as of 1992) who previously died in the Holocaust. As the description of the book on Amazon explains, "Based on the stories of people he counselled, the author sheds new light on the subject of reincarnation and the divinity of the human soul. In addition to the fascinating case histories, Rabbi Gershom includes information on Jewish teachings regarding the afterlife, karmic healing, and prophecies."

I found the thesis of this book so interesting that I bought a copy for myself, curious to see what kind of "compelling" evidence the author presents. Yet despite the fascinating stories Rabbi Gershom did present, my simple question remained: Is there any biblical proof that *gilgul* exists? Is there any evidence for it in the earliest Jewish writings? There is, to be sure, a traditional Jewish statement that all Jewish souls were present at Mount Sinai when the Torah was given.[18] But is that what *gilgul* means?

According to the *Jewish Encyclopedia*, the belief in the transmigration of souls was not part of the early, foundational Jewish faith. This respected reference work states, "This doctrine was foreign to Judaism until about the eighth century, when, under the influence of the Mohammedan mystics, it was adopted by the Karaites and other Jewish dissenters. It is first mentioned in Jewish literature by Saadia [who died in AD 942], who protested against this belief."[19] Similarly the Jewish Virtual Library states that "there is no definite proof of the existence of the doctrine of *gilgul* in Judaism during the second temple period. In the Talmud there is no reference to it (although, by means of allegoric interpretations, later authorities found allusions to and hints of transmigration in the statements of talmudic rabbis)."[20]

What is clear is that the doctrine became popularized by the Jewish mystics, especially in the school of Isaac Luria, starting about six hundred years ago, and from there it became more mainstream, especially in ultra-Orthodox Jewish thought. But it has no support in the Scriptures, and as just noted, virtually no support in early rabbinic literature. As expressed by the learned Conservative rabbi Louis Jacobs:

> Reincarnation is the idea that a soul now residing in a particular body may have resided in the body of another person in an earlier period of time. Theories of reincarnation or metempsychosis are found in many religions and cultures, ancient and modern, but there are no references to the idea in the Bible or the Talmud, and it was unknown in Judaism until the eighth century CE, when it began to be adopted by the Karaites [a sectarian Jewish group] (possibly, it has been suggested, under the influence of Islamic mysticism).[21]

Others, however, would argue that there is, in fact, scriptural support for *gilgul*. Writing in the *New York Jewish Week*, Shmuly Yanklowitz states, "The Torah explains that all of us were present to accept the Law at Mount Sinai (Deuteronomy 29:14). How can this be—if I was not physically present, let alone born, in what way was I present? And, barring a satisfying answer to that question, how can I be bound by a covenant that I didn't make?"[22]

What, then, is his answer? He says, "The Jewish mystical tradition holds that our souls were present, although our bodies weren't. There were three million bodies and souls present at the time, but through reincarnation over time those souls have splintered off and been housed in many bodies. Thus, one may truly have a 'soul mate' out there who is the other part of their fractured soul."[23]

That is certainly a fascinating concept, but is that what Deuteronomy 29:14 is stating? Starting in verse 13, Moses said to Israel, "I make this covenant, with its sanctions, not with you alone, but both with those who are standing here with us this day before the LORD our God and with those who are not with us here this day" (JPS TANAKH). Do these verses state that all generations of Israel were present at Sinai when God made His covenant with the nation (or forty years later, when the covenant was renewed through Moses)? Certainly not. The text simply states that the covenant was made with those who were present, along with future generations. That's it. As Rashi notes, the text is not referring to Israelites who were absent that day but rather to "the generations that will be in the future."[24]

As explained by the commentator Obadiah Sforno, these words contain "a reference to future, as yet unborn generations. You will therefore have to explain to these unborn generations in due course that you yourselves only received this land on the understanding that subsequent generations of Jews would remain loyal to the terms of your acceptance. They will continue to inherit the land from you only on that basis."[25]

This is confirmed by professor Jeffrey H. Tigay, who wrote:

> That is, future generations. The reference cannot be to absentees, since verses 9–10 indicate that all are present. According to Midrash Tanḥuma, the phrase refers to those who were spiritually present: the souls of all future generations of Jews...were present and bound themselves to God by this covenant. In any case, the point of the text is that the mutual commitments made here by God and Israel are binding for all future generations. Ancient Near Eastern treaties likewise stipulate that they are binding on the parties' descendants.[26]

Even if one believed that, in a spiritual matter of speaking, all generations of Israel were present at Sinai (as if represented corporately), this concept is found nowhere in the Torah. And even a metaphorical, spiritual concept like this falls short of a belief in the transmigration of souls.

Simply stated, reincarnation, in any form, is not taught in the Bible, either in the Hebrew Scriptures or in the New Covenant Writings. God speaks of Himself as the God of Abraham, Isaac, and Jacob—all distinct individuals, all dead and buried, yet all spiritually alive to God in an ongoing way as opposed to split up into different souls or migrating into the bodies of others. As stated succinctly in the Letter to the Hebrews, "Just as it is appointed for man to die once, and after that comes judgment" (Heb. 9:27). No wonder, then, that Rabbi Saadia Gaon scorned those Jews who held to the doctrine of metempsychosis (reincarnation)—he actually said they "call themselves Jews!"—which, he notes, they called the "transmigration" of souls. He wrote:

> What they mean thereby is that the spirit of Ruben is transferred to Simon and afterwards to Levi and after that to Judah. Many of them would go so far as to assert that the spirit of a human being might enter into the body of a beast or that of a beast into the body of a human being, and other such nonsense and stupidities.[27]

Every individual is born once, dies once, and will be resurrected once. And at the resurrection each individual will give a final account to God. That's why the father's righteousness (or wickedness) is not transferred to his son, nor the son's righteousness (or wickedness) to his son. As the Lord said through the prophet Ezekiel, "Behold, all souls are mine; the soul of the father as well as the soul of the son is mine: the soul who sins shall die" (Ezek. 18:4).

When people die, they sleep in the dust, metaphorically speaking. (From the perspective of the New Covenant Writings, at death their souls are absent from the body and present with the Lord, if righteous, or separated from Him, if unrighteous.) Then, at the end of the age, "many of those who sleep in the dust of the earth shall awake, some to everlasting life, and some to shame and everlasting contempt" (Dan. 12:2). There is no room for reincarnation here.

But this doesn't preclude the idea that in every generation there is a potential Messiah. In fact, that's how some of the rabbinic texts we previously looked at have been explained. As noted on the Ask Moses website, it's true that the Midrash states that the Messiah was born the same day the second temple was destroyed and that his name was Menachem. But this has been understood traditionally to mean that "had the Jews of that generation merited redemption, Menachem would have been revealed as Moshiach and immediately redeemed the Jews from exile."[28]

A MESSIAH BELIEVED TO BE NEAR

This concept became especially real to the Lubavitcher Hasidim (who, by the way, do believe in the transmigration of souls), but with one additional twist: they became increasingly convinced that during the last years of the

Rebbe's life, they were at the door of the age of redemption. All the signs were there!

According to Harris Lenowitz, a professor of Hebrew studies at the University of Utah:

> Chabad had exposed its official position on messianic matters through various channels, prior to the Rebbe's death. Schneerson's addresses on the topic of the "Imminence of Redemption," delivered over the last two years of his life, were adapted and published in English (as *Sound the Great Shofar: Essays on the Imminence of the Redemption*, ed. U. Kaploun [Brooklyn, 1992]). Briefly, the evidence Schneerson put forth for the approach of the end of the present order of the cosmos included historical events given cosmic interpretation—such as the release of the Jews from the Soviet Union, the fall of Communism, and the events of the Gulf War [in 1991]. These were understood as miracles belonging to the time of redemption. Theologically, the Rebbe's contention was that the messiah is human and is present in every generation, but that his generation was the one most ready to be redeemed since it possessed the merit of all the good deeds of preceding generations. On the practical side, the Rebbe urged everyone to fulfill their part in the redemption by living in constant awareness of its character and in the certainty that the messiah would be made manifest instantly.[29]

According to the Rebbe directly (from talks delivered toward the end of his life), in every generation there is a potential Messiah, someone who is a descendant from the tribe of Judah and is worthy to be Messiah. In support of this he quotes the Chatam (or Chasam) Sofer, a major rabbinic authority who lived from 1762–1839, who wrote: "From the time of the destruction of the *Beis HaMikdash*, there was born one who in his righteousness is worthy of being [Israel's] redeemer."[30] And since according to traditional Judaism, the Messiah's coming could potentially materialize "on any particular day," then such a concept is a "logical imperative."[31]

In other words, if the Messiah could potentially be revealed at any moment in history, then there had to be a potential Messiah waiting in every generation. But this generation, it seemed, was different. Of course, the Rebbe says, there must be someone in this current generation worthy of being the Messiah, but things are different now than before. That's because "when the divine service of the Jewish people over the centuries is considered as a whole," everything that needs to be done to bring the redemption has already been done. Thus, "There is no valid explanation for the continuation of the exile."[32]

So, the Rebbe taught in the last years of his life that nothing was standing in the way of the Messiah being revealed. There was no reason for the exile to continue. The time was at hand! He said:

> Our Sages have described the Redemption as a feast. To speak in terms of this analogy, the table has already been set, everything has been served, we are sitting at the table together with *Mashiach*. All we need to do is open our eyes. Our Sages describe *Mashiach* as waiting anxiously to come. In previous generations, however, his coming was prevented by the fact that the Jews had not completed the tasks expected of them. At present, however, those tasks have been accomplished; there is nothing lacking. All we have to do is accept *Mashiach*.[33]

Can you imagine how these words impacted his followers? Can you imagine how confident they were that the final redemption was indeed near, so close they could touch it? The Messianic era was as close as...the Rebbe himself, who sat before them and taught.

As he said in 1991 (and just months before his first stroke):

> What more can I do to motivate the entire Jewish people to clamor and cry out, and thus actually bring about the coming of *Mashiach*?....All that I can possibly do is to give the matter over to you. Now, *do everything you can to bring Mashiach, here and now, immediately*....I have done whatever I can: from now on, you must do whatever you can."[34]

These words both electrified and shocked his followers, who felt the frustration of their beloved leader along with the invitation to do everything they could "*to bring Mashiach, here and now, immediately*." They would redouble their efforts, working even harder for the Rebbe—and soon enough, the world—to see that he was indeed the Messiah.

And what happened when he became gravely ill? Susan Perlman notes that Pamela Druckerman of the Jewish Telegraphic Agency reported on

March 15, 1994, "As Lubavitch Rebbe Menachem Mendel Schneerson lies unconscious in a Manhattan intensive care unit following a stroke last week, some Lubavitch leaders are viewing his illness, along with the recent shooting of Chasidic students on the Brooklyn Bridge as a sign that redemption is near."[35]

Obviously, redemption is at the door! The final seconds are ticking away. The Rebbe will be raised up! Druckerman continued:

> Neil Gillman, an associate professor of philosophy at the Jewish Theological Seminary in New York and longtime observer of the Lubavitch movement, predicted the Rebbe's death could not be justified along the same theological lines that propelled him into potential Messiah status, without rupturing the movement. "They will quickly conclude that the generation wasn't ready, that they weren't good enough," Gillman said, referring to the Jewish belief that there is a potential messiah in every generation who will be revealed if and when the world is ready. "But for the Lubavitchers—who have invested tremendously in a version of history that many say points to Schneerson as the Messiah—there is a determination to hold onto that vision."[36]

It turns out that Professor Gillman was right on target, as the Lubavitch movement has been ruptured over divisions concerning the Rebbe being Messiah, with the most prominent leaders saying he *could have been* the Messiah—he was the worthiest candidate of the generation—and other zealots saying *he is* the Messiah.

And already, before the Rebbe's death, other Jewish leaders were sharing their deep concerns. As Perlman notes, describing the events surrounding the Rebbe's ninetieth birthday:

> Schneerson's 90th birthday became a media event in April 1992. Among the honors was a celebration in Washington, D.C. with Nobel Laureate Elie Wiesel bringing the tribute and many United States congressmen in attendance. May 1992 produced a "Moshiach Parade" down Fifth Avenue in Manhattan with tens of thousands cheering. The parade was organized by the "International Campaign to Help Bring Moshiach." More full-page advertisements and additional critics such as Rabbi Morris Rubinstein made their sentiments known:

> I urge the Habad Messianism to be categorically rejected. Every Messianic Movement in the past brought nothing but disappointment and grief. This movement has the potential for a spiritual Jonestown disaster with many apostasizing as in the past. Every personal Messiah has sooner or later taken on the persona of divinity—Jesus of Nazareth, Sabbetai Zevi and Jacob Frank. It can very easily happen again....Habad is not an insignificant movement in Judaism—but the time has nevertheless come to call its bluff; to openly and unequivocally reject its messianic pretensions (*National Jewish Post and Opinion*, 23 September 1992).[37]

Today, more than twenty-five years later, the controversy continues to simmer, both within Chabad and without.

TWO MESSIANIC POTENTIALITIES?

Perhaps, though, there is another Talmudic text we should consider. It's found in b. Sanhedrin 98a, and it states:

> *Rabbi Alexandri says: Rabbi Yehoshua ben Levi raises a contradiction* between two depictions of the coming of the Messiah. *It is written: "There came with the clouds of heaven, one like unto a son of man...* and there was given him dominion and glory and a kingdom...his dominion is an everlasting dominion" (Daniel 7:13–14). *And it is written:* "Behold, your king will come to you; he is just and victorious; *lowly and riding upon a donkey* and upon a colt, the foal of a donkey" (Zechariah 9:9). Rabbi Alexandri explains: *If* the Jewish people *merit* redemption, the Messiah will come in a miraculous manner *with the clouds of heaven. If they do not merit* redemption, the Messiah will come *lowly and riding upon a donkey.*[38]

How interesting! Here, then, are two different descriptions of the coming of the Messiah, both of them found in prophecies in the Tanakh. One says the Messiah will come in triumph and glory, riding on the clouds of heaven. The other says he will come in a meek and lowly way, riding on a donkey. This sounds similar to the teaching of Rabbi Saadia Gaon, who wrote that if the Jewish people are worthy, they will only experience the Messiah son of David, but if they are not worthy, they will go through war and suffering, first experiencing the Messiah son of Joseph and then the Messiah son of David. As explained on the official Chabad website:

> Quite significantly, R. Saadiah Gaon (one of the few to elaborate on the role of Mashiach ben Yossef) notes that this sequence is not definite but *contingent!* Mashiach ben Yossef will *not* have to appear before Mashiach ben David, nor will the activities attributed to him or his death have to occur. All depends on the spiritual condition of the Jewish people at the time the redemption is to take place.[39]

But there's a big problem here, since when it comes to the Talmudic text, both Daniel 7 and Zechariah are recognized as Messianic prophecies. In other words, both will come to pass. Both will be fulfilled. This has nothing to do with potential Messiahs or the soul of the Messiah being present in every generation or the people of Israel proving themselves worthy of the Messiah. No, the Messiah will come meek and lowly, riding on a donkey, and he will come in triumphant power, riding on the clouds. Both will happen as surely as God's Word is true.

When it comes to the teaching of Saadia, the problem is that the Bible knows nothing of this Messiah son of Joseph. When it speaks of the redeemer, the Messiah, the anointed one who will deliver his people, it is always the same person: the Messiah son of David.

What then are we to make of these problems and apparent contradictions? The solution is really quite simple. The Messiah will fulfill dual roles—a lowly role and a triumphant role, a dying role and a ruling role. And in order to do both, he has to rise from the dead. It is as simple as it is profound.

Now, to take things one step further, what if the Tanakh gave clear indications that the Messiah was to come at a certain point in history—not potentially, but in actuality—and this time frame was confirmed in the Talmud? What if the Messiah had to arrive almost two thousand years ago to begin his mission, only to die, rise from the dead, and continue his mission to this day? Wouldn't this rule out the idea of a potential Messiah in each generation? Wouldn't this point to one Messiah, ordained by God before the world began, who would come at a specific prophesied time? And if the Messiah was to be revealed, then concealed, then revealed again, couldn't this potentially span a time period lasting many centuries? Couldn't his concealment last indefinitely—at least, a concealment from the eyes of some—while he continued his work behind the scenes?

I have argued at length elsewhere that according to the Hebrew Scriptures, the Messiah had to come and begin his mission of redemption *before* the destruction of the temple in AD 70, meaning that he had to come to our people Israel, die for our sins, and rise from the dead almost two thousand years ago. This is found in the Jewish Bible![40] Not only so, but the Talmud contains a tradition indicating that the Messianic age should have begun roughly two thousand years ago.[41]

Is the picture becoming clearer? Before we bring things into sharp focus, we need to take a slight detour in our investigation to look back at a fascinating but tragic piece of Jewish history. It will shed further light on the topic of this book: resurrection.

CHAPTER 4

THE MYSTICAL MESSIAH WHO CONVERTED TO ISLAM

THE STORY IS bizarre, incredible, unbelievable. It's like a movie with a plot so absurd that it stretches all credulity, only to have an over-the-top, shocking ending that leads to an even more impossible sequel. Except in this case, every word of the story is true. Not a syllable is fictional or exaggerated. What you are about to read is not disputed by historians. They all know that this story, the story of the mystical Messiah, Shabbetai Zevi, is fact, not fiction. (Note that his name is spelled several different ways, as will become evident in some of the quotes that follow.)

Zevi was born in 1626 to upper-middle-class parents in Smyrna (which is now Izmir, Turkey), allegedly on the Ninth of Av (Tisha b'Av), a date of tremendous importance in Jewish history. According to tradition, it was on this day that both the first and second temples were destroyed (respectively, in 586 BC and AD 70) and that the Jews were expelled from England (in 1290) and from Spain (in 1492).[1] It is a day of fasting and mourning. And according to some rabbinic traditions, it is the day on which the Messiah will be born (or *was* born).[2]

Zevi received a strong education in rabbinic texts and was recognized as a scholar while still a young man, specializing in Jewish mysticism (*Kabbalah*). While still in his teens, he began to share his mystical insights with a small group of followers, and as an extreme ascetic, he set himself apart. But Zevi was not simply a precocious (and devoted) Orthodox Jew. He was prone to extreme mood swings, riding a wave of ecstasy for days at a time only to plunge into the depths of depression. Many psychologists today believe he suffered from bipolar disorder and was a manic depressive.[3]

For his followers, though, these ups and downs only added to his uniqueness and charismatic appeal, particularly when he would claim to receive new insights—"illumination"— while in an ecstatic state. But this was not the only thing that happened to him while in a state of ecstasy. Instead, "when 'illuminated' he felt compelled to contravene Jewish law, perform bizarre rituals (*ma'asim zarim* or strange acts), and publicly pronounce the proscribed name of God."[4]

This would be like a Christian leader claiming to receive divine inspiration only to curse the name of Jesus or tear up a Bible. How bizarre! One would think that actions like this would immediately drive his followers away. Instead, this was proof to some of them that he was actually the Messiah, one who had to break the old laws in order to introduce the new Messianic order. Why else would a religious Jewish ascetic act in such ways? This is the power of deception.

As a young man, Zevi was married twice (at ages twenty and twenty-four), but both marriages ended in divorce, as he failed to consummate them. Later he married a Torah scroll—with a public ceremony, as well—to illustrate his devotion to God's holy teaching. (This really happened; as a result, he was expelled from the city of Salonica for this "wedding" ceremony.) Some years later he married again, this time to a woman who had allegedly been promiscuous in her past, similar to Hosea marrying a prostitute, and this wife bore him children. Such were the eccentricities of Shabbetai Zevi, a man of striking features and charismatic character. (In the standard portrait we have of him, he is wearing a turban, his beard and mustache meticulously groomed, with perhaps a soft look in his eyes.)

AN EXPECTANT FERVOR

But Zevi did not live in a vacuum, and it's important to place him in a larger, historical context, locating him within the spiritual and political situation in Turkey at that time. As Matt Goldish notes, "Shabbatai Zvi was a strange man in a strange age—an age of rapid social, political, and religious change, when no certainty about the world and its future seemed possible any longer."[5] And, he continues, in this atmosphere, others also imagined themselves to be the Messiah, including Jewish, Christian, and Muslim pretenders.

Goldish writes that a Messianic fervor was sweeping the Jewish, Christian, and Muslim world, claiming that it was this phenomenon that explained the sudden and dramatic rise of Shabbetai Zevi. Others, like Gershom Scholem, the great scholar of Jewish mysticism, claim that it was the Jewish mysticism of the day (specifically, the kabbalistic teachings of Isaac Luria, whom we mentioned before) that paved the way for belief in Zevi as Messiah. Other scholars claim that, to the contrary, it was Zevi's Messianic movement that caused these mystical beliefs to spread. Either way, there can be no doubt that Jewish history in the previous two centuries helped create the womb out of which this powerful Messianic movement was birthed.

Scholem points back to the expulsion from Spain of all unbaptized Jews in 1492, one of the most traumatic events in Jewish history. This, he believed, was a pivotal moment, leading to developments in Jewish mysticism in the next two centuries that prepared the way for the ascendancy of Shabbetai Zevi.[6] The upheaval experienced by the large and influential Jewish community in Spain cannot be overestimated, and this trauma most certainly impacted Jewish beliefs and Messianic hopes.

As for major events that took place in Zevi's own lifetime, a Jewish website asks why the Jewish world was so ready to accept a false Messiah like Shabbetai Zevi. To answer this question, the website points to the brutal massacre of three hundred thousand Ukrainian Jews by Bogdan Chmielnicki in 1648–49, followed by the devastation Jewish survivors then suffered "in the Russian-Swedish war of 1655. In this context, the Jewish people's historical dream of redemption from the bondage of exile took on a new degree of urgency and desperation. In these communities, Shabbetai Tzvi found a receptive audience."[7]

On the other hand, some Jewish communities around the world were virtually untouched by these tragedies, yet they too embraced Zevi as Messiah. What explains *that*? This remains a subject of ongoing scholarly debate.

What is certain is this: When Zevi declared himself to be the Messiah in 1648, there was not much reaction from his home community of Smyrna, "which had become accustomed to his eccentricities."[8] Nonetheless, he was banished from Smyrna by the local rabbis and traveled through Greece and Turkey through much of the 1650s, after which he was

> expelled from the Jewish communities in Salonika and Constantinople (now Istanbul) for violating the commandments and performing blasphemous acts. In the 1660s he arrived in Egypt via Israel. During

this period he led a quiet life, displaying no messianic pretensions. The turning point in his messianic career came in 1665 as the result of a meeting with his self-appointed prophet, Nathan of Gaza.[9]

Goldish tells us that Nathan, who was already well known as a mystic at the age of twenty-two, made a shocking announcement. Nathan claimed to have received a prophetic vision revealing that Shabbetai Zevi "would be the Jewish messiah."[10] This is when the movement exploded. This is when history took such an unexpected, radical turn. A Messianic fervor spread through the Jewish world. It was the moment of redemption. At long last, the period of exile was about to end. Shabbetai Zevi will redeem us!

And how did Nathan receive the revelation about Shabbetai Zevi? According to a pro-Shabbetai chronicle, Rabbi Nathan had spent the night studying Torah with some colleagues (it was during the festival of Shavuot, Weeks), when he fell into a deep sleep. He began to sleepwalk, reciting an entire tractate of the Talmud from memory (quite a prodigious feat), then giving directives to the other scholars there with him. These men smelled an unusual fragrance in the room, going outside to discover its source.

During this time Rabbi Nathan was leaping and dancing, disrobing himself one garment at a time until he was down to his underwear. Suddenly he jumped into the air, then collapsed to the ground. But when his colleagues went to help him, he was dead like a corpse. Goldish continues:

> They therefore placed a cloth over his face, as is done to the deceased, far be it from us.
>
> Presently a very low voice was heard, and they removed the cloth from his face; and behold, a voice emitted from his mouth, but his lips did not move. And he said, "Take care concerning my beloved son, my messiah Shabbatai Zvi"; and it said further, "Take care concerning my beloved son, Nathan the Prophet." In this way it became known to those sages that the source of that wonderful odor they had smelled was in the holy spiritual spark which came into Rabbi Nathan and spoke all these things.[11]

Afterward, when he came back to his normal senses, he had no recollection of what had happened and was startled to hear the other rabbis relate to him the words he had spoken. And since Nathan was a highly respected man, and there seemed to be no logical explanation for these mysterious events, it was thought they must be confirmation that Shabbetai Zevi really was the Messiah.

AN UPSIDE-DOWN VENERATION

But what of Zevi's continuing pattern of strange behavior? What of his breaking sacred Jewish laws and traditions? Goldish says:

> In the manic phase of his intense mood swings he would pronounce the Tetragrammaton, the ineffable four-letter name of God, as it is spelled (a violation of the Second Commandment in Jewish law), eat forbidden foods, change prayer services, or annul fast days. Such ritualized antinomian conduct had already caused his excommunication from his native city and several others over the previous eighteen years. But Nathan and the other theologians of the movement successfully cast these bizarre episodes in a positive light, explaining that they were necessary mystical exercises by which the messiah would redeem the world.[12]

Light was now darkness, and chaos was now order. The Messiah, whom tradition expected to keep the Torah and traditions perfectly, was now violating that very Torah and those very traditions—and he was doing so in the name of being the Messiah. But now, rather than being excommunicated, he was being venerated. Now wealthy Jews were selling their possessions in anticipation of the inauguration of the Messianic kingdom in Palestine. Now leading rabbis were endorsing him. Now whole Jewish communities were rejoicing because the Messiah had been revealed. Truth is indeed stranger than fiction.

Juan Marcos Bejarano Gutierrez cites Rabbi Jacob Sasportas, who "described the enthusiasm for...Sabbatai's messianic claims in Amsterdam."[13] Sasportas wrote:

> And all of the city of Amsterdam pulsated and was under the fear of the Lord. They increased the joy with drums and dances in the marketplaces and streets and in the synagogue, dancing with joy, and all of the Torah scrolls were taken out of the arks with their beautiful jewels, without paying attention to the danger of the envy and hate of the nations. On the contrary, they would make public declarations and speeches to the nations.[14]

Others, including children, were gripped with prophetic fervor, delivering messages about Shabbetai being the Messiah. As recorded by one of his followers, Baruch Ben Gershon of Arezzo:

> Now, this is the manner of the prophecy which came during those days. A deep sleep would come upon [the prophets], and they would fall upon the ground like dead people with no breath remaining in them. About a half hour later breath would come from their mouths though their lips would not move, and they would recite passages of song and passages of comfort. They would all declare, "Shabbatai Zvi is the Messiah of the God of Jacob." Afterward, they would rise back to their feet knowing not what they had said or done.[15]

In the city of Izmir (Smyrna) alone, as many as 150 reportedly prophesied like this, with some of them also pronouncing the divine name—an act of blasphemy, according to Jewish tradition, but now viewed positively by the followers of Zevi. It was all part of an unprecedented Messianic fervor, and it spread through the Jewish world like wildfire.

People of all classes and backgrounds believed Zevi to be the Messiah. Both educated and uneducated, rich and poor, declared their allegiance. Even Jewish communities that had not experienced hardship and persecution believed that Zevi was the long-awaited redeemer. It's as if a switch was flipped and suddenly, in a moment of time, everything changed.

To be sure, there were pockets of resistance to the movement. There were rabbis who openly opposed Zevi, including the leading rabbis of Jerusalem. But others were afraid to speak out because of Zevi's popularity. To deny his messiahship was to be a rank unbeliever. Such was the atmosphere in the Jewish world in 1666. The feeling was electric.

According to one eyewitness, Rabbi Leib ben Ozer, who had talked to people who had been near Shabbetai Zevi but were not his followers, they told him, "There was none like him in stature and in the way his face looked, like that of one of God's angels."[16] Furthermore they told him that when Zevi sang songs to God, which happened multiple times a day, it was impossible to look directly at him, "for one who looked at it, it was as if he looked into fire."[17]

As for those who prophesied, ben Ozer reports "that prophets arose in hundreds and thousands, women and men, boys and girls and even little children; all of them prophesied in the holy tongue [Hebrew] and in the language of the Zohar as well, and none of them knew a letter of Hebrew and all the less so the [idiosyncratic] language of the Zohar."[18]

The fervor spread throughout much of the Jewish world, with significant portions of the Jewish community following him. As summarized on the Jewish Virtual Library website, the news spread to other communities in Palestine while legendary reports reached Jewish communities in Italy, Holland, Germany, and Poland, impacting parts of the Jewish world that which had undergone intense suffering in recent decades as well parts of the Jewish world that had not: "Repentance alternating with public manifestations of joy and enthusiasm was the order of the day. From many places delegations left bearing parchments signed by the leaders of the community which acknowledged him as the Messiah and king of Israel."[19]

A CONVERSION NO ONE EXPECTED

And so it was time for Zevi to travel to Istanbul to reveal himself to the sultan, who would then bow down to him. But the sultan was not impressed, and rather than bow down to Zevi, he arrested him upon his arrival in the city. Still, finding him somewhat amusing (and apparently a source of tourist income), the sultan allowed Zevi to continue to operate his royal court from prison, entertaining the Jewish guests who traveled from near and far to greet him. Zevi even changed the Ninth of Av from a day of fasting (as it had been for centuries) to a day of celebration in honor of his birthday. And he started signing his letters with, "I am the Lord your God, Shabbetai Zevi." That's how deeply deceived he had become.

Eventually, however, the sultan tired of Zevi's antics and offered him two choices: convert to Islam or die. And what did Zevi do? He converted to Islam! Yes, "Shabbetai Tzvi became Aziz Mehmed Effendi, and, with a royal pension, lived until 1676, outwardly a Muslim but secretly participating in Jewish ritual. His letters reveal that at the time of his death, he still believed in his messianic mission."[20]

But this is only the beginning of the story, which gets stranger by the moment. You see, *it was not just Zevi who converted to Islam.* Many of his followers followed suit. They became Muslims too, but in their private practices they continued to profess their belief that Zevi was the Messiah. This group became known as the Dönmeh (meaning "converts" in Turkish), and as unbelievable as this sounds, *the Dönmeh exist until this day.* I kid you not. Whole books have been written about them, tracing their extraordinary history from the 1660s until the beginning of the twenty-first century.[21] Who would make up something like this?

But for these Sabbateans (as Zevi's followers were known), their Messiah becoming a Muslim was not a matter of spiritual compromise and cowardice. They had a theological explanation for his (and their) conversion, a rationale for this apparent act of apostasy. In accordance with Jewish tradition they believed that in order to usher in the Messianic age, the world would have to become totally righteous or totally wicked. In this case, because the world (specifically, the Jewish world) was not righteous enough, proving itself unworthy to welcome the Messiah, it was Zevi's duty to usher in the final apostasy, with his disciples following his example. What better way to make the world totally wicked than for the Messiah himself to become a Muslim?

This is what Scholem refers to as "redemption through sin," and it has its roots in the Talmud, being further developed in Jewish mysticism.[22] Robert Sepehr notes that, according to Reb Yakov Leib HaKohain, the director of Dönmeh West, a Californian neo-Sabbatean organization founded in 1972:

> It is commonly held conjecture that Sabbatai Zevi's conversion to Islam was an act of cowardice that betrayed the Jewish people. However, this "conversion" was not an act of cowardice, but in fact one of the mystical ma'asim zarim (strange actions) that he and Nathan of Gaza believed the Messiah was destined to perform, based on their reading of the Kabbalah.[23]

We will have more to say about Reb HaKohain in a moment, but allow me first to explain more about this concept of "redemption through sin," beginning with a lengthy passage in the Talmud that focuses on the coming of the Messiah and the Messianic age.

In one part of the Talmudic discussion, two passages of Scripture are contrasted: Daniel 7:13, where the Messiah comes in the clouds of heaven, and Zechariah 9:9, where the Messiah comes riding on a donkey. For a Christian reader, there's no difficulty with these passages at all. First, Jesus the Messiah comes riding on a donkey; He will return riding on the clouds of heaven. For a Jewish reader, however, the verses presented a problem: Will the Messiah come riding on a donkey, or will he come in the clouds of heaven? Which will it be? According to the Talmud, the answer is simple:

if we are worthy, he will come in the clouds; if we are not worthy, he will come riding a donkey.[24]

So, according to the followers of Shabbetai Zevi, because their generation was not worthy to receive him as the exalted Messiah, he had to suffer abasement. He would not be revealed in glory but rather in humiliation. As the Talmud stated, "The son of David [meaning the Messiah] will come only in a generation that is entirely innocent [meaning worthy]...or...entirely guilty [meaning unworthy]."[25]

Another important text, part of the same extended Talmudic discussion, taught that the world would apostatize into heresy before the Messiah would come. (The italicized text represents the exact words of the Talmud; the rest of the text is the expanded translation and commentary of Rabbi Adin Steinsaltz.) The Talmud states:

> *During the generation that the son of David comes, arrogance will proliferate and the cost* of living *will corrupt* people so they will engage in deceit. *The vine will produce its fruit, and* nevertheless, *the wine* will be *costly. And the entire* gentile *monarchy will be converted to* the *heresy* of Christianity, *and there will be no* inclination among the people to accept *rebuke.* This...*supports* the opinion of *Rabbi Yitzḥak, as Rabbi Yitzḥak says: The son of David will not come until the entire kingdom will be converted to heresy. Rava says: What is the verse* from which this statement is derived? It is the verse: *"It is all turned white; he is ritually pure"* (Leviticus 13:13). One is a leper and ritually impure only if he has a leprous mark, however small, but not if his skin is completely leprous. Similarly, the world will be redeemed only when the Jewish people reach their lowest point.[26]

You can see how Shabbetai's followers could take a text like this and say, "Our sacred books tell us that before the Messiah can be received and the world can be redeemed, 'the entire kingdom will be converted to heresy.' Our righteous Messiah is hastening that day, leading the descent into heresy. What a courageous, self-sacrificing act!"

Jewish mystical thought, however, went much further, with concepts like the *sefirot* (divine emanations), the *shevirat ha-kelim* (the shattering of the vessels), the *qelippot* (the demonic, worldly husks), and the act of *tikkun olam* (the repairing of the world), concepts that, to be candid, are highly esoteric. In fact, many readers would find these mystical concepts bizarre, if not incomprehensible. And yet somehow these concepts made their way into popular Jewish thought, to be grasped and understood by the masses.

This stream of mystical teaching, much of which was developed in the previous one hundred years, also emphasized that the final redemption was near and the way had been prepared for the Messiah to complete the work of spiritual restoration. This apparently contributed to the spiritual fervor of the hour. The signs of the times indicated that the end was near. Shabbetai Zevi was the final piece to the puzzle. But when his generation proved unworthy to receive him, he had no choice but to apostasize, thus pioneering the only other path to redemption.

To give you an idea of just how esoteric these concepts are, let me share a summary provided by Gershom Scholem. And as you read this, remember that Scholem intended to clarify and simplify these mystical thoughts, not make them more complex. He wrote:

> The redeemer will not appear at the head of an army to fight the messianic war; he will come "without hands" and without military strength. His real war will be against the demonic powers of the *qelippah* [singular of *qelippot*, husks], and it will be waged essentially on the "inner," spiritual levels of the cosmos, although it might eventually manifest itself on the material level as well. The messiah struggles in the depths of his soul to extract the sparks of the divine light from the embrace of the *qelippah*. Hence also the mystery of his suffering. He will subdue Pharaoh, the great dragon; but he is also himself the true Pharaoh and the "holy serpent." He is locked in combat with the very principle that is his own metaphysical source, subduing it, but at times also subdued by it and falling into its bottomless abyss. His ultimate messianic task consists, apparently, not merely in the defeat and annihilation of the power of evil, but in raising it up to the sphere of holiness, that is, in the *tiqqun* of the *qelippah*.[27]

Were you able to follow that at all? Perhaps this will bring further clarity: "This was a case of apostasy for the sake of redemption. One had to become a Muslim to initiate the process of repairing the order of the universe to the way it had been prior to Creation and the breaking of the vessels that had contained the sparks of God's emanation."[28]

Harris Lenowitz put it like this:

> His conversion to Islam was interpreted as if it echoed the conversion
> of the Jews of Iberia to Catholicism, but in his case it would come to
> be seen not as forgivable in one facing death but as required for the
> messiah, who had to reach the lowest depths of baseness in order to
> gather there the sparks of light that, once raised up, would complete
> the repair of the cosmic order.[29]

You could say that, according to these mystical concepts, the Messiah
had to enter into the depths of darkness in order to rescue the scattered
and hidden light. (Yes, this is an oversimplification, but hopefully it helps
to clarify.) The Messiah, so to say, would go into exile himself in order to
liberate the exiles. (Again, this is an oversimplification.)

As explained by Gad Nassi:

> Shabbetai Tzvi's task as a Muslim was to gather the "holy sparks"
> that were dispersed among the gentiles—a necessary step toward
> redemption. Only the messiah could fulfill this mission, so the expla-
> nation went, and to do so he must hide his identity and act within the
> heart of the enemy. This explanation appeared plausible to those who
> still believed in the messianic mission of Shabbetai Tzvi because it fit
> into the prevalent Lurianic view of kabbalah.[30]

In other words, Zevi's actions fit into the kabbalistic teachings of Rabbi
Isaac Luria, which had become quite popular at that time. (This, again, was
a major thesis of Scholem.) That's why so many initially embraced him as
Messiah, and that's why many of his disciples followed him into Islam.

To give you an analogy (again, oversimplified), it's as if a woman lost a
precious family heirloom, a gorgeous necklace made up of the most expensive jewels. Somehow, the necklace was accidentally thrown out with the
garbage, and in order to find it, someone would have to search through the
garbage dumb, heap by heap, until the necklace was recovered. In order to
find the jewels, you had to get filthy. In order to find the necklace, you had
to enter the garbage dump yourself. And perhaps while there, you would
find other costly items as well. Your abasement meant their liberation.

This is how the Dönmeh continued for so many generations. Shabbetai
Zevi *was* the Messiah, but the work of redemption was still ongoing. The

sparks of light still had to be redeemed. The process of *tikkun* still had to be completed.

A WOULD-BE MESSIAH WHO DIDN'T RISE

But there is something remarkable that I must point out, especially in the context of this book. It is obvious that there was massive spiritual deception surrounding Shabbetai Zevi, both before and after he converted to Islam. The deception was so great that it split the Jewish world in two, representing the largest false Messianic movement in Jewish history. And the deception was so great that even after Zevi became a Muslim, he was still hailed as Messiah by some of his followers, with many of them becoming Muslims as well. *Yet no one ever claimed that Zevi rose from the dead. There were no claims of dozens, let alone hundreds, of his followers seeing him alive from the grave. As we noted earlier, this simply doesn't happen.*

It's true that he did not circulate teachings that he would die (or be killed) and rise from the dead. It's true that this was not part of his Messianic vision. But it's also true that his followers were able to believe the most far-fetched things about him, both while he was alive and then after he died. Yet, to repeat, none of them reported seeing him alive from the dead. No one claimed that his tomb was empty.

And this is in keeping with a common pattern. No matter how much people wish that their loved ones (or their leaders) were still alive, physical death has a certain finality about it, and it's not hard to guard a tomb. The bereaved may feel that their deceased loved ones are somehow "present" with them. They may believe that they can communicate with each other. They may even speak of the deceased appearing to them in visions and dreams. But they do not suffer mass hallucinations that their loved ones or leaders have risen from the dead and are appearing in bodily form.

That's why there are not numerous claims about the resurrection of spiritual leaders of the past. It's a myth that doesn't stick. It's a myth that can easily be refuted. And it's a myth that was never associated with Shabbetai Zevi, which is quite remarkable given the fanatical nature of his followers. If they could concoct the theory that his conversion to Islam was God's plan to bring in the redemption, surely they could concoct a theory that they saw him rise from the dead. Yet he didn't rise, and they never claimed that he did.

A PERVERSE LEGACY

But before we close out this tragic and bizarre chapter in Jewish history, there are two more sub-stories to tell—the first from the 1700s, and the second from our own generation. We will begin with the story of Jacob Frank, a story that is beyond strange and even perverse.

Jerry Rabow writes:

> Although Jacob Frank...was born fifty years after the death of Shabbatai Zevi, he deserves to be regarded as Shabbatai's true successor....
>
> He...extended the paradoxical teachings of Shabbatai Zevi and Baruchya Russo that the coming of the messianic age had transformed sexual prohibitions of the bible into permissions (Shabbatai) and even obligations (Russo). According to Frank, engaging in sexual orgies became the means to purify the soul from its sins. Debauchery became therapy....
>
> Shabbatai Zevi had descended into the Sultan's place. The Donmeh had descended into the world of Islam. Now Jacob Frank planned a similar journey—the Frankists must descend into the world of Christianity.[31]

As Sepehr summarizes, Frank was a heretical rabbi who was born in 1726 to a Polish follower of Shabbetai Zevi, whose reincarnation Frank later claimed to be. (He also claimed to be the reincarnation of the patriarch Jacob.) Sepehr writes, "Frank created a new religion, now referred to as Frankism, which was instigated by the Lurian Kabbalah, and expanded on the 'redemption through sin' philosophy made popular by Zevi."[32]

And how far did Frank and his followers go? Frank claimed the God who created the universe was different than the God of the Bible, whom he viewed as evil, in harmony with similar gnostic beliefs. But that was only the beginning. Frank rejected all the moral laws of the Scriptures, claiming that "the only way to a new society was through the total destruction of the present civilization. He insisted that child sacrifice, rape, incest and the drinking of blood were perfectly acceptable and necessary religious rituals."[33] Not surprisingly, he was quickly excommunicated, along with his followers, by the Polish Jewish authorities, since he not only made himself into a god but also taught the concept of "purification through transgression."[34]

Yes, Frank went so far as to convert to both Catholicism and Islam, plus have sex with his followers (even his own daughter!), "while preaching a doctrine that the best way to imitate God was to cross every boundary, transgress every taboo, and mix (as he claimed God did) the sacred with the profane."[35] Despite all this, at one point in time Frank had as many as fifty thousand followers, including some of "Europe's royalty, nobility, and richest bankers."[36] Did I tell you that the contents of this chapter would be beyond belief?

Frank's life represented the worst possible articulation of "redemption through sin," and in keeping with our illustration above about searching in the garbage dump for an expensive necklace, Frank said this about his philosophy:

> No man can climb a mountain until he has first descended to its foot. Therefore we must descend and be cast down to the bottom rung, for only then can we climb to the infinite. This is the mystic principle of Jacob's Ladder, which I have seen and which is shaped like a V.[37]

And:

> I did not come into this world to lift you up but rather to cast you down to the bottom of the abyss. Further than this it is impossible to descend, nor can one ascend again by virtue of one's own strength, for only the Lord can raise one up from the depths by the power of His hand.[38]

Indeed, wrote Frank, a professing Christian, "This much I tell you: Christ, as you know, said that he had come to redeem the world from the hands of the devil, but I have come to redeem it from all the laws and customs that have ever existed. It is my task to annihilate all this so that the Good God can reveal Himself."[39]

How radically different this is from the Christian message, in which the Messiah descends into the depths of human suffering and sin, taking our guilt on His own shoulders, dying in our place and then rising from the dead, that we might obtain forgiveness of sins and a new life marked by holiness. Through the cross, then, God's laws are not annihilated. Instead, those laws are now written on our hearts, and it becomes our nature to obey rather than disobey. *There is nothing holy about lawless anarchy.*

At this point you might say, "I can't imagine there's yet another chapter to the story of Shabbetai Zevi," and yet there is. It's the story of a contemporary group of the followers of Zevi, a modern version of the Dönmeh. They are not historically descended from these Turkish, crypto-Jewish Muslims, but they share a belief in the Messianic role of Shabbetai Zevi.

Their leader was Dr. Lawrence G. Corey, a poet, author, and teacher who earned a doctorate in Jungian Studies and Comparative Religion. As for his own spiritual journey, he said this:

> First off, there are absolutely no dogmas in anything I practice or teach. As a matter of fact, I really am a great subversive and my belief is in destroying all religious dogmas by not following them. I've converted to Islam, Christianity and Hinduism, and I was born Jewish. I literally and legally converted to those religions—not so much to practice them, but for mystical reasons. It's not so much the religions themselves, but the great teachings of those religions that I'm interested in. The only reasons for the conversions were the same as 17th century Kabbalist Sabbatai Zevi and his 18th century successor Jacob Frank, as well as Ramakrishna, who also practiced all religions to release the holiness—the "sparks of God"—that were trapped within the religious practices. So that was my intention for the multiple conversions.[40]

Corey, then, was given the Hebrew name Yakov Leib HaKohain at birth, while his English name was Lawrence G. Corey. Upon his conversion to Muslim he was given the name Aziz Mehemed Effendi (just like Shabbetai Zevi), while he received the name John-Francis after converting to Catholicism and the name Kali Dass after converting to Hinduism.[41]

According to his official biography page:

> Before his retirement in 1992, he was scholar-in-residence, for over twenty years, at the Center for Transpersonal Studies of Hermosa Beach, California—during which time he was a frequent guest lecturer at the South Bay Kehilla (a covertly Sabbatian Jewish congregation), The Vedanta Society of Southern California, and the Roman Catholic Archdiocese of Los Angeles. He is now the founder and moderator of the Donmeh of the Internet, a world-wide virtual community of over 300 scholars and lay-people dedicated to the teaching, learning and practice of 16th century Lurianic Kabbalah as

reconfigured in the 17th century by the Jewish Messiah and Avatar, Sabbatai Zevi and his prophet and chief exegete, Nathan of Gaza.[42]

Did I say that truth was stranger than fiction?

And yet, in the midst of this madness, there's one more point to make, an important observation about this larger story that we dare not miss. Despite the fervent, even fanatical belief in Shabbetai Zevi, his followers never claimed that he rose from the dead. It is because he did not get out of the grave. Fact.

CHAPTER 5

THE REBBE DIDN'T RISE

JUST THINK. MANY of the followers of Rabbi Schneerson were convinced he would not die, or that if he did die, he would overcome death. After all, they were sure he was the Messiah. Death itself could not stop him. Yet despite their religious fervor and deep faith, to this day none of them claims that he or she witnessed his physical resurrection from the dead. That is highly significant.

Why didn't his followers simply imagine that he rose in front of their eyes? Why didn't they experience mass hallucinations and claim they saw him in the flesh and talked with him face to face? Why didn't their religious fervor override reality?

Some of the Rebbe's followers claim his death was not a real death, that it was merely a test for their earthly eyes. Some claim that if you dug up his grave, his body would not be there. But no one, of course, has ever tried to do such a thing.

Some claim that the Rebbe is spiritually present in their prayer gatherings—as we saw, they even pray to his chair, claiming they can feel him come into the room—while virtually all his followers attest to his ongoing guidance and help (which, to be sure, is commonly claimed for other deceased rabbinic leaders). And there are still others who claim that in some way, the Rebbe is physically alive. *Yet no one claims to have interacted with him physically, face to face, after his alleged resurrection.*

Interestingly, many critics dismiss the New Testament accounts of the resurrection of Jesus, arguing that His followers simply imagined that He rose. "It's what you call cognitive dissonance," they say, "when people believe the opposite of reality because they can't bear to face the facts."

As explained on a psychology website:

The term cognitive dissonance is used to describe the feelings of discomfort that result when your beliefs run counter to your behaviors and/or new information that is presented to you. People tend to seek consistency in their attitudes and perceptions, so when what you hold true is challenged or what you do doesn't jibe with what you think, something must change in order to eliminate or reduce the dissonance (lack of agreement). A classic example of this is "explaining something away."[1]

In other words, the critics allege, Yeshua's followers suffered from some sort of mass delusion, experiencing group hallucinations and imagining that they saw Him in His resurrected state. They were sincere, but they were deceived. Could this be true?

In his 2014 article "Cognitive Dissonance and the Resurrection of Jesus," Kris Komarnitsky wrote:

The conviction that Jesus was raised from the dead is among the earliest of all Christian beliefs. Paul, the earliest known Christian author, reports the resurrection of Jesus was proclaimed by those who came before him in the Jesus movement (1 Cor 15:3–4). How does one account for the rise of this belief if the gospel accounts of a discovered empty tomb and corporeal postmortem appearances of Jesus are legends, as many scholars propose?

The most popular answer to this question is that belief in the resurrection came about due to a post-mortem bereavement hallucination of Jesus by Peter, and possibly others. Another largely overlooked possibility for the rise of the resurrection belief is the extraordinary phenomenon of cognitive dissonance reduction.[2]

Interestingly, Komarnitsky also discusses beliefs about the Lubavitcher Rebbe, writing, "The Lubavitcher example is especially relevant to the study of Christian origins because of how close it comes to Christian beliefs."[3] He even devotes a section of his article to the subject of Shabbetai Zevi, just as we devoted a chapter of this book to this prominent false Messiah. "In conclusion," he writes, "cognitive dissonance reduction is a powerful human phenomenon that seems fully capable of explaining the rise of the resurrection belief among Jesus' followers."[4]

Then why, pray tell, didn't the same thing happen with the Rebbe (or with other revered spiritual leaders)? Why didn't the Rebbe's followers, who so fervently expected him to rise from the dead, also hallucinate his resurrection?[5]

Simon Dein writes:

> [The] Lubavitch are not a group of fanatics....They are sane people trying to reason their way through facts and in the pursuit of understanding....Like many groups whose messianic expectations fail to materialize, resort is made to eschatological hermeneutics to explain and reinforce the messianic ideology....The Rebbe's illness and subsequent death posed cognitive challenges for his followers. They made two predictions that were empirically disconfirmed: that he would recover from his illness and that he would usher in the Redemption. In accordance with cognitive dissonance theory...they appealed to a number of post hoc rationalizations to allay the dissonance.[6]

Yet with all their rationalizations, some of which are quite complex and esoteric, they did not rationalize that they encountered the Rebbe after his physical resurrection from the dead.

WHAT THEY HAVEN'T CLAIMED

I pointed out in the first chapter how deeply devoted the Rebbe's followers were to him. They clung to his every word. They hung on his every teaching. They looked to him as the apex of spirituality, the most righteous human being on the planet, "the ultimate Jew."[7] Some even felt that, on a certain level, he was the embodiment of God in earthly form. They attributed all kinds of supernatural powers to him and to this day feel deeply connected to him, more than twenty-five years after his death. Some even pray to him and say, "May he live forever!" Yet they do not claim that the Rebbe physically rose from the dead and that they saw him in the flesh, resurrected and alive, with their very own eyes. Take a minute to let that sink in.

In 1993, one year before the Rebbe's death, his followers wrote an adoring book about him titled *Wonders and Miracles*. From his birth, we are told, there was something unique about him, as recognized by other significant leaders at that time. His mother was even instructed to wash his hands before he nursed, and so "he never ate in his life without first washing his hands."[8] So, we are told, he followed Jewish tradition right out of the womb! And according to this same book, already at the age of three he showed exceptional fortitude and focus, climbing a tree the other boys were afraid to climb, saying, "They look down, so they are afraid of falling, but I look up so I am not afraid."[9]

All types of miracles are attributed to him in the pages of this volume, including visions, prophetic revelations, supernatural guidance, healings, and the opening of barren wombs. There was seemingly nothing the Rebbe could not do, at least in the eyes of his followers, so great was their veneration for their leader. And yet, to say it once more, even these followers do not claim that the Rebbe physically rose from the dead. They too still await his resurrection.

One of my colleagues visited the main synagogue in Brooklyn and talked to some of the Rebbe's disciples. He asked, "Do you believe the Rebbe is alive?" One replied, "Yes, and he's here right now."

My friend asked, "You mean, you sense his presence?"

"No," the Rebbe's follower replied. "He's right over there," he said, pointing to a far wall.

This man truly believed the Rebbe was actually there, in that synagogue, along with his followers. Yet this man also knew the Rebbe was not bodily present. He was not there physically, in a resurrected state. Instead, he was invisible, yet somehow "there." That's how much this follower believed in the Rebbe, and that's how much many of his other followers believe in him.

Yet, to say it again, *neither this man nor any of the Rebbe's other followers claim to have seen and met with the Rebbe in the flesh after his bodily resurrection.* No group or individual claims to have seen and interacted with Menachem Mendel Schneerson in the flesh since he died in 1994. And that's why they have concocted so many theories about his "concealment." That's also why many of his followers stopped believing he was the Messiah once he died. (A potential Messiah for the last generation, yes; but because the generation wasn't worthy, therefore *not* the Messiah overall.) Even the most fervent believers that the Rebbe is the Messiah, like Rabbi Shmuel Butman, cited in chapter 1, have become much quieter as the years have gone on. In contrast, the followers of Jesus became much bolder and more vocal in the decades following His resurrection, to this very day.

A BELIEF THAT PERSISTS

Professor David Berger wrote that he first realized that belief in the Rebbe as Messiah had survived his death when he saw a full-page ad in the *Jewish Press* four or five days after the Rebbe's passing. It advertised an all-afternoon event that was to take place on the Sunday marking one week since his death:

> The text ended, "With broken hearts we reaffirm our faith that we will at once witness Techiyas Hameisim [the resurrection of the dead] and we will have the Rebbe lead us out of Golus [exile] immediately, and together we continue to proclaim, *Yechi adonenu morenu verabbenu melech hamoshiach leolam voed* [May our Master, Teacher, and Rabbi, the King Messiah, live forever].[10]

Indeed, in the days following the Rebbe's death, one of his eighteen-year-old adherents opined, "All Lubavitchers believe the Rebbe is *Moshiach*. We still believe this. It is not impossible that the Rebbe will be resurrected. The Rebbe has great power now. His spiritual presence is even greater now in all the worlds. People still write to him for a blessing, although, of course, they do not get a reply but there is a response. Things are happening."[11] Another suggested, "I think that the Rebbe will come back to life soon. I think that he will look as he did before he died. He will be dressed in the same clothes. He will be well and will be able to speak again. His body will be like it was before his stroke."[12]

And they believed this to the core of their being. They were not expecting him to die. As Messiah he could not die. He would soon be healed and revealed as Messiah. Any moment now it was going to happen. And then he died. Not to worry! He is about to be raised from the dead and revealed as Messiah. But that never happened.

That's why his followers have so many different explanations and theories: he didn't really die; he remains spiritually alive although concealed physically; his presence is embodied invisibly when they meet; he will still resurrect; he will come again; he was the potential Messiah; he had the soul of the Messiah, which is passed on from leader to leader through the generations; etc. But, to repeat, the Rebbe's followers were originally expecting his resurrection.

Berger wrote:

On the third anniversary of the Rebbe's death, a full-page advertisement appeared in *The New York Times* declaring that "The third of Tammuz is not the Rebbe's yahrzeit [day of death]," a word denoting the anniversary of an ordinary human being's demise. In this case, we were informed, the date marks the time when the Rebbe "was liberated from the limitations of corporeal existence." In the absence of such limitations, he "is accessible to all of us, everywhere, at any time.... Anyone, however great or humble, can turn to him with their deepest prayers. There are no barriers. There is no need to make a pilgrimage or stand on line to receive his blessing....Amazing stories keep pouring in from all corners of the globe. People are experiencing miracles large and small....And all this because of a personal connection to the Rebbe who is with all of us."[13]

This alone puts a great divide between Rabbi Schneerson and Rabbi Yeshua (Jesus). Rabbi Schneerson's followers expected him to rise and he didn't, so many of them deny he really died. Rabbi Yeshua's followers did not expect Him to rise, but He did, and to this day they celebrate both His death and His resurrection. What a contrast!

As Shaul Magid pointed out:

Some liken the notion of the dead Messiah to Christianity, but this is, in my view, an error. Christianity has no dead Messiah—it has a resurrected Messiah. As Paul made clear, Christianity rests on the belief in Jesus's resurrection as an overcoming of death (1 Corinthians 15:1, 15:11; Romans 1:4). Jesus did indeed die on the cross at Calvary, for if not, he could not have been resurrected. It was only by dying that Jesus could overcome death. The claim that Schneerson did not die— or did not die in the way humans die—is something else.[14]

It is something else indeed. And that's why on billboard after billboard, on website after website, and on publication after publication you will see references to "The Rebbe, SHLITA," with the word SHLITA serving as an acronym for the Hebrew phrase "May he live a good, long life, Amen." But in Judaism this acronym is only put after the name of *a living person*. If the person is deceased, a different acronym is used, such as Z'L ("May his memory be a blessing") or ZT'L ("May the memory of the righteous be a blessing"). To the most fervent devotees, the Rebbe never died.

TWO LEADERS, DIFFERENT OUTCOMES

Again, a number of scholars have suggested that charting the development of the Lubavitch movement after the Rebbe's death can help us understand the rise of early Christianity. But the opposite is actually true. The Christian movement was based on the absolute certainty that Jesus rose from the dead and that He was seen by hundreds of eyewitnesses over a period of forty days. In contrast, while still growing and vibrant as a whole, the Lubavitch movement has splintered when it comes to beliefs about the Rebbe, with the majority publicly denying belief that he is the Messiah, and with none of his followers claiming to be eyewitnesses of the physically resurrected Rebbe. *That's because one rabbi rose from the dead, and the other rabbi did not.* This is the gospel truth.

Just imagine what would have happened if the Rebbe actually rose from the dead—literally came out of the grave—and some of his followers saw him in the flesh. Alive again. Walking and talking. No longer sickly and silent. Alive! Can you imagine it? Even if he forbade his followers from taking pictures or recording videos, the effect would have been absolutely electric, especially if he appeared in the flesh to his most trusted disciples. And what if he appeared to them again and again for a period of several weeks, teaching them and instructing them face to face, and then, to add to the miracle, he appeared to as many as five hundred of his followers at one time?

The whole movement would have known for sure that their Rebbe was indeed the Messiah, never to doubt it again. The whole movement would have been galvanized around this fact: "The Rebbe rose! Our top rabbis saw him with their own eyes! The grave really is empty! The Rebbe is Moshiach! Go tell the whole world!" The testimony of these leaders would have sealed the deal, especially if miracles continued to occur on a daily basis in the Rebbe's name.

But that is not what happened. The Rebbe did not rise. And no amount of religious fervor or cognitive dissonance can manufacture a resurrection. Death, indeed, can be quite stubborn.

It would be difficult to imagine a more brilliant man than the Rebbe. Difficult to imagine a more loved man—indeed, revered man—than the Rebbe. Difficult to imagine a man who raised any loftier expectations among his followers. Difficult to imagine a man who inspired as many people after his death as before his death. So, it is no insult to him to say that he failed to rise. It is only a reminder of his humanity.

He died, like the rest of us will, and must await the future resurrection of all the dead, both the righteous and the wicked. Not so Yeshua. He rose on the third day, just as He said He would, never to die again. And as noted by theologian Christopher Rowland, with reference to the first accounts of what happened to Jesus after His death, "The earliest documents stubbornly use the language about resurrection."[15]

In 1998 a *New York Times* headline announced, "Messiah Fervor for Late Rabbi Divides Many Lubavitchers." Yes, "Four years after the death of Rabbi Menachem Mendel Schneerson, the charismatic Hasidic leader, his Lubavitch movement finds itself embarrassed by a persistent group of his followers, mostly in Brooklyn, who stubbornly proclaim the rabbi as the Moshiach, or Messiah, and eagerly await his resurrection."[16]

So, even his most devoted followers did not claim that he physically arose. They were still awaiting his resurrection, four years after his death. Why? *It's because he did not rise.* Not only so, but these fervent believers were considered an embarrassment to the rest of the movement, which had moved on after the Rebbe died. Of particular embarrassment were those who were guilty of deifying the Rebbe, as reported in a March 6, 1997, article: "In a blow to the thousands of Lubavitchers who believe that Rabbi Menachem Mendel Schneerson is the Messiah, the highest national Lubavitch rabbinical body for the first time has condemned the 'deification' of any human being, saying it is 'contrary to the core and foundation of the Jewish faith.'"[17] According to the guidelines set forth, "Conjecture as to the possible identity of Moshiach is not part of the basic tenet of Judaism. The preoccupation with identifying [the deceased] rebbe as Moshiach is clearly contrary to the rebbe's wishes."[18]

Indeed, one of the most respected Lubavitcher leaders, Rabbi Yehuda Krinsky (who was very close to the Rebbe), found it necessary to issue this statement in 1998: "We must pray for the arrival of Messiah, increase our personal goodness and kindness and encourage an awareness and anticipation of our redemption. No one can know with certainty, and clearly should not campaign about, who Moshiach may or may not be."[19] And yet just a few years earlier, in 1989, Rabbi Krinsky said, "'I don't know of anyone around now more suitable to fill the shoes of the Messiah than the Rebbe' (*The Wall Street Journal*, 21 December 1989)."[20]

In stark contrast, four years after the death (and resurrection!) of Yeshua, His core, founding followers were not divided about His rising from the dead. And rather than their faith being an embarrassment to the larger Jesus movement, it provided the foundation. That's because one rabbi rose from the dead, and the other rabbi did not.

Writing in 2011, Simon Dein stated:

> Lubavitcher messianism is a complex phenomenon.... It is impossible to know how many people still privately hold the Rebbe to be *Moshiach* or even consider this as a possibility. Some may indeed hold to this position but are wary of voicing their opinions for fear of criticism, ridicule or ostracization from the wider Lubavitch community.[21]

Had the Rebbe truly risen from the dead, the opposite would be true. The whole movement would be celebrating him as Messiah, and those who denied it would be criticized, ridiculed, or ostracized.

EXAMINING THE HALLUCINATION CLAIMS

At the outset of this book I wrote, "Perhaps by comparing what happened to these two movements—the movement that proclaimed Yeshua as Messiah and the movement that proclaims the Rebbe as Messiah—after the deaths of their leaders, we can shed light on what really happened two thousand years ago." As we continue down this road, comparing these two movements, we can now sharpen the focus of our investigation and ask some probing questions: If the followers of Jesus engaged in cognitive dissonance, causing them to believe that their leader rose from the dead, why didn't the Rebbe's followers do the same? And if the followers of Jesus experienced some type of group hallucination, why didn't the Rebbe's followers experience this?

Professor Michael Licona, a respected scholar of the resurrection of Jesus, pointed to Gary Sibcy, "a licensed clinical psychologist with a Ph.D. in the subject [of group hallucinations] and [who] has a great interest in whether hallucinations can be shared by groups."[22] Dr. Sibcy wrote:

> I have surveyed the professional literature (peer-reviewed journal articles and books) written by psychologists, psychiatrists, and other relevant healthcare professionals during the past two decades and have yet to find a single documented case of a group hallucination,

that is, an event for which more than one person purportedly shared in a visual or other sensory perception where there was clearly no external referent.[23]

How extraordinary. Group hallucinations seem to be as rare as the proverbial dodo bird.

Licona then illustrated just how far-fetched it is to suggest that all the disciples had the same hallucination at the same time, rebutting some of the arguments of Michael Goulder:

> In order to avoid the implausibility of a group hallucination, Goulder would have to suggest that the appearance to the Twelve, which is perhaps the most strongly attested of Jesus' postresurrection appearances, involved each disciple experiencing an individual hallucination at the same time. Although grief, life-threatening stress and fatigue can contribute to an emotional state where a hallucination may result, the reality of such a proposal is initially problematic, since each of the Twelve were males who probably belonged to various age groups and almost certainly possessed different personality types. Far more punishing to such a proposal, however, is the requirement of mind-boggling coincidences. Despite the fact that hallucinations are experienced by roughly 15 percent of the general population and a much larger 50 percent of recently bereaved senior adults (only 14 percent of which are visual in nature), an incredible 100 percent of the Twelve would have experienced a hallucination, of the risen Jesus (rather than something else such as guards), simultaneously, in the same mode (visual) and perhaps in multiple modes. It would be an understatement to claim that such a proposal has only a meager possibility of reflecting what actually occurred. Embracing it would require an extraordinary amount of faith.[24]

As New Testament scholar Craig Keener summarized, "If 'group hallucinations' occur, they are very rare, as Mike Licona's research has shown.... Many cited cases of supposed group hallucinations are misattributed, belonging instead to categories such as optical illusions, legend, or fraud."[25] He then cites an article by J. O'Connell, "Jesus' Resurrection and Collective Hallucinations,"[26] and notes that O'Connell acknowledges that group hallucinations are unusual, but on 75–83 [he] offers six documented cases in the past 425 years (all in spiritually charged contexts), plus several cases that he regards as more questionable, showing that in some religious contexts collective hallucinations have occurred. These cases share common elements: visions are *expected* (84); sometimes stress (84); not everyone present sees the vision (85); those who see it do not all see the same thing (85–86); and the vision does not converse (86). Using these and other criteria, O'Connell distinguishes these cases from Jesus's resurrection appearances (87–105).[27]

As Professor N. T. Wright noted in response to those who claimed that it was common for people to have visions of people after their death, "The more 'normal' these 'visions' were, the less chance there is that anyone, no matter how cognitively dissonant they may have been feeling, would have said what nobody had ever said about such a dead person before, that they had been *raised from* the dead."[28]

The Orthodox Jewish scholar Pinchas Lapide put it like this:

> When this scared, frightened band of the apostles which was just about to throw away everything in order to flee in despair to Galilee; when these peasants, shepherds, and fishermen, who betrayed and denied their master and then failed him miserably, suddenly could be changed overnight into a confident mission society, convinced of salvation and able to work with much more success after Easter than before Easter, then no vision or hallucination is sufficient to explain such a revolutionary transformation.[29]

As we will see in the next chapter, the accounts of the appearances of Jesus after His death do not resemble these group hallucinations in the least. And to say it once more, this attempt to explain away the reality of the resurrection of Jesus completely falls apart when we realize that no such group hallucinations have been reported among the followers of the Rebbe. They *wanted* him to rise. They *expected* him to rise. But he did not rise, which is why they did not see him physically after his death, let alone sit and talk with him or have a meal with him. Yet this is the very thing the first followers of Jesus did for a period of weeks after His resurrection.

Rabbi J. Immanuel Schochet, a philosophy professor and leader in the Lubavitcher movement, was a staunch critic of professor David Berger, whom, you will recall, denounced the idea that the Jewish Messiah could be someone who rose from the dead. Schochet wrote, "Citing Talmudic-Midrashic statements which aver that the redeemer may arise from the dead, these hasidim support their claim that the Rebbe may be resurrected in due time and then fulfill the messianic prophecies."[30] Note carefully those words: "the Rebbe may be resurrected in due time." To this day, more than twenty-five years after his death, the Rebbe has still not risen from the dead.

Writing in 2011, Michael Freund noted, "It might sound fanciful, or even far-fetched, but after all these years, there are still people who believe that [Shabbetai Zevi, the false Messiah who converted to Islam and died in 1676] will yet return to redeem Israel."[31] And yet here, in the midst of such deep deception, Zevi's followers didn't claim that he rose from the dead and that they witnessed it with their own eyes. There is a reason for this!

The bottom line, then, is this: Despite fervent (and at times, fanatical) belief in the Rebbe, his followers have not claimed to have seen him alive and in the flesh. And ultimately, public belief that the Rebbe is Messiah has faded (or become muted). That's because the Lubavitcher Rebbe, for all his greatness and brilliance and devotion, did not rise from the dead. If God had raised him from the grave, the discussion would be totally different. It is hard to argue with resurrection.

CHAPTER 6

THE RABBI WHO REALLY ROSE

IN A SCHOLARLY article published in 2001, New Testament scholar Joel Marcus noted:

> The recent history of the modern Chabad (Lubavitcher) movement of Hasidic Judaism provides insight into the development of early Christianity. In both movements successful eschatological prophecies have increased belief in the leader's authority, and there is a mixture of "already" and "not yet" elements. Similar genres of literature are used to spread the good news (e.g. miracle catenae and collections of originally independent sayings). Both leaders tacitly accepted the messianic faith of their followers but were reticent about acclaiming their messiahship directly. The cataclysm of the Messiah's death has led to belief in his continued existence and even resurrection.[1]

As we have seen, the parallels between these two movements are real and obvious. And while it's still too early to predict what will happen to the Lubavitch movement in the years ahead, it has survived the Rebbe's death and continues to grow, even dramatically. In that sense it parallels the early Messianic Jewish movement, which became known as Christianity in the centuries that followed. But as we have also seen, there is a massive difference between these two movements, and it boils down to one word: resurrection.[2] Only one of these potential Messiahs rose again.

AN UNEXPECTED MESSIAH

Matthew Novenson, a scholar in Christian origins, noted that "James Charlesworth argues that, although early Christian writers inherit the concept 'messiah' from their Jewish heritage, they decisively 'remint' it to correspond to the life, death, and resurrection of Jesus. He concludes, 'Suffice it to be stated now that Jewish messianology does not flow majestically into Christian christology.'"[3]

Put simply, Charlesworth was saying that Jesus did not fit conveniently into an already existing Jewish template. He did not meet the most common expectations about the role of the Messiah, as varied as they may have been in the first century of this era. In short, despite some arguments to the contrary, it seems that virtually no one was expecting a crucified Messiah. No one was expecting the Savior of Israel (and the world) to die an ignominious, criminal's death. *Had Jesus not risen from the dead, despite the many miracles He had performed and despite His personal charisma, His Messianic movement would have ended two thousand years ago.* The resurrection changed everything.

Looking at this through a wider lens, it's not surprising that biographies about religious leaders in past generations celebrate their accomplishments, often presenting them in saintlike, even supernatural terms. They were bigger than life and better than other humans. They were transcendent. They were ultra-spiritual. They were unique.

In stark contrast, the New Testament writings talk candidly about the failures of their early leaders, the founders of the church. These writings tell us that the first followers of Jesus, the men whose lives and testimonies laid the foundation for this movement, were full of doubt and fear, often misunderstanding Yeshua's words and intentions while He was alive, even though they were with Him day and night for a period of several years.

Matthew, Mark, and Luke all record how these Jewish men reacted when Jesus began to talk about His impending suffering and death:

> And he began to teach them that the Son of Man must suffer many things and be rejected by the elders and the chief priests and the scribes and be killed, and after three days rise again. And he said this plainly. And Peter took him aside and began to rebuke him. But turning and seeing his disciples, he rebuked Peter and said, "Get behind me, Satan! For you are not setting your mind on the things of God, but on the things of man."
>
> —MARK 8:31–33

Peter, who became one of the key leaders of the movement, could not possibly believe that Yeshua, the Messiah, would suffer a fate like this. It was so preposterous to him that he actually *rebuked* his Master. In turn, Yeshua rebuked him, stating that Peter was seeing things through a satanic, worldly perspective rather than a divine, heavenly perspective. What a serious gaffe!

And how did Mark get this information? How did he learn about Peter's embarrassing error?

Some scholars claim that the author of Matthew was an eyewitness, so he was there when this happened, and he recorded it in his Gospel. (Others believe that the author of Matthew relied on eyewitness testimony.) And we know that Luke did extensive research of the earliest witnesses, so he would have learned this from oral or written sources before recording the event in his Gospel. But what was Mark's source? This is an important question because many scholars believe that Mark's Gospel was the first one written, and to our knowledge, he was not there when this event took place. Well, according to traditional information, it was Peter who gave the information to Mark.[4] Yes, *Peter*, the one who so royally put his foot into his own mouth and stepped so far out of line. He was the one who shared this information with Mark.

But Peter was not alone in his unbelief and spiritual dullness. After Jesus cleansed the temple, He was challenged by the local leadership:

> The Jewish leaders demanded, "What are you doing? If God gave you authority to do this, show us a miraculous sign to prove it."
>
> "All right," Jesus replied. "Destroy this temple, and in three days I will raise it up."
>
> "What!" they exclaimed. "It has taken forty-six years to build this Temple, and you can rebuild it in three days?" But when Jesus said "this temple," he meant his own body. After he was raised from the dead, his disciples remembered he had said this, and they believed both the Scriptures and what Jesus had said.
>
> —JOHN 2:18–22, NLT

Do you see that? The theme of bodily resurrection was on Jesus' lips from early in His public ministry, and right off the bat it was misunderstood, especially when He expressed Himself in semi-mystical terms, speaking of "this temple"—which, to the Jewish leaders, would have suggested *the* temple—but really meaning His physical body. It was only after He rose that His disciples understood and believed. And note carefully what is written: "They believed both the Scriptures and what Jesus had said." Yes, the Jewish Scriptures actually predicted the Messiah's rejection, violent death, and resurrection, and after Yeshua rose from the dead, the light went on and everything became clear. It was written there all the time!

HIS UNSUSPECTING FOLLOWERS

We'll explore what is actually written in these Scriptures in the next chapter, but first let's look again at how dense the first disciples were, as recorded in the Gospels. They knew that Yeshua was the promised Messiah—it was undeniable to them that He was *the man*—but His suffering and death completely threw them. They were expecting a very different outcome.

So, after reading about Peter rebuking Jesus in Mark 8, in the very next chapter of Mark's Gospel we read that Jesus took His three closest followers, Peter, Jacob (James),[5] and John, up onto a mountain to pray. And as they prayed, He was transfigured, His face shining with the glory of God. Moses and Elijah appeared and spoke with Him, the cloud of God's presence came, and the Father spoke from the cloud. It was an absolutely glorious and extraordinary experience, a clear manifestation of the Messiah's supernatural stature.

Yet Mark records, "And as they were coming down the mountain, he charged them to tell no one what they had seen, until the Son of Man had risen from the dead. So they kept the matter to themselves, questioning what this rising from the dead might mean" (Mark 9:9–10; Jesus often referred to Himself as the Son of Man, a Messianic title.)[6] What, they wondered, does He mean by "rising from the dead"? And note that this is recorded in Mark 9, which means the disciples had already heard Jesus talk about His death and resurrection (as recorded in Mark 8), but they still had no idea what He meant.

Then in this very same chapter in Mark we read, "They went on from there and passed through Galilee. And [Jesus] did not want anyone to know, for he was teaching his disciples, saying to them, 'The Son of Man is going to be delivered into the hands of men, and they will kill him. And when he is killed, after three days he will rise.' But they did not understand the saying, and were afraid to ask him" (Mark 9:30–32).

They still could not figure out what He was talking about, even though He was now repeating the same information over and again: "I'm going to be killed, but after three days, I will rise from the dead." They just didn't get it.

Once more, and almost unbelievably, in the very next chapter of Mark we read:

> And they were on the road, going up to Jerusalem, and Jesus was walking ahead of them. And they were amazed, and those who followed were afraid. And taking the twelve again, he began to tell them what was to happen to him, saying, "See, we are going up to Jerusalem, and the Son of Man will be delivered over to the chief priests and the scribes, and they will condemn him to death and deliver him over to the Gentiles. And they will mock him and spit on him, and flog him and kill him. And after three days he will rise."
>
> —MARK 10:32–34

And Luke adds this: "But they understood none of these things. This saying was hidden from them, and they did not grasp what was said" (Luke 18:34). Their minds were still dull. They simply did not understand, which, when you think of it, is really quite odd.

After all, if I told you repeatedly, "I'm going to be killed, but on the third day I will rise from the dead," you would easily understand my words. You might think I was crazy. You might think I had a death wish and would do your best to prevent me from being killed. But the words themselves would not be that mysterious: "I'm going to be killed, and I'm going to rise again." All the more would this be clear if I stated exactly *when* I would rise again: on the third day.

Of course, if I was the leader of some religious cult, my followers might actually believe me. "Yes, great leader, we believe you will rise!" And as we have seen, many of the followers of the Lubavitcher Rebbe fervently believed he would rise. But it was quite the opposite with the followers of Yeshua. They had no template in which the Messiah, the King of the Jews, the mighty Deliverer, would die a violent criminal's death, let alone rise from the dead. The thing was hidden from their eyes.[7]

This is hardly the way you write the stories of your founding leaders. You praise them rather than embarrass them. But it gets worse.

The night that Jesus was betrayed, all His disciples—meaning His closest followers, His core group—got up and ran, despite His telling them moments before exactly what would happen. (See Matthew 26:20–56.) At

77

this very late juncture, immediately before His crucifixion, they still didn't get it. And what happened after He died, even after there were reports of His resurrection? They were in great despair, their hopes dashed to pieces. As expressed at that time by two of His early followers (although not in the innermost circle), they thought Jesus of Nazareth was

> a man who was a prophet mighty in deed and word before God and all the people, and...our chief priests and rulers delivered him up to be condemned to death, and crucified him. But we had hoped that he was the one to redeem Israel. Yes, and besides all this, it is now the third day since these things happened. Moreover, some women of our company amazed us. They were at the tomb early in the morning, and when they did not find his body, they came back saying that they had even seen a vision of angels, who said that he was alive. Some of those who were with us went to the tomb and found it just as the women had said, but him they did not see.
>
> —LUKE 24:19–24

To paraphrase, "We had hoped He was the one to redeem Israel, but then He was killed. We must have been wrong! We admit that things are a bit confusing now, with reports that He rose from the dead. But to tell the truth, we're pretty bummed."

And what about the closest disciples, the first eleven?[8] John records that on the very night that these resurrection reports were circulating—meaning the Sunday of the resurrection—and even after some of these men had seen that Yeshua's tomb was indeed empty, "the disciples were meeting behind locked doors because they were afraid of the Jewish leaders. Suddenly, Jesus was standing there among them! 'Peace be with you,' he said" (John 20:19, NLT).

What a contrast between their attitudes and the attitudes of the followers of the Rebbe, who so fervently expected him to rise. For these men, the death of Jesus meant it was all over. So much for His being the Messiah! *But then He rose from the dead, and everything changed. Everything!*

One of those eleven, however, was not there. His name was Thomas, and he refused to believe what the other ten (along with the women who had seen Jesus) said. He exclaimed, "Unless I see in his hands the mark of the nails, and place my finger into the mark of the nails, and place my hand into his side, I will never believe" (John 20:25). This was the level of skepticism, doubt, and hopelessness that had to be overcome.

The narrative continues:

> Eight days later, his disciples were inside again, and Thomas was with them. Although the doors were locked, Jesus came and stood among them and said, "Peace be with you." Then he said to Thomas, "Put your finger here, and see my hands; and put out your hand, and place it in my side. Do not disbelieve, but believe." Thomas answered him, "My Lord and my God!" Jesus said to him, "Have you believed because you have seen me? Blessed are those who have not seen and yet have believed."
>
> —JOHN 20:26–29

This actually went on for a period of several weeks—almost six full weeks, to be exact—until there was no more room for doubt. Jesus the Messiah rose from the dead![9] His followers didn't expect it, but it happened. They had lost all hope when He died, but His resurrection not only restored their hopes; it gave them a confidence they never had before, with most of them subsequently dying for their faith.

According to reliable tradition, Peter, the one who rebuked Yeshua for saying He was going to be crucified, was himself crucified for his testimony. And tradition tells us that once-doubting Thomas took the message of Jesus to India, dying as a martyr there. (According to tradition, he was either stoned to death or speared to death.)[10] These doubting, fearful, depressed, and hopeless disciples became the nucleus of a world-changing, faith-filled, fearless, and victorious army. And as they presented the message of their crucified and risen Messiah, He made Himself real to the hearers in many different ways, as He continues to do to this very moment.

Professor N. T. Wright paints an excellent picture of just how deeply these disciples had adjusted their lives to the apparent fact that their leader, Jesus, had died and was no more. Their hopes were dashed to pieces, only to be shockingly brought back to life when Jesus arose from the grave. This led to massive modifications in their outlook and actions, as Wright explains:

> The reason the early Christians gave for these modifications was not that they had received a fresh private message which had made them realize their mistake, but that something had *happened*, something

which was not at all what they expected or hoped for, something around which they had to reconstruct their lives and in relation to which they had to redirect their energies. They were not refusing to come to terms with the fact that they had been wrong all along. On the contrary, they were indeed coming to terms with, and reordering their lives around, dramatic and irrefutable evidence that they had been wrong. They were not so much like confused Japanese citizens refusing to reconcile themselves to the events of 1945, and continuing to cling to their belief that they "must have" won the war, and that all evidence to the contrary was cunning enemy propaganda. They were more like people who, discovering that they had been fighting for the wrong side, at once changed their allegiance and applied for citizenship in the victorious country. They were more like Herod the Great, who backed Mark Antony in the Roman civil war, and then, after Augustus had won, went at once and offered to back him with the same energy. They were like someone who had been deeply asleep, and would have preferred to stay that way, but who, on hearing the alarm clock, sprang out of bed at once and got on with the business of the day.[11]

When Yeshua arose, that alarm clock started ringing, causing those disciples to spring out of bed and get on with the business of the day.

A WHOLE NEW TEMPLATE

In the year 2000, professor Israel Knohl, a respected Israeli biblical scholar, authored a controversial book, claiming that there were hints of a suffering-rising Messiah in Jewish writings (the Dead Sea scrolls) before the time of Jesus. He wrote:

I propose to show that Jesus really did regard himself as the Messiah and truly expected the Messiah to be rejected, killed, and resurrected after three days, for this is precisely what was believed to have happened to a messianic leader who had lived one generation before Jesus....Thus, for the first time in the history of Judaism, a conception emerged of "catastrophic" messianism in which the humiliation, rejection, and death of the Messiah were regarded as an inseparable part of the redemptive process. The hero of our book, this slain Messiah, is the missing link in our understanding of the way Christianity emerged from Judaism.[12]

As stated, this was a highly controversial thesis, in particular when it came to interpreting the texts he was referencing, texts that allegedly spoke of the death of a Messianic figure and his resurrection on the third day. In Knohl's words, "This is precisely what was believed to have happened to a messianic leader who had lived one generation before Jesus."

The problem, however, is that outside of these ancient texts, whose interpretation remains highly disputed, there are no other records of this purported Messianic leader who allegedly rose from the dead. Nowhere is there a mention of his death and his supposed resurrection. Not a word.

We can conclude, then, that whoever this man was (if Knohl is rightly reading the texts) and whatever his followers thought, he never rose from the grave. That's why we're largely in the dark in terms of his identity.

Not so with Jesus of Nazareth. He is the best-known Jew in history and the most famous rabbi of all time. And He has brought multiplied hundreds of millions of Gentiles into the worship of the God of Israel. No one else compares with Him.

The Jewish New Testament scholar Paula Fredriksen offered her thoughts on the disciples' claims that Jesus rose from the dead. She wrote:

> Why his followers had this experience is an interesting question. After all, many other Jews in this period followed other charismatic, prophetic figures (John the Baptizer comes readily to mind); but none of their movements outlived the death of their founder. Why was this group different?
>
> These postmortem visitations tell us something about Jesus and something about his followers, and the two are linked. "The resurrection" gives us a measure of the degree to which Jesus of Nazareth had successfully forged his followers into a group intensely, indeed singularly, committed to himself and to his prophecy of the coming Kingdom. His death—unexpected, traumatic, bewildering—threw the whole journey to Jerusalem into sudden reverse, inflicting on them a grinding cognitive dissonance: If Jesus were dead, how could his prophecy be true? If Jesus' prophecy were true, how could he be dead? Resurrection both resolved this dissonance, and reinforced the prophecy. If Jesus were raised, then the Kingdom truly must be at hand.[13]

Writing less than twenty-five years after the Messiah's resurrection, Paul put it like this. (And remember that Paul, also called Saul, was a devout and zealous Jew who had been a rabid persecutor of this Jewish Jesus movement until the risen Messiah appeared to him personally and literally turned his world upside down.) He wrote:

> For I also passed on to you first of all what I also received—that Messiah died for our sins according to the Scriptures, that He was buried, that He was raised on the third day according to the Scriptures, and that He appeared to Kefa, then to the Twelve. Then He appeared to over five hundred brothers and sisters at one time—most of them are still alive, though some have died. Then He appeared to Jacob, then to all the emissaries, and last of all, as to one untimely born, He also appeared to me.
>
> —1 CORINTHIANS 15:3–8, TLV

This is absolutely remarkable. The risen Messiah did not simply appear to a select few. He appeared to all His first followers repeatedly, as Acts records: "He presented himself alive to them after his suffering by many proofs, appearing to them during forty days and speaking about the kingdom of God" (Acts 1:3). And then, somewhere during this forty-day period, He presented Himself to *more than five hundred at one time*. Not only so, but Scripture records that He ascended to heaven in the presence of some of these very same men (Acts 1:6–11).

No wonder they then preached with such boldness. No wonder those who fled for their lives when Jesus was betrayed now joyfully gave their lives to stand for Him. No wonder they were fearless in the face of intimidation and threats and beatings and persecution and imprisonments and even death. Yeshua rose from the dead, and they saw it with their own eyes. Their fear turned to faith, and their cowardice turned to courage. He was alive, and they could never doubt it again.

What's more, Jesus told them that when He ascended to heaven, He would send the Holy Spirit down upon them and that, empowered by the Spirit, they would do the same works that He did. (See Luke 24:49, John 14:12, and Acts 1:8.) And they did! They too saw the same miracles take place. They too saw blind eyes open. They too saw lame people walk. They too saw the dead raised—all through the merit of (and in the name of) Yeshua, the King of the Jews, the Messiah of Israel, and the Savior of the world.

MIRACLES UPON MIRACLES

What's even more, these same miracles are taking place *to this very day* through prayer that is offered in Jesus' name. He really is alive! And it's not just the "special people" who can work these miracles. It's not just the charismatic, superstar leaders who have seen such remarkable answers to prayer. To the contrary, it's often through the most common, ordinary people that these miracles take place. That's because the power is in the name of Yeshua the risen Messiah, not the power of His followers.

This too is in contrast with reported miracles performed through the Rebbe, which are certainly many. The hasid must somehow connect to the Rebbe, perhaps by going to the Rebbe's grave site or by presenting a question in the form of a letter, which is then placed at random into one of the Rebbe's many writings, with the result being that the page on which the letter is placed provides the answer to the question. But the hasid himself cannot perform similar miracles.

It is the opposite with the followers of Yeshua. Any of them, at any time, and in any place, through His merit and in His name, can see God's miraculous power demonstrated. This should certainly get our attention.

Randy Clark, a Christian leader who often teaches on the subject of divine healing, wrote a doctoral dissertation titled "A Study of the Effects of Christian Prayer on Pain or Mobility Restrictions From Surgeries Involving Implanted Materials." In his mind, a study like this could provide indisputable evidence about God's healing power—through the name of Jesus—since you were dealing with something tangible like a metal implant. Did the implant disappear after prayer? Did the implant remain intact but the condition heal so the implant was no longer necessary? This is what he documented in his thesis.

Randy also takes teams with him to pray for the sick, teaching them what the Scriptures say and then giving them some simple guidelines for prayer. And remember, these are ordinary Christians he takes along with him, not simply the cream of the crop and the elite.

He recounts what happened on one of his trips to Brazil, when at the end of a church meeting he called his team forward and asked them to stand in the front, ready to pray for anyone needing a healing. For many of them this would be the first time they had done such a thing. He writes:

As the people were coming forward, one of the team members—
we'll call him Sam—became very nervous. He had never prayed for
anyone in his life. In fact, he had joined the team to gain the experience of praying for the sick. His wife had been with us on other
trips, and she had returned home telling him of all the healings she
witnessed.

A recovering alcoholic, he had wanted to come for three years,
but each year, shortly before the trip, he would fall off the wagon.
Ashamed, he would not go on the trip. This year he had maintained
his sobriety.

As the people were coming forward, he prayed this prayer: "God,
You know I have never prayed for anyone, I don't know what I am
doing, so please bring me an easy one—a headache or a bellyache."

Sam looked out into the crowd and saw a young man in a wheelchair coming toward him. He prayed, "No, Lord, not that! An easy
one, a headache or a bellyache." He looked away, not wanting to
make eye contact with the young man. But moments later, the young
man tugged on his trousers.[14]

Can you imagine how Sam felt? He had never done anything like this
before, and the first person who wanted prayer was a crippled man in a
wheelchair! Randy continues, "Though Sam had never prayed for anyone,
all the team members had been given instruction through videos and books
on how to pray for the sick. He interviewed the paraplegic and found out he
was a twenty-five-year-old police officer. He had been shot in the stomach,
and the bullet had severed his spinal cord."[15]

Of all things! Sam was about to pray for a man with a severed spinal
cord. Good luck with that!

But there's more:

Sam's flight had been canceled in Atlanta, and he had been up all
night in the airport and then flew to Saõ Paulo and on to Manaus. He
had not slept in almost forty-eight hours. As he was praying for the
paraplegic, he was growing sleepy. He interviewed him again to see
if anything was happening in response to his prayer. The paraplegic
told him, "No, nothing is happening." Sam, who had only a little
faith to start with, now realized he had no faith.

Then he remembered a statement I had written in the *Ministry
Team Training Manual*: "I don't expect you to heal anyone, only God

can heal, but I do expect you to love the people, and to treat them with respect." He thought to himself, *I haven't prayed very long for this young man; if I stop now, he will feel like he isn't valued. Even though I don't have faith for him to be healed, I can take the time to pray for him so he will feel valued and loved.*

As the night was getting later, Sam was becoming sleepier. He said, "My head was now resting on the paraplegic's shoulder, and just before I started to snore, the young man jumped out of the wheelchair, grabbed me, put his face on my shoulder, and wet my shirt with his tears. Then he walked off, pushing the wheelchair."...The next day we videoed the young man's testimony.[16]

Yes, Jesus really rose from the dead, and He continues to perform miracles to this day. Book after book has been written on the subject, recounting these extraordinary acts, often with detailed documentation.[17] In fact, not only did Randy Clark document such miracles in his dissertation, but other scientific studies have provided similar documentation, including healing of the blind and deaf after prayer.[18]

For example, in the April 2019 edition of the peer-reviewed journal *Complementary Therapies in Medicine*, Clarissa Romez, David Zaritzky, and Joshua W. Brown wrote an article titled, "Case Report of Gastroparesis Healing: Sixteen Years of a Chronic Syndrome Resolved After Proximal Intercessory Prayer." According to the abstract:

A male infant at two weeks of age was hospitalized vomiting forcefully. He had a pyloromyotomy. He did not improve with medical therapy. The diagnosis of gastroparesis was made after a nuclear medicine gastric emptying study and intestinal manometry. He required a gastrostomy tube (g-tube) and a jejunostomy tube (j-tube) for feeding. At 11 months of age, the j-tube was converted into a feeding jejunostomy with Roux-en-Y limb. For 16 years he was completely dependent on j-tube feeding. In November 2011, he experienced proximal-intercessory-prayer (PIP) at a church and felt an electric shock starting from his shoulder and going through his stomach. After the prayer experience, he was unexpectedly able to tolerate oral feedings. The g- and j-tube were removed four months later and he did not require any further special treatments for his condition as all symptoms had resolved. Over seven years later, he has been free from symptoms. This article investigates a case of PIP as an alternative intervention for resolving severe idiopathic gastroparesis when maximal medical management is not effective.[19]

He is risen, indeed!

Randy Clark shares another amazing story of God's healing power through Jesus the Messiah, again through a common, average believer. It involved a man who had been totally blind for fifty years: "His eyes were white from about an eighth of an inch thickness of scar tissue that covered the entire pupil and cornea. Instead of Hispanic brown eyes, his were milky white. He was totally blind, having not seen a thing for fifty years," and he went blind as "a five-year-old boy... [when a] man had accidently spilled muriatic acid in his eyes."[20]

The man came for prayer in one of Randy's meetings, and a woman prayed for his healing, but nothing happened. So she prayed again and again and again—for four hours, even though the healing team members had been instructed not to stay too long with any one person, since there were about six thousand people in the meeting. But she felt a strong impression in her heart to keep on praying for him, so she did.

Three days later Randy received a call from the man's pastor, who said, "This man could not see anything when the night was over. Neither could he see anything the next day and night, but on the third morning, though he went to bed totally blind, he woke up with brand-new eyes and clear vision."[21] The doctors at the hospital, where his records were kept and where his story was well known, were absolutely astonished, and they kept asking him, "Tell us again, how is it you see?"

And to repeat: These are just two examples of literally *millions* of miracles of healing and deliverance experienced by ordinary people after other ordinary followers of Jesus prayed for them in His name. *There are even documented accounts of people being raised from the dead*—and I mean in this very century.

Perhaps the most remarkable story took place in Nigeria, where a man who had been dead for more than two days was raised from the dead and healed. The man, who was a pastor, was killed in a car accident, and rigor mortis had set in. So he "was embalmed, but not the way it is done in America with the removal of organs. They injected chemicals into the body to slow down decay, since there was no refrigeration."[22]

Everyone thought the man's wife was crazy when she insisted on continuing to pray for him, but she could not be stopped, demanding that his body be taken from the local morgue and brought to a meeting where a German evangelist was speaking. The whole story could make an incredible movie, but the bottom line is that this woman managed to get her husband's corpse to the meeting, and he was raised from the dead that day. There's even a video of the first moments after he came back to life. I kid you not.

You might say, "I still have a hard time believing this. After all, it took place all the way over in Nigeria. Why don't miracles like this happen in America?"

Well, they do, sometimes right in a hospital and witnessed by doctors and nurses. Here's one well-known example involving a man named Jeff Markin, who collapsed from a massive heart attack after driving himself to the emergency room of a Florida hospital on October 20, 2006. The emergency medical team went to work immediately on Mr. Markin, along with the supervising cardiologist, Dr. Chauncey Crandall, trying to shock his heart back to life. But after working feverishly for forty minutes—including "using defibrillator pads more than a dozen times"[23]—they called the time of death and walked away from Markin's corpse.

Normally that would have been the end of it. But as Dr. Crandall "was walking away after filling out some paperwork he sensed the Holy Spirit's voice saying that he should pray for the now officially dead heart attack victim."[24] So Dr. Crandall obeyed the Spirit's prompting, even though Markin's body was getting readied for the morgue, persuading another doctor to try shocking Markin's heart one more time, but only over this other doctor's protests. Really now, the man is clearly dead! But this time, Markin's heart revived with "a perfect heartbeat,"[25] and he began to breathe again.

And what happened to Jeff Markin's brain after being dead for forty minutes? How did the lack of oxygen affect him? Not only was Markin's brain perfectly normal after being dead for so long, but he became a follower of Jesus as a result of this miracle, having been a nonbeliever before. The Messiah is still raising the dead to this day.

Professor Craig Keener, one of the most respected New Testament scholars in the world today and a man of tremendous learning, has estimated that at least 200 million people have witnessed a miracle in Jesus' name—and he means people alive today.[26] Some of these are miracles occurring in nature, some physical healings, some miraculous prophecies. The list is almost endless and incredibly impressive.

Some of the most amazing miracles involve the Muslim world, where, on a regular basis, Muslims are having visions of Jesus and as a result, converting to Christianity. (Whole books have been written on this as well, and even those books barely scratch the surface.[27]) In other cases these Muslims have a dream about someone they have never met, but they are told in the dream that this person will bring them a message that will change their life. Then shortly after having the dream, for the first time in their life they meet the person they saw in the dream, and it just so happens that the person is a Christian missionary.

Things like this are happening all the time in the Muslim world, to the point that millions of Muslims are now coming to faith in Jesus. To say it again, He is risen!

As Reza Safa explains:

> One of the ways that God has chosen to communicate the message of the gospel to the Iranian people is through dreams and visions. This is the fulfillment of Isaiah's declaration:
>
> *So shall He sprinkle many nations.*
> *Kings shall shut their mouths at Him;*
> *For what had not been told them they shall see,*
> *And what they had not heard they shall consider.*
> —ISAIAH 52:15, NKJV
>
> A great majority of the thousands of converts who are coming to Christ in Iran have had a dream or vision from the Lord. At times the Lord Jesus Himself has appeared to them and spoken with them. Antioch Ministries in San Jose, California, which reports fifty thousand Iranian Muslim conversions through its satellite TV ministry begun in 2002, reports: "Almost 50 percent of those who call the office have had a dream about Jesus."[28]

We have a team from our ministry school serving in northern Iraq, doing an amazing work among the local communities as well as the refugees who have poured in from Syria. The wife of one of our graduates befriended a young Muslim woman who was deaf in one ear. She asked if she could pray for her healing in the name of Jesus. The young woman responded, "I love Jesus!" She then shared her story with our team member.

As a Muslim, this woman had believed that Jesus was a prophet and even the Messiah, but she did not believe He was the Son of God, she did not believe He was crucified, and of course, she did not believe He rose from the dead. She and a number of other women had been badly burned in a fire, and they were hospitalized together in the same location.

One by one the other women died of their injuries, and she sensed that she was next. Then she had a vision in which a man whom she knew was Jesus washed her body in a river. When the vision ended, she was healed of her burns. Yes, this really happened!

But she had little idea of who Jesus really was until our team member shared the full story with her, also praying for her hearing to be restored. She was instantly healed and gave her life to Yeshua, the living Savior, a light to the Gentiles and the Messiah of Israel.

At the end of his Gospel account John wrote, "There are also many other things that Yeshua did. If all of them were to be written one by one, I suppose that not even the world itself will have room for the books being written!" (John 21:25, TLV).

He wrote these words more than 1,900 years ago. How much more would this be the case today!

The one and true Messiah has risen from the dead. That is undeniable. But His death was not an interruption in His mission. Instead, it was an integral, absolutely central part of His mission. When you understand this, you understand it all.

CHAPTER 7

REDISCOVERING ISRAEL'S SUFFERING AND RISING MESSIAH

A S WE NOTED in chapter 1, on June 1, 1996, in direct response to claims that the Lubavitcher Rebbe—now deceased for two years—was the Messiah, the Rabbinical Council of America (RCA) issued this statement: "In light of disturbing developments which have recently arisen in the Jewish community, the Rabbinical Council of America in convention assembled declares that there is not and has never been a place in Judaism for the belief that Mashiach Ben David [Messiah son of David] will begin his Messianic Mission only to experience death, burial, and resurrection before completing it."[1]

Thirteen years later, in 2009, the RCA went one step further, banning any rabbis who held to such a belief.[2] Considering that the RCA is one of the world's largest organizations of Orthodox rabbis, this is highly significant.[3]

But what if this belief in a dying and rising Messiah was actually biblical? And what if rather than the Messiah's death interrupting his mission, his death was an essential part of that mission? What if the Scriptures *required* the Messiah to die on behalf of the sins of the world, only to be raised from the dead, vindicated by God? And what if part of the Messiah's mission included him being rejected by his own Jewish people, then becoming a light to the nations of the world, only to be accepted by his people at the end of the age? What if all of that was actually written in the Tanakh, the Hebrew Scriptures?

Before we look to the Scriptures, let me share a famous Jewish story with you, one used to argue that Jesus was not the Messiah. It goes like this. A rabbi was on a train one day when he was approached by a Jewish

91

follower of Jesus, who sat down with the rabbi and tried to convince him that Jesus was the Messiah.

The rabbi would have none of it, explaining that he took the word of the Jewish leaders who lived in Jesus' day. "If they didn't believe in him, why should I? They were far more learned than I am, and yet they saw He could not be the Messiah."

The Jewish Christian replied, "But the greatest rabbi of his era, Rabbi Akiva, who died one hundred years after Jesus, believed that Bar Kochba, one of his contemporaries, was the Messiah! So if Rabbi Akiva could be wrong, maybe the other ancient rabbis were wrong."

The rabbi replied, "Well, maybe Bar Kochba *was* the Messiah!"

The believer answered, "But Bar Kochba was killed by the Romans in AD 135! He obviously couldn't be the Messiah."

The rabbi smiled and said, "Aha!"

That's the end of the story, but it's obviously quite flawed, since any true follower of Jesus would have had an immediate answer to the rabbi's "Aha!" It's true, he or she would say, that Bar Kochba was killed by the Romans and has been dead ever since. But Jesus was killed by the Romans and rose from the dead. There's quite a difference! One is dead; the other is very much alive. The comparison does not hold. Aha, indeed!

Not only so, but Bar Kochba was a warring general whose goal was to kill as many Roman soldiers as possible, thereby defeating the Roman Empire and liberating his Jewish people. His goal for himself was anything but death. He wanted to kill the enemy and live.

In stark contrast, Yeshua's goal *was* to die, to be the Good Shepherd who laid down His life for the sheep, who gave Himself to pay the ransom for our souls and to take our sins away by the power of His righteous life. That's why He said that no one took His life from Him; rather, He laid it down of His accord and then took it back up again (John 10:11–18).

And all this is found right within the pages of the Jewish Scriptures. The suffering, rising, and dying Messiah is not a concept that is alien to the biblical Jewish faith. To the contrary, it is found right at the heart of that faith. The biblical Messiah must die and rise to complete his mission. Without his atoning death, the mission would remain incomplete.

As expressed by the respected rabbinic scholar Daniel Boyarin, "The notion of the humiliated and suffering Messiah was not at all alien within

Judaism before Jesus' advent, and it remains current among Jews well into the future following that—indeed, well into the early modern period."[4]

He continues, "Whether or not one accepts [Messianic Jewish] theology, it remains the case that they have a very strong textual base for the view of the suffering Messiah based in deeply rooted Jewish texts early and late. Jews, it seems, had no difficulty whatever with understanding a Messiah who would vicariously suffer to redeem the world."[5]

But let's put aside for a moment the question of a suffering Messiah. Let's see what traditional Judaism says about the atoning power of the death of the righteous, a concept I have written about at length elsewhere.[6] It is a concept that remains deeply embedded in traditional Jewish thinking to this very day, and it is often invoked at the funeral of a beloved rabbinic leader.

THE DEATH OF A RIGHTEOUS ONE

You can think of it like this. A hostile army surrounds an ancient city where the king lives, threatening to kill all the men. The king offers his life instead, knowing that in the eyes of this army, his life is more valuable than the lives of all the men combined. By offering his life, he saves the rest.

Or on a more mundane level, imagine that you and one hundred of your friends go to an expensive restaurant and run up an incredibly large bill, including rare bottles of wine costing tens of thousands of dollars, resulting in a bill far beyond anything any of you could pay. When the management finds out, they are about to have you arrested until a super-wealthy diner stands up and says, "I have a one-million-dollar credit limit on my card. I'll pay for all their dinners." He is so rich that he is able to cover all your bills. That's a lot of money!

In the same way, in Jewish theology, when an especially righteous person dies, it is believed that his death can atone for the sins of the generation. He is so righteous that he doesn't deserve to die, but because of his very righteousness and the worth of his life, he can cover the sins of the entire generation. Or, to change the image, he is so spiritually rich that he can pay off everyone else's debt. God will forestall the judgment and give the generation time to repent. As the Talmud states, "*At a time when* there are *righteous people in the generation*, the *righteous are seized*, i.e., they die or suffer, *for* the sins of *the generation. If there are no righteous people in the generation, school children*, who are also without sin, *are seized for* the sins of *the generation.*"[7]

Abraham Cohen offers this useful summary:

> Occasionally we find it stated that the good suffer on behalf of the bad; e.g. "When there are righteous in a generation, the righteous are punished for the sins of that generation."...(Shab. 33b). Even the thought of vicarious atonement occurs, as in the question why the account of Miriam's death...immediately follows the law of the red heifer....The answer given is, "As the red heifer brought atonement for sins, similarly does the death of the righteous bring atonement for sins" (M.K. 28a). Other extracts which point in the same direction are: "Moses spake before the Holy One, blessed be He, 'Will not a time come when Israel will have neither Tabernacle or Temple? What will happen to them (as regards atonement)?' He replied, 'I will take a righteous man from amongst them and make him a pledge on their account, and I will atone for their iniquities'" (Exod. R. 35:4). When Moses said to God, in connection with the incident of the Golden Calf, "Blot me, I pray Thee, out of Thy book" (Exod. 32:32), he offered his life as an atonement for the sin of his people (Sot. 14a).[8]

Further contributing to this concept is the idea in Judaism that a guilty person's death would serve as the atonement for all their sins. So, the Talmud teaches, if a man is about to be put to death for his crimes and he doesn't know what to confess, he should simply say, "Let my death be an atonement for all my sins."[9] Accordingly, the undeserved death of a righteous person could theoretically atone for the sins of the guilty.

The Zohar, the foundational book of Jewish mysticism, gives further spiritual insight into this traditional Jewish concept:

> The children of the world are members of one another. When the Holy One desires to give healing to the world, he smites one just man amongst them, and for his sake heals all the rest. Whence do we learn this? From the saying, "He was wounded for our transgressions, bruised for our iniquities" [Isa. 53:5], i.e. by the letting of his blood— as when a man bleeds his arm—there was healing for us—for all the members of the body. In general a just person is only smitten in order to procure healing and atonement for a whole generation.[10]

This concept has also given comfort to the grieving, helping explain why some people, including innocent little children, die unexpected or premature deaths. The concept was even invoked by an ultra-Orthodox leader in 2014 with reference to the massacre of four rabbis who were praying in their synagogue in Har Nof, a neighborhood on the outskirts of Jerusalem. The men were slaughtered in cold blood by Palestinian terrorists—in their house of worship, during early morning prayer—making their deaths all the more horrific. Why were they not protected? Why did God allow them to perish?

Rav Moshe Sternbuch, delivering a eulogy at one of the funerals, explained that God was angry with the nation of Israel, which deserved judgment. But instead of pouring out His wrath, He took the lives of these godly men instead. In Sternbuch's words, "Each of these four *kedoshim* [holy men] who were killed is a *korban olah* [whole burnt offering], and it is their blood that has stopped the *middas hadin* [the attribute of justice] from taking vengeance on all of *Klal Yisrael* [the people of Israel]."[11] In other words, God accepted the violent, undeserved death of these four righteous men as a payment for the sins of rest of the generation, a generation that deserved to be judged. This, then, would open up the door of mercy if the generation would repent. As rabbinic literature states repeatedly, "The death of the righteous atones."[12]

Rabbi Moshe Chaim Luzzatto (1707–1746) dealt with this subject in his classic book *Derech Hashem* (*The Way of God*). He wrote:

> All men were originally bound to each other, as our Sages teach us, "All Israel are responsible for one another." As a result of this, each individual is bound to everyone else, and no man is counted separately. God's Attribute of Good is the stronger, however, and if the guilt for sin is shared by others, this must certainly be true of the merit associated with good deeds.
>
> As a result of this principle, suffering and pain may be imposed on a *tzaddik* (righteous person) as an atonement for his entire generation. This *tzaddik* must then accept this suffering with love for the benefit of his generation, just as he accepts the suffering imposed upon him for his own sake. In doing so, he benefits his generation by atoning for it, and at the same time is himself elevated to a very great degree. For a *tzaddik* such as this is made into one of the leaders in the Community of the Future World, as discussed earlier.

Such suffering also includes cases where a *tzaddik* suffers because his entire generation deserves great punishments, bordering on annihilation, but is spared via the *tzaddik*'s suffering. In atoning for his generations through his suffering, this *tzaddik* saves these people in this world and also greatly benefits them in the World-to-Come.[13]

Why, then, can't this be an essential part of the mission of the Messiah, the ultimate *tzaddik* (righteous man)? Why can't his suffering and death pay for the sins of the rest of the world, not for one generation only but for all generations? After all, in the Talmud (b. Sukkah 45b), Rabbi Shimon bar Yochai made this astonishing claim (and note that he was famous in Talmudic lore for both his righteousness and his suffering):

[Because of the troubles I have known], I can free the entire world from punishment from the day on which I was born to this very moment, and were my son, Eliezer with me, it would be from the day on which the world was made to this moment, and were Yotam ben Uzziah [a famous, righteous sufferer] with us, it would be from the day on which the world was made to its very end.[14]

In the expanded translation of Rabbi Adin Steinsaltz, we get even more insight into the rabbi's claims (as before, the words in italics represent the actual Talmudic text; the rest is the explanatory translation):

And Ḥizkiya said that *Rabbi Yirmeya said in the name of Rabbi Shimon ben Yoḥai: I am able to absolve the entire world from judgment* for sins committed *from the day I was created until now.* The merit that he accrued through his righteousness and the suffering that he endured atone for the sins of the entire world. *And were* the merit accrued by *Eliezer, my son,* calculated along *with my* own, we would absolve the world from judgment for sins committed *from the day that the world was created until now. And were* the merit accrued by the righteous king, *Jotham ben Uzziah,* calculated with *our* own, we would absolve the world from judgment for sins committed *from the day that the world was created until its end.* The righteousness of these three serves as a counterbalance to all the evil deeds committed throughout the generations, and it validates the ongoing existence of the world.[15]

As explained in a modern commentary:

> R. Shimon b. Yohai now talks about his own merit, and that of his
> sons. This line is related to a famous aggadah [story] about R. Shimon
> b. Yohai and his son (Shabbat 33b) and their time in the cave. Their
> suffering there was sufficient to protect the whole world from its sins.
> Also their Torah learning was great enough to save the whole world
> from the consequences of their lack of dedication to the Torah.[16]

How much more, then, can Israel's Messiah, the perfectly righteous one
and the very Son of God, pay for the sins of the whole world? How much
more, then, can his suffering, which included being rejected by his generation, being brutally beaten and flogged, then crucified, atone for all generations? How much more effective is the merit of the Redeemer? As stated
in the expanded translation just cited, but here, applying it to Yeshua, "The
merit that he accrued through his righteousness and the suffering that he
endured atone for the sins of the entire world." Indeed!

With reference to extremely righteous individuals who suffer in this
world, Rabbi Luzzatto also wrote:

> The merit and power of these *tzaddikim* is also increased because of
> such suffering, and this gives them even greater ability to rectify the
> damage of others. They can therefore not only rectify their own gen-
> eration, but can also correct all the spiritual damage done from the
> beginning, from the time of the very first sinners.[17]

This sounds like the gospel to me! *The Messiah died for our sins. The
Messiah paid for our guilt. The Messiah is our Redeemer.*

In an interesting passage in the Mishnah, discussing different afflictions
of the skin, Rabbi Ishmael exclaims, "May I be the atonement for Israel!"
(Or, "I am the atonement for Israel!") As the commentators explain, this
reflected his great love for his people, as he was saying, "All the punishment that would come upon them, I receive on myself in order to atone for
them."[18] Or in the words of another commentary, "Rabbi Ishmael offers to
take upon himself vicarious atonement for Israel's sins."[19]

This is exactly what our Messiah has done, as written in the prophet
Isaiah. And note carefully that when He was suffering for the sins of the
Jewish people, they thought He was suffering for His own sins. They

thought *He* was guilty. They failed to understand He was taking *our* guilt. As Isaiah wrote:

> He was despised and rejected by men, a man of sorrows, acquainted with grief, One from whom people hide their faces. He was despised, and we did not esteem Him. Surely He has borne our griefs and carried our pains. Yet we esteemed Him stricken, struck by God, and afflicted. But He was pierced because of our transgressions, crushed because of our iniquities. The chastisement for our *shalom* was upon Him, and by His stripes we are healed. We all like sheep have gone astray. Each of us turned to his own way. So ADONAI has laid on Him the iniquity of us all.
>
> —ISAIAH 53:3–6, TLV

Shalom Paul, an Israeli biblical and Semitic scholar, says it well: "We were totally taken by surprise when we realized that his maladies were actually in atonement for our own wrongdoings, for he (הוא—the pronoun is emphatic) was, in effect, bearing the sickness that we should have suffered....The Lord exacted payment from the servant for our iniquitous ways."[20]

As Rav Shaul (better known as the apostle Paul) stated concisely, "For while we were still helpless, at the right time Messiah died for the ungodly" (Rom. 5:6, TLV). Or, in the words of Peter (and with reference to Isaiah 53), "He Himself bore our sins in His body on the tree, so that we, removed from sins, might live for righteousness. 'By His wounds you were healed'" (1 Pet. 2:24, TLV). And again, "For Messiah once suffered for sins also—the righteous for the unrighteous—in order to bring you to God" (1 Pet. 3:18, TLV).

This was the Messiah's mission: not simply to come as a godly teacher and powerful warrior, but to come first as the perfect substitute, the ideal atonement, the righteous one taking the place of a world of unrighteous ones. Messiah lived a perfect life to cover all of our imperfections. He died so we could live. He suffered so we could be forgiven. Then God raised Him from the dead so that we too could enjoy eternal life together with Him. And so, rather than His death interrupting His mission, His death formed the foundation of His mission.

A RELATABLE REALITY

Is there anything "un-Jewish" about these concepts? More specifically, is there anything that a follower of the Rebbe could not relate to, at least on some level? Indeed, do not the Rebbe's own words point in this direction?

At a pivotal time in the Chabad movement, one year after his father-in-law's death, when the Rebbe finally assumed the mantle of leadership for his community, he delivered his inaugural discourse. And it was that night—January 17, 1951—and that discourse that remain famous in Hasidic lore.

As he came toward the end of his teaching, he made reference to his late father-in-law, the sixth Rebbe, a man who suffered much under the Russian Communists as the leader of his flock, refusing to bow or compromise even when imprisoned and facing death. He was also physically sick in his final years. Speaking of this revered leader, the Rebbe said:

> Let it be that he who has "borne our sicknesses and endured our pains...who was wounded for our transgressions and afflicted by our iniquities"—just as he has witnessed our hardship—quickly and in our time should redeem his flock from spiritual and physical Exile combined, and let us all merit to see and meet with the Rebbe, in a physical body and within our reach, and he will redeem us![21]

Did you grasp the significance of his words?

First, he was applying the description of the suffering servant of the Lord in Isaiah 53 to his father-in-law, Yosef Yitzchak Schneersohn. Second, he was looking for Yosef Yitzchak to return and redeem the people of Israel, physically and spiritually. Third, he was expecting to see him face to face again, "in a physical body and within our reach."

Remarkably, this is where the title of the book *And He Will Redeem Us* comes from, except that it is now applied to the seventh Rebbe rather than the sixth. And it is his followers—the followers of the seventh Rebbe—who now say, "Let us all merit to see and meet with the Rebbe, in a physical body and within our reach, and he will redeem us!" As professor Elliot Wolfson notes, "Precisely what the seventh Rebbe said about his father-in-law's passing in a talk on 8 Adar I 5710 (February 25, 1950) came to be applied to him."[22]

That's why it is not surprising that the Rebbe's followers were quick to apply Isaiah 53 to him after his second, more serious stroke. In fact, "After his stroke in March 1994 they placed ads proclaiming him to be Messiah. One ad in the *Manhattan Jewish Sentinel* (20–24 April 1994) entitled 'How Can the Rebbe Be Moshiach, If He is Ill?' applied Isaiah 53 as an explanation to Schneerson's sufferings. They felt that his death would not invalidate his messiahship."[23]

So, the seventh Rebbe, Menachem Mendel Schneerson, applied Isaiah 53, the prophecy of the vicarious suffering of the servant of the Lord, to the previous Rebbe, saying that his father-in-law carried the pains of his Jewish people. Then the followers of the seventh Rebbe applied Isaiah 53 to the Rebbe himself when he was sick and suffering.

And these were not the first religious Jews to apply Isaiah 53 to suffering Jewish leaders (or even to the Messiah himself). That's why Rabbi Immanuel Schochet, who was one of the most respected scholars in the Lubavitch movement, spoke of the "validity of the pervasive Talmudic-Midrashic-Zoharic interpretation that the subject of that chapter is indeed Mashiach."[24] Yes, Isaiah 53, this chapter that so graphically describes the substitutionary suffering of God's servant, has been widely applied to the Messiah in traditional Jewish literature. In fact, the Jewish anthropologist Raphael Patai wrote, "It is quite probable that the concept of the suffering Messiah, fully developed in the Talmud, the Midrash, and the Zohar, has its origin in the Biblical prophecies about the Suffering Servant."[25]

Did you follow that? Patai argues that the concept of the suffering Messiah, which is well attested in classic rabbinic literature, can be traced back to biblical passages like Isaiah 53. But this is where things become really exciting. This same passage, Isaiah 53, not only speaks of the Messiah's sufferings on our behalf. *It also speaks of his death.* Yes, it clearly predicts the death of the Messiah, a death that was central to his redemptive mission. Not only so, but *Isaiah 53 predicts his resurrection.* It's all written down here for us, right on the pages of the Hebrew Scriptures.

Earlier in this chapter we looked at Isaiah 53:4–6. Now let's look at the verses that follow, without commentary or explanation. Read this text slowly, and let it sink in:

> He was oppressed and He was afflicted yet He did not open His mouth. Like a lamb led to the slaughter, like a sheep before its shearers is silent, so He did not open His mouth. Because of oppression and

judgment He was taken away. As for His generation, who considered? For He was cut off from the land of the living, for the transgression of my people—the stroke was theirs. His grave was given with the wicked, and by a rich man in His death, though He had done no violence, nor was there any deceit in His mouth. Yet it pleased Adonai to bruise Him. He caused Him to suffer. If He makes His soul a guilt offering, He will see His offspring, He will prolong His days, and the will of Adonai will succeed by His hand. As a result of the anguish of His soul He will see it and be satisfied by His knowledge. The Righteous One, My Servant will make many righteous and He will bear their iniquities. Therefore I will give Him a portion with the great, and He will divide the spoil with the mighty—because He poured out His soul to death, and was counted with transgressors. For He bore the sin of many, and interceded for the transgressors.

—Isaiah 53:7–12, TLV

Now, let's go back and review what we just read. In verses 4–6 the servant was described as smitten, afflicted, wounded, crushed, and bruised. In verses 7–12 the servant is like a lamb going to slaughter, taken away to judgment. He is cut off from the land of the living, he exposes himself to death, he is put in a grave, and indeed, he dies.

Yet there is a purpose to his suffering. He makes himself "a guilt offering." He bears the punishment of the wicked and makes them righteous by his righteousness; he intercedes for sinners. The servant stands in for the unrighteous, suffering on their behalf, and through his self-sacrifice, the ungodly are redeemed. So it is written in the Hebrew Scriptures, the Tanakh.

But there's more. The servant will rise again! He will "see His offspring. He will prolong His days." That means resurrection! Yes, God Himself will vindicate His servant, giving him "a portion with the great" and dividing "the spoil with the mighty." So it is written in Isaiah 53.[26]

But Isaiah 53 does not stand alone. The passage actually begins in Isaiah 52:13–15, a section frequently cited with reference to the Messiah in Jewish tradition. There the prophet declares:

Behold, My servant will prosper, He will be high and lifted up and greatly exalted. Just as many were appalled at You—His appearance was disfigured more than any man, His form more than the sons of men. So He will sprinkle many nations. Kings will shut their mouths because of Him, for what had not been told them they will see, and what they had not heard they will perceive.

—ISAIAH 52:13–15, TLV

We see, then, that this righteous servant of the Lord will not only die, he will also suffer terrible disfigurement. This is exactly what happened to Yeshua, who was brutally beaten, severely flogged, then nailed to a cross. But just as his sufferings were intense, so also was his exaltation, as these same verses make clear. The Messiah will not only rise from the dead, he will be highly exalted. Just how high?

I'll allow a traditional Jewish text called Midrash Tanchuma to tell us just how high Messiah's exaltation will be: "HE SHALL BE EXALTED...more than Abraham, LIFTED UP more than Moses, AND BECOME EXCEEDINGLY TALL, more so than the ministering angels."[27]

As explained in the New Testament writings, just as the Messiah humbled himself on our behalf, his Father will give him the highest name in the universe:

He emptied Himself—taking on the form of a slave, becoming the likeness of men and being found in appearance as a man. He humbled Himself—becoming obedient to the point of death, even death on a cross. For this reason God highly exalted Him and gave Him the name that is above every name, that at the name of *Yeshua* every knee should bow, in heaven and on the earth and under the earth, and every tongue profess that *Yeshua* the Messiah is Lord—to the glory of God the Father.

—PHILIPPIANS 2:7–11, TLV

So, according to the Midrash, the Messiah, who would suffer so terribly, would one day be more highly exalted than Abraham, Moses, or even the ministering angels. According to Paul, who was quite familiar with Isaiah 53, the Messiah, who would die a lowly, criminal's death, would one day be so highly exalted that every created being would confess him as Lord, "to the glory of God the Father."

Isaiah, by the inspiration of the Spirit, predicted it all centuries before it happened, and Jesus the Messiah lived it out for the watching world to see. And because He died, as the Scriptures said He would, and because He rose from the dead, as these same Scriptures said He would, we are sure that He will come again to complete His mission, just as the Scriptures said.

And yet the story gets more fascinating and complex. Did you know that according to many Jewish traditions, there will be *two* Messiahs, one of whom is killed and raised from the dead? Yes, Jewish tradition teaches that the one known as Messiah son of Joseph will die fighting for his people, only to be raised from the dead by Messiah son of David. This is taught in the Talmud![28]

Now, you would think that with the rise and expansion of Christianity, Talmudic Judaism would distance itself from any notion of a suffering Messiah, let alone a dying Messiah, let alone a dying and rising Messiah. That would sound too much like Yeshua! Yet there are many rabbinic texts that speak of the Messiah's suffering, along with other texts that speak of his death and resurrection (even if the latter refer to the Messiah son of Joseph). How do we explain this?

According to Raphael Patai, "When the death of the Messiah became an established tenet in Talmudic times, this was felt to be irreconcilable with the belief in the Messiah as the Redeemer who would usher in the blissful millennium of the Messianic age. The dilemma was solved by splitting the person of the Messiah in two."[29]

Somehow, Patai reasons, it could not be denied that the Messiah had to die, yet since this didn't seem to fit with the Messiah being the Redeemer, Judaism invented a second Messiah. So, one Messiah would suffer and die (and rise); the other Messiah would triumph and rule and reign.

The only problem is that according to the Bible, there's only one Messiah. And that's where we find the solution as well: It is one and the same Messiah who suffers, dies, rises, then returns to rule and reign. One Redeemer only!

Now, a traditional Jew would quickly protest and say, "But there's a massive flaw with your theory. The death of the Messiah son of Joseph is not redemptive. It doesn't atone for sins, like the death of your Jesus supposedly does. Your analogy breaks down."

Actually, it was no less an authority than Rabbi Moshe Alsheikh, the famous sixteenth-century commentator, who interpreted Zechariah 12:10 with reference to *the atoning death of Messiah son of Joseph*. He wrote:

> I will do yet a third thing, and that is, that "they shall look unto me,"
> for they shall lift up their eyes unto Me in perfect repentance, when

they see Him whom they pierced, that is, Messiah, the Son of Joseph; for our Rabbis, of blessed memory, have said that He will *take upon Himself all the guilt of Israel*, and shall then be slain in the war *to make atonement in such manner that it shall be accounted as if Israel had pierced Him, for on account of their sin He has died; and, therefore, in order that it may be reckoned to them as a perfect atonement*, they will repent and look to the blessed One, saying that there is none beside Him to forgive those that mourn on account of Him *who died for their sin*: this is the meaning of "They shall look upon Me."[30]

And is it any surprise that this same verse, Zechariah 12:10, is applied to the crucifixion of the Messiah in the New Testament in John 19:37?

In order to complete his mission, the Messiah had to die. And in order for the whole world to know he was really the Messiah, he had to be raised from the dead. Since then, his mission has continued, just as predicted in the Jewish Scriptures, which teach that this rejected Messiah will also be a light to the Gentiles until his salvation reaches to the ends of the earth. Only then will he return and set up his kingdom on the earth.

So, in total contrast with those who believe the Rebbe is Messiah and must deny or explain away his death, followers of Yeshua the Messiah celebrate and commemorate the Messiah's death. In fact, one thing that all the different Christian and Messianic Jewish denominations have in common is what is called the Lord's Supper, or Communion. (It's also known as the Eucharist.) It is based on Yeshua's last meal with His disciples before He was crucified, where He told them that the bread symbolized His body, which was about to be broken for us, and the wine represented His blood, which was about to be poured out for us. (See Luke 22:14–20.) He encouraged us to partake of the bread and wine on a regular basis, thereby proclaiming His death until He returns. (See 1 Corinthians 11:23–26.)

And do you know the main thing the Messiah is waiting for today, before He comes back? He is waiting for His own people to embrace Him. The Jewish people must welcome back the Jewish Messiah. What stops my dear people from doing that today?

Perhaps this prayer, found in some traditional Yom Kippur (Day of Atonement) prayer books, can take on new meaning today:

Messiah our Righteousness has turned away from us, we were per-plexed and there is no one to justify us. He bears our iniquities and the yoke of our crimes upon himself. And was pierced because of our iniquities. He carries our sins on his shoulder, to find forgiveness for our misdeeds. We were healed by his bruises.[31]

Let healing come to the people of Israel!

CHAPTER 8

THE MYSTERY OF THE DIVINE ANGEL AND THE MESSIAH

E VEN MORE CONTROVERSIAL than the claims that the Lubavitcher Rebbe was the Messiah are the claims that he was somehow divine. As Rabbi Dan Cohn-Sherbok observed in 1997, "Some followers of the *Rebbe* have even gone so far as to use incarnational terminology [meaning God taking on human form] in describing his mission. During his lifetime, the *Rebbe* was referred to as the 'Essence of the Infinite'; today some Lubavitcher Hasidim talk of him as 'Master of the Universe.'"[1]

As evidence for these beliefs professor David Berger refers to the writings of some Lubavitch rabbis, including Rabbi Levi Yitzhak Ginsberg, who claimed, "The Rebbe is the 'master of the house' with respect to all that happens to him and all that happens in the world."[2] Nothing can take place without his explicit agreement, and he can bring to pass whatever he desires. No one can tell him what to do! "In him the Holy One Blessed be He rests in all His force just as He is (because of his complete self-nullification to God, so that this becomes his entire essence)."[3]

Berger also cites Rabbi Sholom Charitonow, who Berger claims asserted "that the Rebbe manifests the Essence of the unlimited God,"[4] explaining why it follows that even his physical body remains alive in the deepest sense. As Charitonow explained, there are no borders or limitations concerning the divine Essence, for which no interruptions are possible: "In other words—not only is the interruption unnecessary, it is in fact impossible. This can apply to something which has a form (whether of a physical or a spiritual nature); it cannot, however, apply to something that is eternal by nature, having no form whatsoever."[5]

To be sure, some of these concepts tie in with the exalted view that

Hasidic Jews have of a *tzaddik*, a deeply righteous man, in particular, a rebbe. In their view the *tzaddik* doesn't actually die. Rather, he is freed from the restrictions of time and space, existing on a totally spiritual plane. As Wolfson explains (with reference to the Lubavitcher Rebbe's predecessor):

> The death of the sixth Rebbe actually augmented his efficacy, since he was not restricted anymore by a corporeal body and therefore he could accomplish greater providential feats, including returning to the world to lead the Jewish people to welcome the Messiah. The physical demise of the sixth Rebbe is merely a test of faith, the concealment of truth, which is part and parcel of the "birth pangs" that precede the coming of the savior. The intent of the test is to empower the hasidim "to push away and to destroy the concealment and withdrawal, so that the truth will be revealed."[6]

As laid out in one of the foundational writings of the Chabad movement:

> And this is what is written in the holy Zohar, that the righteous one, who has passed away, is found in all the world more than in his life…this is with respect to the worship of God, in heavenly matters, and with respect to mundane matters, it says explicitly in the holy Zohar, that the righteous protect the world, more in their deaths than in their lives, and if not for the prayer of the righteous in that world, the world would not exist even for a moment.[7]

But it is quite a jump from believing in the ongoing power of a (deceased) righteous person to calling that person God incarnate. That's why very few followers of the Rebbe make this claim, even while believing he will return one day as the Messiah. Those who make this claim leave other religious Jews quite surprised.

This is what happened in January 2008 when radio host Zev Brenner hosted a debate between a Lubavitcher rabbi who believed that the Rebbe was the Messiah and a modern Orthodox rabbi who did not. During the show Brenner spoke with a devout Lubavitch woman and asked her, "Did the Rebbe die?"

She responded, "God forbid. The Rebbe is *atzmus me'elokus* [the very essence of God] in a *guf* [body]. He cannot die."

He asked, "Where is the Rebbe right now?"

She responded, "All over," which left Brenner startled.[8]

But, a critic notes:

> What Zev Brenner heard is normative Chabad messianist theology.
>   The Rebbe, no longer confined to his body, is everywhere. He
> is omnipresent and almost, but not quite, omnipotent, as well. He
> answers your prayers and intercedes for you on high. He watches you
> and he watches over you.[9]

Outlandish, you say? I concur. The Rebbe was just a man, even if an exceptional, extraordinary man. He does not become God after death.

Yet this belief that almighty God can manifest Himself in a physical form, right before our eyes, is not as odd as it may sound. As we'll see in a moment, such a concept has precedents within the Hebrew Bible itself. And the question of God manifesting Himself in some kind of tangible form begs a larger question, namely, how can the infinite, eternal, unknowable God be known and experienced by finite, mortal human beings? It's a question that Jewish mysticism addressed head-on.

CAN GOD BE KNOWN?

As explained by the Jewish literary critic Adam Kirsch, every monotheistic faith has to deal with the question of how an infinite God can relate to a finite creation. If He is transcendent and beyond our reason, how can we have a relationship with Him? The gulf between the Creator and the creation is vast, which leads the Zohar to come up with a highly imaginative solution:

> God, the *Zohar* grants, is in the ultimate sense unknowable. This
> is the aspect of God that it refers to as *En Sof*, "without end," the
> Infinite. *En Sof*, like the Maimonidean God, is completely beyond
> the power of the human mind to understand or express. "*En Sof*
> cannot be known," the *Zohar* explains, "and does not produce end
> or beginning...there are no end, no wills, no lights, no luminaries
> in *En Sof*. All these luminaries and lights depend on it for their exis-
> tence, but they are not in a position to perceive."[10]

Instead, the *En Sof* (or, as commonly spelled, the Ein Sof) makes Himself known to human beings through a series of emanations known as *sefirot* (plural; the singular form is *sefira*), each one representing a different attribute of God. As Kirsch explains, the *sefirot* are "the ten stages, or attributes, or aspects of God's self-disclosure. These can be seen as the successive phases by which God transitions from the unknowability of *En Sof* to the God we recognize and worship in this world. They are, in the *Zohar*'s image, the vessels that enclose God's being so that we can come to recognize it."[11]

A popular website explains that a major concept in Jewish mysticism is that the *Ein Sof*, the Endless One, is revealed through what are called the *sefirot*, which are "vessels or spheres related to the Creator only through resemblance, and are the ten most common names for the varying aspects of Divinity. Though they are one with the Creator, they are also the Creator's garments and the 'beams of light which it sends out.'"[12] And since the root of the word *sefira* (singular of *sefirot*) comes from the Hebrew verb "to tell," these *sefirot* are thus seen as aspects of God through which He communicates with His earthly creation.

In the Zohar, the first of these three "stages" of divine disclosure are Keter (the Divine Crown), followed by Chokhmah (Wisdom), then Binah (Understanding). Yet even still, according to the Zohar, even after these three stages of divine self-disclosure, God remains too transcendent for human interaction. "It is with the next stage of the *sefirot*," Kirsch explains, culminating in the sixth *sefira*, called Tiferet (Beauty) "that we reach the aspect of God with whom we have some kind of relationship, the God of the Bible to whom we pray. (Another name for Tiferet is 'the Blessed Holy One.')"[13] So, it is only six stages removed from the infinite essence of God when human beings can know Him and encounter Him. What a novel concept!

The Zohar teaches that these stages of self-disclosure continue until we reach the last of the *sefirot*, called either Shekhinah (God's Presence in the World) or Malkhut (Kingdom), and ultimately, "It is through the *Shekhinah* that humans can experience the Divine."[14] As Kirsch explains:

> When the divine realm is in proper harmony, God's influence descends to the world through this chain until it reaches Malkhut, which in turn passes on the divine blessing to our world. In this aspect, Malkhut is known as the Shekhinah, the divine presence that dwells with the people of Israel and protects them in their journey through history; one synonym for the Shekhinah is "the assembly of

Israel." The Shekhinah is the key mediator between the *sefirot* as a whole and the world below, which is our world. (Although, to be precise, the *Zohar* posits several layers of reality between the *sefirot* and our world, filled with angels and other supernatural beings.)[15]

To be candid, I do not see this complex system supported in the Scriptures, and the more you read the Zohar, the more fantastic (and even bizarre) the speculation becomes. At the same time, there is something these Jewish mystics were right about, namely, that the eternal and transcendent God does not reveal Himself to human beings in direct and unmediated form. As the Lord told Moses in Exodus 33, "You cannot see My face, for man may not see Me and live" (Exod. 33:20, JPS TANAKH). Or as stated by Paul, God is "the blessed and only Sovereign, the King of kings and Lord of lords, who alone has immortality, who dwells in unapproachable light, whom no one has ever seen or can see" (1 Tim. 6:15–16).

WHO IS THE ANGEL OF THE LORD?

How, then, do we explain the many times in Scripture that God seems to reveal Himself directly to His people? How is it that some of these encounters are described as being face to face? I've addressed that question at different times over the years, looking for insights into the Hebrew Bible, the New Covenant Writings, and rabbinic literature. But I want to focus here on one particular being described in the Bible as "the angel of the LORD." Why is this angelic messenger so important? (In Hebrew, the word *angel* simply means "messenger" and can refer to earthly beings or heavenly beings. In the cases we'll look at here, the angel is a heavenly being.)

This angel is first mentioned in Genesis 16, when Hagar has been sent away by Abraham and Sarah. As Hagar is despairing for her life, the angel appears to her and speaks to her as if he were God Himself:

> The angel of the LORD found her by a spring of water in the wilderness, the spring on the way to Shur. And he said, "Hagar, servant of Sarai, where have you come from and where are you going?" She said, "I am fleeing from my mistress Sarai." The angel of the LORD said to her, "Return to your mistress and submit to her." The angel of the LORD also said to her, "I will surely multiply your offspring so that they cannot be numbered for multitude."
>
> —GENESIS 16:7–10

The angel speaks to Hagar once more, after which the text says, "So she called the name of the LORD who spoke to her, 'You are a God of seeing,' for she said, 'Truly here I have seen him who looks after me'" (verse 13). In Hagar's mind, hearing the voice of this angelic messenger who spoke for God was the same as hearing His voice, and seeing the angelic messenger was like seeing God's face.

This special messenger is next mentioned in Genesis 22, where God tests Abraham by commanding him to sacrifice his beloved son Isaac. As Abraham is about to comply, he is suddenly interrupted by this angel: "But the angel of the LORD called to him from heaven and said, 'Abraham, Abraham!' And he said, 'Here I am.' He said, 'Do not lay your hand on the boy or do anything to him, for now I know that you fear God, seeing you have not withheld your son, your only son, from me'" (Gen. 22:11–12).

Then a few verses later this angel speaks again, and note that he speaks as if he were God Himself:

> By myself I have sworn, declares the LORD, because you have done this and have not withheld your son, your only son, I will surely bless you, and I will surely multiply your offspring as the stars of heaven and as the sand that is on the seashore. And your offspring shall possess the gate of his enemies, and in your offspring shall all the nations of the earth be blessed, because you have obeyed my voice.
>
> —GENESIS 22:16–18

Commenting on these verses, Rabbi Bahya ben Asher (1255–1340) made some startling observations, pointing out first that if this was a mere angel, Abraham would not have listened to him, as the angel would have been countermanding God. Not only so, but the angel does not say to Abraham, "You did not withhold your son from Him," but rather, "You did not withhold your son from Me." Rabbi Bahya wrote:

> You also need to know that the apparently strange phenomenon in this paragraph, i.e. that G'd is the one who subjects Avraham to the trial whereas the angel prevented him from going through with it, needs to be understood as follows: The "angel" mentioned in our paragraph is not of the category of the נפרדים, "disembodied spiritual creatures," but it belonged to what are known as the נטיעות, "the emanations of G'd."[16] Had the angel who called out to Avraham and

instructed him to desist belonged to the category known as נפרדים [disembodied spiritual creatures], Avraham would have ignored him, would not have allowed himself to be countermanded by a subordinate of the One who had instructed him in the first place. Moreover, it is quite unthinkable that an angel of the "lower" category נפרדים [disembodied spiritual creatures] would have been allowed to say to Avraham ולא חשכת את בנך ממני, "and you did not withhold your son from Me." He would have had to say: "you have not withheld your son from Him."[17]

Precisely so. There is something different about this "angel," something divine. Rabbi Bahya continues:

All of this proves that the voice which the Torah describes as emanating from an "angel of G'd," was of a superior divine level. This "angel" is also known as the "great angel," who manifested himself in Exodus 14,19 when the Torah describes him as traveling in front of the encampment of the Jewish people (performing all kinds of miracles)....When the Torah describes this divine emanation as מלאך, the meaning is that G'd is "contained, present," within this divine emanation.[18]

So in a unique way, this angel is a "divine emanation," and the Lord is somehow "contained" or "present" within the angel. Indeed, he notes, "We encounter something similar in Exodus 23,21 where G'd explains to Moses that the מלאך [angel] who will be accompanying the Jewish people needs to be related to with the utmost reverence as 'My Name is within him.'"[19]

Then, commenting on the last verses from Genesis 22, which we cited above, Rabbi Bahya notes that the angel, who is directly identified with the LORD (Hebrew, YHWH), swears by Himself: "By myself I have sworn, declares the LORD." Who is this angel? For a traditional Jew like Rabbi Bahya, the angel could not be confused with God. And yet, as he indicated, there is clearly a special connection between God's essence and this angel. Who, then, is this angelic messenger?

We don't have to go far to find the answer. In fact, we find it right within the pages of Genesis, this time on the lips of the patriarch Jacob as he was close to death. Praying a blessing over his two grandsons, he said:

> The God before whom my fathers Abraham and Isaac walked, the God who has shepherded me throughout my life to this day, the Angel who redeemed me from all evil, may He bless the boys, and may they be called by my name, and by the name of my fathers, Abraham and Isaac. May they multiply to a multitude in the midst of the land.
>
> —GENESIS 48:15–16, TLV

Do you grasp the significance of what you just read? *Jacob is equating the angel with God Himself.* This is the most natural, unforced, and logical way to read the Hebrew, since 1) The parallel structure of the verses makes this clear, referring to God, God, and the angel. The text is straightforward and unambiguous to anyone fluent in biblical Hebrew. And 2) The Hebrew verb for *bless* is in the singular: May "He" bless the boys—not "they." This angel was somehow God Himself! Not surprisingly, Rabbi Bahya cited these very verses to support his reading of Genesis 22. He was quite right in doing so, even if he did not recognize the full force of these verses.

There are rabbinic commentaries that seek to minimize God being identified with the angel in Genesis 14, as in this statement in the Talmud:

> *And Rabbi Yoḥanan said:* The task of providing *a person's food is more difficult than the redemption. While, with regard to the redemption, it is written: "The angel who has redeemed me from all evil"* (Genesis 48:16), indicating that *a mere angel* is sufficient to protect a person from all evil; *whereas, with regard to sustenance, it is written: "The God who has been my shepherd* all my life long to this day" (Genesis 48:15). This verse implies that only God can help one who is struggling to earn a living.[20]

But this is hardly a fair reading of the biblical text. Instead it is a forced attempt to deny that Jacob refers to God as "the Angel who has redeemed me from all evil."

According to Rabbi Obadiah Sforno (1475–1550), the word "the" before "the Angel" is not a definitive article identifying a specific angel. Rather, it refers to angels "who in the past on different occasions had been Yaakov's guardian angels. Yaakov appeals to his own guardian angels to bless the children if their own merit does not suffice for the guardian angels assigned to them to do the job."[21]

Once more, however, this interpretation breaks down on several levels.

First, Jacob *does* reference "the" Angel, not "the angels"; second, as we noted, the blessing is in the singular. It is one being—God!—who blesses Jacob's grandchildren, not God and His angels.

According to the Chizkuni commentary (composed in the thirteenth century, likely in France):

> In verse 15 Yaakov had commenced the blessing by referring to G-d by His name of "האלוהים" [God], whereas in this verse he has switched to an angel as the source of the blessing. How are we to account for this? The two verses have to be understood as follows: "The G-d before Whom I and my forefathers have walked by means of His angel who protected me against all harm; may He arrange for that same angel also to protect the lads who are your sons."[22]

Now go back and read Genesis 48:15–16 and ask yourself: Is this really what Jacob was praying? Is this really what these verses are saying? The answer is, obviously not. Jacob spoke of God and the angel interchangeably, asking this God/divine angel to bless his grandsons. And he did so with good reason, recognizing, "In the expression *the angel*...he calls to mind God's visible encounters with him at turning-points of his life, above all at Peniel [in Genesis 32]."[23]

Yes, when Jacob speaks of this special angel, he speaks of coming face to face with God in visible form. As a number of biblical scholars have explained, "the angel of God," or more specifically, "the angel of YHWH," is regularly used in the Old Testament to speak of God manifest in human form. And "The *mal'ak yhwh* [angel of Yahweh] incarnates the discourse and activity of God as it affects the world."[24]

And here's something really fascinating. While there are many references to angels in the plural in the Old Testament, including the phrase "angels of God," whenever the word *angel* is used with YHWH, the divine name, it is always in the singular. There is one distinct angel of YHWH![25]

What, then, did Jacob have in mind when he spoke of this angel? When he was in Bethel in Genesis 28, he had a dream in which he saw angels descending and ascending, recognizing a special divine presence there. So, there was angelic activity there, although the text does not mention one angel in particular. But in Genesis 32 we read that during a critical night in his life, Jacob wrestled with "a man" until dawn, and he knew that this "man" had the power to bless him and change his life. Hosea tells us that this "man" was an angel (Hos. 12:4), but that's not the end of the story. In the morning Jacob named the place "Peniel," which means "face of God," for he said, "I have seen God face to face" (Gen. 32:30). How striking! Somehow this angelic messenger, in the form of a man, carried the very presence of God.

This is similar to the account we read in Judges 13, where an angel of the Lord appeared to Manoah and his wife, the parents of Samson, and Manoah offered a sacrifice to the Lord in the presence of His angel—except that Manoah didn't realize he was a divine messenger. The text records:

> And when the flame went up toward heaven from the altar, the angel of the LORD went up in the flame of the altar. Now Manoah and his wife were watching, and they fell on their faces to the ground.
>
> The angel of the LORD appeared no more to Manoah and to his wife. Then Manoah knew that he was the angel of the LORD. And Manoah said to his wife, "We shall surely die, for we have seen God." But his wife said to him, "If the LORD had meant to kill us, he would not have accepted a burnt offering and a grain offering at our hands, or shown us all these things, or now announced to us such things as these."
>
> —JUDGES 13:20–23

So they too, just like Jacob, had an encounter with an angelic messenger in the form of a man, and Manoah, just like Jacob, claimed to have "seen God."[26]

This brings us to Exodus 3, where Moses encounters "the angel of YHWH." Look carefully at what the Torah teaches:

> Now Moses, tending the flock of his father-in-law Jethro, the priest of Midian, drove the flock into the wilderness, and came to Horeb, the mountain of God. An angel of the LORD appeared to him in a blazing fire out of a bush. He gazed, and there was a bush all aflame, yet the bush was not consumed. Moses said, "I must turn aside to look at this marvelous sight; why doesn't the bush burn up?" When the LORD saw that he had turned aside to look, God called to him out of the bush: "Moses! Moses!" He answered, "Here I am." And He said, "Do not come closer. Remove your sandals from your feet, for the place on which you stand is holy ground. I am," He said, "the God

of your father, the God of Abraham, the God of Isaac, and the God
of Jacob." And Moses hid his face, for he was afraid to look at God.

—EXODUS 3:1–6, JPS TANAKH

What a passage! Notice that the text first states that it is the *angel of
Yahweh* who appeared to Moses in a blazing fire out of a bush but then
states that *God* called to him out of the bush. And as the voice speaks, it is
the voice of the Lord Himself, to the point that the voice tells Moses not to
get any closer, since this is holy ground. In response, "Moses hid his face,
for he was afraid to look at God."

Now, you might say, "The angel was speaking on God's behalf, just like
the prophets did. We all understand that. So when the angel said, 'I am the
God of your father,' that would be no different than a prophet speaking for
God and saying, 'I am the God of your father.' Everyone would know that
the prophet was not claiming to be God, and no one would mistake the
prophet for God. He, like the angel, would be recognized as God's messenger, nothing more."

But that argument simply doesn't work, for two obvious reasons. First,
the prophet would not say to his audience, "Don't come near me, for the
place where you're standing is holy ground." Of course not! Second, the
people would not be afraid to look at the prophet because they were afraid
to look at God. They would recognize he was merely God's messenger.

That is not the case here. The angel is directly associated with Yahweh
in His message and His holiness. That's why Moses could not approach the
angelic messenger in the burning bush, and that's why he was afraid to look.
How could a mortal man look at God?

What's interesting is that in Genesis 32:30 and Judges 13:22, the JPS
Tanakh translation rendered it, respectively, "I have seen a divine being
face to face, yet my life has been preserved," and, "We shall surely die,
for we have seen a divine being." Yet in both of these verses, just as in
Exodus 3:6, the Hebrew word is *'elohim*, God. And just as the right and
obvious way to translate the word in Exodus 3:6 was "God," that's the right
way to translate it in these other verses. Jacob and Manoah and Moses all
felt that when they had seen the angel of the Lord, they had seen God.[27]
As a Jewish tradition, quoted by professor Elliot Wolfson, states, "Know
that... 'An angel of the Lord appeared to him in a blazing fire out of a bush'
(Exod. 3:2)...*refers to God Himself.*"[28]

As noted in one theological wordbook, this angelic messenger "seems to be God, since those who see him marvel that they have seen God (Jud 13:21–22) and he speaks for God in the first person (Gen 16:10; Ex 3:2, 6; Jud 2:1)."[29] Or, in the words of another theological lexicon, "The determination of the relationship between Yahweh and his *mal'āk* [angelic messenger] is particularly difficult because a series of texts do not precisely distinguish between Yahweh and [the angel of Yahweh] (Gen 16:7ff.; 21:17ff.; 22:11ff.; 31:11ff.; Exod 3:2ff.; Judg 6:11ff.; 13:21f.)."[30]

Now, look back once more to Genesis 48:15–16, and things are making much more sense:

> Then he blessed Joseph and said,
> "*The God* before whom my fathers Abraham and Isaac walked, *the God* who has shepherded me throughout my life to this day, *the Angel* who redeemed me from all evil, may *He* bless the boys, and may they be called by my name, and by the name of my fathers, Abraham and Isaac. May they multiply to a multitude in the midst of the land."
>
> —GENESIS 48:15–16, TLV, EMPHASIS ADDED

Commenting on this verse, professor Nahum Sarna, a highly respected contemporary Jewish scholar, said this:

> The capitalization reflects the fact that the parallelistic structure of verses 15–16 strongly suggests that "angel" is here an epithet of God. No one in the Bible ever invokes an angel in prayer, nor in Jacob's several encounters with angels is there any mention of one who delivers him from harm. When the patriarch feels himself to be in mortal danger, he prays directly to God, as in 32:10–13, and it is He who again and again is Jacob's guardian and protector (28:15, 20; 31:3; 35:3). Admittedly, "Angel" as an epithet for God is extraordinary, but since angels are often simply extensions of the divine personality, the distinction between God and angel in the biblical texts is frequently blurred (cf. Gen. 31:3, 11, 13; Exod. 3:2, 4).[31]

What an incredible statement: the word *angel*, which is capitalized in this Jewish translation, "is here an epithet of God," and, "No one in the Bible ever invokes an angel in prayer." In other words, Jacob was directing his prayer to the angel, whom he equated with God. As noted by Dr. Y. Moshe

Imannueli in his Hebrew commentary on Genesis, "The author senses no difference between the three names [mentioned in vv. 15–16]....There is no difference between 'God' and 'angel,' for the second comes to represent the first."[32]

WHO IS METATRON?

Explaining this from a Christian perspective, the Old Testament scholar C. F. Keil wrote:

> This triple reference to God, in which the Angel who is placed on an equality with *Ha-Elohim* [God] cannot possibly be a created angel, but must be the "Angel of God," i.e. God manifested in the form of the Angel of Jehovah, or the "Angel of His face" (Isa. lxiii. 9), contains a foreshadowing of the Trinity, though only God and the Angel are distinguished, not three persons of the divine nature. The God before whom Abraham and Isaac walked, had proved Himself to Jacob to be "the God which fed" and "the Angel which redeemed," i.e. according to the more fully developed revelation of the New Testament, ὁ Θεός [God] and ὁ λόγος [the Word], Shepherd and Redeemer. By the singular יְבָרֵךְ (bless, *benedicat*) the triple mention of God is resolved into the unity of the divine nature.[33]

And this brings us to Isaiah 63:9, a text just cited by Keil, speaking (literally) of the angel of God's "face," normally translated as "the angel (or messenger) of His presence." The verse reads, "In all their troubles He was troubled, and the angel of His Presence delivered them. In His love and pity He Himself redeemed them, raised them, and exalted them all the days of old" (Isa. 63:9, JPS TANAKH). Now, this is the only time in the entire Old Testament that the phrase "angel of His presence" occurs, and the wording is significant. As explained by the nineteenth-century biblical scholar Franz Delitzsch (a colleague of C. F. Keil):

> This mediatorial angel is called "the angel of His face," as being the representative of God, for "the face of God" is His self-revealing presence (even though only revealed to the mental eye); and consequently the presence of God, which led Israel to Canaan, is called directly "His face" in Deut. 4:37, apart from the angelic mediation to be understood; and "my face" in Ex. 33:14, 15, by the side of "my

angel" in Ex. 32:34, and the angel in Ex. 33:2, appears as something incomparably higher than the presence of God through the mediation of that one angel, whose personality is completely hidden by his mediatorial instrumentality.[34]

What are we to make of this? In the centuries between the Tanakh and the New Covenant Writings, there was much Jewish speculation about the world of angels and their hierarchy. At the top of the list was an angel called Metatron, a being not mentioned in the Bible but spoken of often in Jewish literature. As explained in a dictionary of ancient Judaism:

> Metatron may derive from the Greek *metathronos*, the one enthroned with God, or from the Latin *metator*, the title of the officer who went ahead of the Roman army to prepare the camp, hence, more generally, a forerunner....3 Enoch designates him "the lesser YHWH," in contrast to God himself, "the greater YHWH," who withdraws from the world, leaving Metatron in charge....He is sometimes identified with the archangel Michael (Israel's celestial representative). He also functions as the Prince of Torah, the Heavenly Scribe and the Heavenly High Priest, serving in the celestial tabernacle, the Tabernacle of Metatron.[35]

Who exactly was this Metatron? And could he have been the one described in Isaiah 63:9 as "the angel of God's presence"? A Jews for Jesus website has some fascinating observations, all based on traditional Jewish sources:

> Several kabbalistic [meaning, mystical] texts reveal that Metatron is not merely an angel, but a manifestation of the Shekhinah in human form; in other words, God himself. For example:
>
>> And R. Tam commented that the Holy One blessed be He is himself called *Metatron*, as is said in the *Pesiqta* [Exod 23:13] "and the Lord walked before them all the day." The Holy One said, "I was the guide [Heb. *Metatron*] for my children," that is, their guard.
>
> Metatron is also spoken of as "the voice of God" in a reference of *Midrash Tehillim* to the passage penned by King David: "The voice

of the Lord was over the waters..." (Psalm 29:3). Keeping in mind that Metatron is held by kabbalists to be the embodiment of the Shekhinah, note the following observation by Chabad founder Rabbi Zalman:

> [It] has been stated in the *Zohar* and *Etz Chayim*, that the *Shechinah*...is called the "word of God"...as in the case of human beings, by way of example, speech reveals to the hearers the speaker's secret and hidden thought.[36]

The website then points to a medieval Jewish prayer recited on Yom Kippur (the Day of Atonement), which states, "May it be Thy will that the sounding of the shofar may be embroidered in Thy Heavenly Curtain by the Angel who is appointed for it, as Thou has accepted the prayers by the hand of Elijah of blessed memory and through Yeshua the Prince of the Face."[37] (Note again that "angel of His presence" in Isaiah 63:9 is literally "angel of His face.") Who is this Yeshua?

According to one of the foremost scholars of Jewish mysticism in the world, Yehudah Liebes, professor of Jewish mysticism and Kabbalah in the Department of Jewish Thought at the Hebrew University of Jerusalem, this Yeshua is actually Jesus! Yes, he "traces references to Yeshua in traditional Jewish liturgy to Jewish believers in Jesus in the first century AD! [Professor] Daniel Abrams of Bar-Ilan University writes of Liebes's observations, 'Yehuda Liebes has brought to our attention the striking identification of Metatron with Jesus in the liturgy.'"[38] Yes, in the traditional Jewish liturgy!

To be clear, Professor Liebes was not claiming that the medieval Jews who prayed this prayer were followers of Jesus. Rather, he believes that early followers of Yeshua, themselves Jews, had a role in shaping some of the Jewish liturgy and that through their influence the wording became so well known that it could not be easily removed. Instead, the meaning of the prayer was changed, but not the wording. And can you imagine what happens to a Messianic Jew who learns about this prayer for the first time, finding it on the pages of a traditional Jewish prayer book, and says, "Wait a second! That's a prayer to God through the mediation of Jesus!" And what happens to a traditional Jew who has prayed the words many times before and then realizes one day, "Wait a second! That's talking about Yeshua— the one the Christians worship—and He is called here 'the Prince of God's face'!" Can you imagine the spiritual upheaval this revelation would bring? Could it be true?

It was Liebes' opinion that this prayer was originally introduced by Jewish followers of Yeshua who saw Him as a unique, highly exalted intermediary between man and God, a figure like Metatron but not fully equal to God.[39] But all this is speculation.

What we do know is that the invisible, transcendent, eternal God often made Himself known in visible, physical form, all while remaining hidden in His heavenly glory. This is what is often meant by the angel (or messenger) of Yahweh, or in Isaiah 63:9, the angel (or messenger) of His presence (or face). The New Covenant Writings put it like this:

> In the beginning was the Word. The Word was with God, and the Word was God. He was with God in the beginning. All things were made through Him, and apart from Him nothing was made that has come into being. In Him was life, and the life was the light of men.... And the Word became flesh and tabernacled among us. We looked upon His glory, the glory of the one and only from the Father, full of grace and truth.
>
> —JOHN 1:1–4, 14, TLV

And then this: "No one has ever seen God; but the one and only God, in the Father's embrace, has made Him known" (v. 18, TLV). What was pointed to in the writings of the Hebrew Bible was fully revealed when the Messiah came into the world! That's why He could say to His disciples, with reference to the miracles He performed, "He who has seen Me has seen the Father. How can you say, 'Show us the Father'? Don't you believe that I am in the Father and the Father is in Me? The words I say to you, I do not speak on My own; but the Father dwelling in Me does His works. Believe Me that I am in the Father and the Father is in Me—or at least believe because of the works themselves" (John 14:9–11, TLV).

It is this truth, namely, Yeshua the Messiah was, in a unique sense, the very essence of God in human form, that explains why death could not defeat Him. As He said to the Jewish crowds who came to hear Him and to challenge Him, "For this reason the Father loves Me, because I lay down My life, so that I may take it up again. No one takes it away from Me, but I lay it down on My own. I have the authority to lay it down, and I have the authority to take it up again. This command I received from My Father" (John 10:17–18, TLV).

You can crucify the Prince of Life, the Messenger of God's Presence, but you cannot keep Him in the grave. He was not only resurrected from the dead and brought back to life; He Himself *is* the resurrection and the life. Is the picture becoming clearer?

CHAPTER 9

WAS THE RESURRECTION A TEST?

IF JESUS DID not rise from the dead, there can be no such thing as the Messianic Jewish (or Christian) faith. Absolutely none at all. In contrast, Islam does not require the resurrection of Muhammad. It views him as the seal of the prophets, and it considers the Quran the literal Word of God. Yet Islam neither believes in nor requires Muhammad's resurrection from the grave. It's the same with Buddha and Buddhism and with Moses and Judaism. None of these religions requires their leader to rise from the dead. But if Yeshua did not rise, then our faith in Him is misguided and His teachings should be disregarded.

Almost two thousand years ago, some of the Christians in Corinth were questioning whether there would be a future resurrection of the dead. Paul addressed this head-on, writing:

> But if there is no resurrection of the dead, not even Messiah has been raised! And if Messiah has not been raised, then our proclaiming is meaningless and your faith also is meaningless. Moreover, we are found to be false witnesses of God, because we testified about God that He raised up Messiah—whom He did not raise up, if in fact the dead are not raised. For if the dead are not raised, not even Messiah has been raised. *And if Messiah has not been raised, your faith is futile*—you are still in your sins. Then those also who have fallen asleep [meaning, died] in Messiah have perished. If we have hoped in Messiah in this life alone, we are to be pitied more than all people.
> —1 CORINTHIANS 15:13–19, TLV, EMPHASIS ADDED

That one sentence sums it up well: *if Jesus the Messiah has not been raised, our faith is futile.*

It's different when it comes to the Lubavitcher Rebbe, as he continues to impact his followers through his writings and videos and personal example, now more than twenty-five years after his death. And the Lubavitcher movement continues to grow worldwide, even though the Rebbe did not rise from the dead. This means that, despite the fragmentation within the movement regarding him being the Messiah, the movement does not require his resurrection.

This, again, is in contrast with the Jesus movement, which absolutely requires the resurrection, even though His personal example was extraordinary and His teaching on another level entirely. But if He did not rise from the dead, then He cannot be the Messiah. If He did not rise from the dead, then His death did not provide atonement for the sins of the world. If He did not rise from the dead, then He was either a liar or He was deceived (or His followers were liars or were deceived). If He did not rise from the dead, then He did not bodily ascend to heaven. If He did not rise from the dead, He is not performing miracles today through His followers, in His name. If He did not rise from the dead, He will not return at the end of the age.

The good news—really, the absolutely wonderful news—is that Yeshua the Messiah *did* rise from the dead, guaranteeing that we too will be resurrected in the future. (That's why Paul stated that Yeshua was "the firstfruits" of those who previously died—meaning, the first to rise from the dead; 1 Corinthians 15:20, 23.) It is the fact of His resurrection that has led countless millions of people to faith over these last two millennia. The grave, indeed, was empty.

But what if there's another angle to this entirely? What if the resurrection of Jesus was only a test? What if God really did raise Him from the dead, but only as a test to see if His Jewish people would follow Him? What if this was just another miracle—albeit an extreme miracle—performed by God to see whether His people would abandon the Torah to follow this alleged Messiah?

As outlandish as it seems, I've heard that argument raised by rabbis. One said to me, "The resurrection would just be another miracle. We don't put our trust in miracles." Another said to me, "Deuteronomy 13 already addresses this. Any miracle that leads us away from the God of our forefathers is just a test of our obedience."

Could it be that these rabbis are right? Let's start by examining Deuteronomy 13, after which we'll consider the larger logic of these arguments. Could the resurrection of Jesus be a test?

We read in Deuteronomy 13:

> If there appears among you a prophet or a dream-diviner and he gives
> you a sign or a portent, saying, "Let us follow and worship another
> god"—whom you have not experienced—even if the sign or por-
> tent that he named to you comes true, do not heed the words of that
> prophet or that dream-diviner. For the LORD your God is testing you
> to see whether you really love the LORD your God with all your heart
> and soul. Follow none but the LORD your God, and revere none but
> Him; observe His commandments alone, and heed only His orders;
> worship none but Him, and hold fast to Him. As for that prophet or
> dream-diviner, he shall be put to death; for he urged disloyalty to the
> LORD your God—who freed you from the land of Egypt and who
> redeemed you from the house of bondage—to make you stray from
> the path that the LORD your God commanded you to follow. Thus you
> will sweep out evil from your midst.
>
> —DEUTERONOMY 13:2–6, JPS TANAKH[1]

So, could this important text in the Torah be used as an argument that
the resurrection of Jesus was simply a test? Certainly not, for at least three
major reasons.

NO, BECAUSE HE MADE GOD KNOWN

First, Yeshua never said, "Let us follow and worship another god." Perish
the thought. All that He did, He did in harmony with His heavenly Father.
All that He did brought glory and honor to the God of Israel. All His miracles and all His teaching drew attention to HaShem, the eternal Lord, the
King of Israel. This is a typical account:

> Jesus went on from there and walked beside the Sea of Galilee. And
> he went up on the mountain and sat down there. And great crowds
> came to him, bringing with them the lame, the blind, the crippled, the
> mute, and many others, and they put them at his feet, and he healed
> them, so that the crowd wondered, when they saw the mute speaking,
> the crippled healthy, the lame walking, and the blind seeing. *And
> they glorified the God of Israel.*
>
> —MATTHEW 15:29–31, EMPHASIS ADDED

When He was asked by a Jewish teacher what the greatest commandment was, Yeshua replied, "'You shall love ADONAI your God with all your heart, and with all your soul, and with all your mind.' This is the first and greatest commandment. And the second is like it, 'You shall love your neighbor as yourself.' The entire Torah and the Prophets hang on these two commandments" (Matt. 22:37–40, TLV).

Did He teach that, in a unique way, the Father was in Him and He was in the Father? Absolutely. (See John 14:8–11.) Did He teach that, in a unique way, He and the Father were one? Certainly. (See John 10:30.) But everything He said and did and taught and modeled was in complete harmony with the absolute monotheism of the Tanakh. He pointed everyone upward, to the Father, and it was His mission to make the Father known to the Jewish people and the world. (See further chapter 8 on the mystery of the divine angel and the Messiah.)

The Letter to the Hebrews puts it very powerfully:

> At many times and in many ways, God spoke long ago to the fathers through the prophets. In these last days He has spoken to us through a Son, whom He appointed heir of all things and through whom He created the universe. This Son is the radiance of His glory and the imprint of His being, upholding all things by His powerful word. When He had made purification for our sins, He sat down at the right hand of the Majesty on high. Thus He became as far above the angels as the name He has inherited is more excellent than theirs.
>
> —HEBREWS 1:1–4, TLV

So, a plain reading of Deuteronomy 13 makes clear that it was not a warning about following Jesus, since Jesus was here to make the God of Israel known. (See John 1:18.)

Counter-missionary rabbi Yisroel Blumenthal differs with this assessment, writing:

> In that passage God clearly instructs us that even if a miracle is performed which seems to substantiate the claims of a prophet, we are not to take this as a sign that God wants us to worship another god. God is testing us to see if we truly love Him with all our hearts. So, even if Jesus were to resurrect himself in front of our eyes, still this cannot serve as a sign that we are to worship him. Since he is

not the one who was revealed to the Jewish people at Sinai, then he is *"another god,"* all his claims to the contrary notwithstanding. So the entire claim of the resurrection, even if it could be backed by solid evidence, does not have the strength to prove the veracity of any brand of trinitarian Christianity.[2]

This, however, represents a fundamental misunderstanding of God's complex unity (called the Trinity by Christians), as it can be demonstrated that *the God of the New Testament is one and the same as the God of the Old Testament.* Put another way, the God of Sinai was the God of Jesus,[3] and as noted by a Jewish author, through the lens of Jewish mysticism, "The Torah, read properly, reveals that God is not a negative abstraction but a complex and dynamic system, full of movement and possibility, which it is possible to understand in great detail."[4] Jesus made this God known.

NO, BECAUSE HE UPHELD THE TORAH

But what if Yeshua simply called on His people to reject the Torah of Moses? What if He didn't call Israel to worship a different God but rather called them to follow a different law? When an interviewer in Israel asked Orthodox Jews whether the Lubavitcher Rebbe could still be the Messiah even though he died, some said that yes, he could. When he then asked them, "Then what about Yeshu [Jesus]?" they seemed surprised by the question. "But Yeshu was a lawbreaker," they said. "He led Israel away from Torah."[5]

As expressed by professor and rabbi Allan Nadler:

> One of the most dangerous consequences of the messianic carnival
> that has overtaken Lubavitch society during the past two decades
> has been its exploitation by fundamentalist Christian missionaries.
> Reporting on a California highway billboard with the phone number
> of a Christian mission to the Jews, a picture of Schneerson and the
> words "Right Idea: Wrong Person," Rabbi Berger concludes with sad-
> ness that "the profound theological differences between Judaism and
> Christianity have been reduced to a matter of mistaken identity."[6]

Maimonides wrote:

> We require only a miracle as [the prophet's] credentials, although it
> may be wrought by stratagem or magic, just as we accept the evidence

of witnesses although there is a possibility of perjury. For we are divinely commanded through Moses to render judgment in a suit at law in accordance with the testimony of two witnesses, the possibility of false swearing notwithstanding. Similarly we are enjoined to yield obedience to one who asserts that he is a prophet provided he can substantiate his claims by miracle or proofs, although there is a possibility that he is an impostor. However, if the would-be-prophet teaches tenets that negate the doctrines of Moses, then we must repudiate him.[7]

As argued on a Chabad website:

The rejection of Yeshu HaNotzri [Jesus the Christian], as the Rambam [Maimonides] calls him, had nothing to do with his death, or his being killed, or the likes thereof. Everyone in those times, including the non-Jews of the time, knew that Jewish rejection of him was precisely because he went against Torah and *mitzvos* [commandments], because he abolished Torah and *mitzvos*. There was nothing about him to indicate that he was a representative of the concept of a Moshiach. This has nothing to do with the fact that he died.

He definitely was misrepresenting [Torah], and definitely had nothing to do with somebody that could have [been Moshiach, but was disqualified] because he died. That's for sure.[8]

But Jesus did *not* teach "tenets that negate the doctrines of Moses." It is false to say that Jesus "abolished Torah and *mitzvos*." As He stated emphatically at the outset of His public ministry:

Do not think that I came to abolish the Torah or the Prophets! I did not come to abolish, but to fulfill. Amen, I tell you, until heaven and earth pass away, not the smallest letter or serif shall ever pass away from the Torah until all things come to pass. Therefore, whoever breaks one of the least of these commandments, and teaches others the same, shall be called least in the kingdom of heaven. But whoever keeps and teaches them, this one shall be called great in the kingdom of heaven. For I tell you that unless your righteousness exceeds that of the Pharisees and Torah scholars, you shall never enter the kingdom of heaven!

—MATTHEW 5:17–20, TLV[9]

That's why Yeshua's first followers, all of them Jews, continued to live as Jews. They only taught that Gentile followers of Jesus were not required to follow the Law of Moses. Then, over the passage of time, and with the destruction of the temple and the scattering of my own Jewish people, rather than following the innovations of the rabbis, who devised new traditions to make up for the loss of temple and national sovereignty, they used the teaching of Jesus and New Covenant Writings as their guide, living out Torah in the newness of the Holy Spirit. They understood that in accordance with the prophecy of Jeremiah, they were under the New Covenant, not the Sinai Covenant, which required a functioning temple and priesthood and sacrificial system, among other things.

The fact is that no one alive today practices Second Temple Judaism. Things have changed dramatically, on the one hand leading to Rabbinic Judaism and on the other hand leading to Messianic Judaism (which ultimately gives birth to Christianity, through which God reaches out to the whole world).

As explained by Dr. Immanuel Jakobovits, former chief rabbi of the United Kingdom:

> When our Sages asserted that "the Holy One, Blessed be He, did not make His covenant with Israel except by virtue of the Oral Law" (Gittin 60B), they not only propounded a cardinal Jewish belief, they also expressed a truth as evident today as it was in Talmudic times. The true character of Judaism cannot be appreciated except by an intimate acquaintance with the Oral Law. The Written Law, that is the Five Books of Moses, and even the rest of the Hebrew Bible, we share with other faiths. What makes us and our faith distinct and unique is the oral tradition as the authentic key to an understanding of the written text we call the Torah.[10]

Or, as Orthodox Jewish author Chaim Schimmel states:

> The Jewish people are frequently called "The People of the Book," yet if one were to search out a people who follow literally the Bible's behest, one might be led to the Samaritans, who still practise their religion on the outskirts of Shechem, or the Karaites who are now settled to the south of modern Tel-Aviv, but never to the Jewish people. *They do not follow the literal word of the Bible, nor have they ever*

done so. They have been fashioned and ruled by the verbal inter-
pretation of the written word, more particularly by the "Torah,"
which embraces both the written and the oral law.[11]

So then, traditional Jews relate to Torah based on the Mishnah and
Talmud and Law Codes and Commentaries and Responsa literature.
Messianic Jews relate to Torah based on the New Covenant Writings and
the Holy Spirit. And they see the fullness of the Torah expressed through
the life and death and resurrection and teaching and example of Yeshua,
who was *not* killed because "everyone in those times, including the non-
Jews of the time, knew that Jewish rejection of him was precisely because
he went against Torah and *mitzvos*."

No, He was killed as an essential part of His mission, part of His ful-
filling the Torah's requirements for blood sacrifices and atonement. (For
more on this, see chapter 7, "Rediscovering Israel's Suffering and Rising
Messiah.") As He said in His very own words, He came not to abolish the
Torah or the prophets but to fulfill them.

NO, BECAUSE THE RESURRECTION HAS MEANING

Second, there is a massive difference between someone working a miracle
or delivering an accurate prophecy and that same person being raised from
the dead. If someone is raised from the dead and does not die again, that
means God is making a statement about that person. He is vindicating that
person, sustaining that person, performing an ongoing miracle by which he
or she defies death. This is clearly an entirely separate category, especially
if this same person ascended bodily to heaven.

That's why elsewhere in Scripture we have examples of pagan miracle
workers duplicating some of Yahweh's miracles (Exod. 7–8) and there
are many references to false prophets. (See, for example, 1 Kings 22 and
Jeremiah 23.) Making an accurate prediction about the future is not that
hard, and giving an accurate interpretation of a dream does not always
require divine wisdom. That's how fortune-tellers, palm readers, and other
charlatans stay in business, while some of them even rely on satanic power.

But throughout the Bible *only God raises the dead*. Satan cannot do it.
Demonic spirits cannot do it. Human beings cannot do it. Why, then, would
God perform an act that only He could perform to back the message of a
false prophet?[12] This would be similar to God parting the sea or sending

fire from heaven or speaking from another mountain (like Sinai) to back the message of a false teacher. To do so would be to undermine the uniqueness of the exodus and the Sinai event (or the uniqueness of Elijah calling down fire from heaven to prove that Yahweh alone was God). In the same way, for God to raise a false teacher from the dead (never to die again) to test His people would be to undermine His uniqueness. (See, for example, Deuteronomy 32:39, which says only God can kill or make alive.)

NO, BECAUSE HIS DEATH AND RESURRECTION WERE FORETOLD

Third, as we saw in chapter 7, the Scriptures predicted the Messiah's death and resurrection. How, then, could God expect His children *not* to believe in the resurrected Yeshua when 1) Yeshua pointed the Jewish people to worship and love their God, not other gods; 2) the miracles He performed exalted the God of Israel; and 3) He declared that He would die and rise in accordance with the words of Israel's prophets?

And that's where the fundamental logic of this argument that "the resurrection is a test" breaks down. In short, if Jesus was not the Jewish Messiah, then the Jewish people did the right thing in rejecting Him. Even rabbinic writings confirm this. As I noted elsewhere, "Both the Talmud and Moses Maimonides speak freely of Jewish participation in Yeshua's death."[13] And even though there is some dispute regarding the Talmud's statements concerning Jesus,[14] there is no dispute regarding what Maimonides wrote. As I pointed out:

> The latter writes explicitly of "Jesus of Nazareth who aspired to be the Messiah and was executed by the court"—meaning the Jewish court, otherwise known as the Sanhedrin. As explained by Rabbi Eliyahu Touger, "The Jews did not actually carry out the execution, for crucifixion is not one of the Torah's methods of execution. Rather, after condemning him to death, the Sanhedrin handed him over to the Roman authorities who executed him as a rebel against Roman rule."[15]

So, according to Maimonides, one of the most respected voices in Judaism, Jesus was a false Messiah and was rightly rejected and condemned by the Sanhedrin, the Jewish leadership at that time. Why, then, would God raise Him from the dead, confirming the very words that Jesus spoke? This would not be a matter of divine testing. This would be a matter of divine deceit, of almighty God going out of His way to trick people into believing in a false Messiah, of saying to them, "You were wrong to reject Him and kill Him!"

Maimonides didn't even believe that Jesus raised people from the dead, even though they subsequently died again (like Lazarus in John 11), writing, "You know that the Christians falsely ascribe marvelous powers to Jesus the Nazarene, may his bones be ground to dust, such as the resurrection of the dead and other miracles."[16] How much less would he accept Yeshua Himself being raised from the dead, never to die again?

Yet a number of leading Jewish scholars, including professor Yehezkel Kaufmann, accepted the accounts of the empty tomb, writing, "On the third day after the crucifixion...the body of Jesus vanished from the grave. Just how that happened is unknown, but the disappearance of the corpse was certainly the occasion of the renewal of the messianic movement."[17] How interesting! As noted by the Jewish historian Ellis Rivkin, "But it was not Jesus' life which proved beyond question that he was the Messiah, the Christ. It was his resurrection. It was only when his disciples were convinced that Jesus had indeed risen from the dead that they were stunned into awareness that Jesus was the Christ."[18]

This is in perfect harmony with what we discovered in the last two chapters, and it reinforces what we stated at the outset of this chapter: without the resurrection, there is no Messianic Jewish (or Christian) faith. And it drives home the question yet again: If Jesus was not the Messiah and the Jewish people did the right thing in rejecting him, why would God raise him from the dead, giving the appearance of vindication and divine backing? Why wouldn't God commend His people for their discernment and courage?

To take this one step further, Jesus predicted the destruction of both the temple and the city of Jerusalem as a divine judgment for His rejection. As Luke records:

> And when he drew near and saw the city, he wept over it, saying, "Would that you, even you, had known on this day the things that make for peace! But now they are hidden from your eyes. For the days will come upon you, when your enemies will set up a barricade around you and surround you and hem you in on every side and tear

you down to the ground, you and your children within you. And they will not leave one stone upon another in you, *because you did not know the time of your visitation.*"

—LUKE 19:41–44, EMPHASIS ADDED

Not only so, but Jesus predicted that His people—the Jewish people—would be scattered from Jerusalem and exiled into the nations. "They will fall by the edge of the sword," He said, "and be led captive among all nations, and Jerusalem will be trampled underfoot by the Gentiles, until the times of the Gentiles are fulfilled" (Luke 21:24).

Was this a test too? Would anyone dare argue that not only did God raise Yeshua from the dead to test His people's obedience, but He also caused His holy temple and holy city to be destroyed and His own children to be killed or exiled to give the appearance of divine judgment? This is madness.

It would also mean that rather than God telling His children, "Well done! You have rejected that dangerous false prophet Jesus," He decided to test them by 1) raising him from the dead; 2) taking him up to heaven, in full view of many witnesses; 3) continuing to perform miracles in his name; 4) destroying the temple; 5) destroying Jerusalem; 6) slaughtering hundreds of thousands of His people (Josephus says one million Jews died in the war against Rome from AD 66–74); and 7) scattering His people around the world. Can anyone possibly believe this? Can even the most devout, ultra-Orthodox, Jesus-rejecting Jew countenance such a scenario?

It would not only make God into the Arch Deceiver. It would make Him the Liar in Chief, since the Torah promised divine blessing for national obedience and divine cursing for national disobedience. Yet here, when Israel allegedly acted in obedience to God by rejecting the supposedly false Messiah Jesus, He cursed them instead. Preposterous!

Of course, a religious Jew could argue that there were other reasons for the destruction of Jerusalem and the exile and that Jesus didn't really rise from the dead. As to the denial of Yeshua's resurrection, Rabbi Yisroel Blumenthal wrote, "It is also possible that some of the disciples removed the body from the grave. Matthew tells us that this is what the general population believed at that time. If this were the case it is obvious that the disciples who actually removed the body would not believe the resurrection story, but the rest of the following would have no problem believing it."[19]

This argument, however, refutes itself, since the disciples who allegedly

135

removed Jesus' body from the grave are the very ones who most fervently believed in His resurrection. Does Rabbi Blumenthal actually think that they were fooled by their very own alleged hoax?

ONLY ONE EXPLANATION SUFFICES

As we have seen, there is only one explanation for the universal belief among the first followers of Jesus that He rose from the dead, namely, that He rose. And if He rose, that means God raised Him. The idea that this was a divine test simply doesn't work.

Moreover, the rabbinic explanations for the destruction of the temple and the subsequent exile are very weak. As we read in b. Yoma 9b, the Talmud asks: *"Due to what* reason *was* the *First Temple destroyed?* It was destroyed *due to* the fact *that there were three matters* that existed *in the* First Temple: *Idol worship, forbidden sexual relations, and bloodshed."*

These are very serious violations, yet the exile lasted only seventy years. What about the destruction of the second temple? At the time the Talmud was compiled, the temple had been destroyed for several hundred years (five hundred at most), meaning the destruction of the second temple had lasted multiple centuries longer than the destruction of the first temple. Now we're looking at the destruction lasting *almost two thousand years.* That's almost *thirty times* as long as the first destruction. What, then, was the reason? The Talmud explains:

> *However,* considering that the people during *the Second Temple* period *were engaged in Torah* study, observance of *mitzvot [commandments], and acts of kindness,* and that they did not perform the sinful acts that were performed in the First Temple, *why was* the Second Temple *destroyed?* It was destroyed *due to* the fact *that there was wanton hatred* during that period. This comes *to teach you that* the sin of *wanton hatred is equivalent to the three* severe *transgressions: Idol worship, forbidden sexual relations and bloodshed.*[20]

So, the Talmud claims that the Jewish people in Yeshua's day were not like their forefathers. They did not engage in idol worship or forbidden sexual relations and bloodshed. Instead they were engaged in Torah study, in keeping the commandments, and in acts of kindness. Their great sin was "wanton hatred" (better rendered "baseless hatred"). And for this, the temple remains destroyed for almost two thousand years? For this, our people have been scattered around the world for multiplied centuries? How can this be?

The Talmud even acknowledges that there was baseless hatred during the days of the first temple as well, which once again begs the question: Why such a severe destruction and such a lasting judgment, when one generation earlier the Jewish people allegedly passed a great test by rejecting a dangerous false Messiah? Why would God give the impression that Jesus was right in predicting this judgment? And to add divine insult to divine injury, why would He raise Jesus from the dead, never to die again?

To say it again, this would not be a test. It would be an act of divine sadism. Perish the thought.

Not only so, but according to this scenario, God would *still* be deceiving His Jewish people, along with multitudes of Gentiles worldwide, by performing miracles in Jesus' name to confirm His resurrection. The thought is beyond absurd.

Could it be, then, that the second temple was in fact destroyed because of baseless hatred, only it was because of our baseless hatred of the Messiah? Could it be?

But there is good news. Even if the Jewish people, my own people, were guilty of rejecting the Messiah on a national level, His death is not the end of the story. Instead, His crucifixion is the beginning of the most amazing story ever told, providing the platform for the greatest event in history, the event that changed the world.

CHAPTER 10

WHY NOT JUDAISM FOR JEWS AND CHRISTIANITY FOR GENTILES?

COULD IT BE that there's a simple solution to our problem? Could it be that we're missing the forest for the trees? What if God's purpose in raising Jesus from the dead was to send Him as a prophet to the nations, the *goyyim*? What if His mission was not to Israel but to the world? That would mean Jews could reject Him as Messiah and practice Judaism, and God would be pleased with this, while Gentiles could embrace Him as Savior and practice Christianity, and God would be please with that.

Put another way, we would each have our own religion and our God-ordained path of faith, and so we would live and let live with tolerance and respect. Is this the way to solve our either-or dilemma? The Lubavitchers can even have the Rebbe as their Moshiach if they like, while the Gentiles can follow Jesus. No more arguing. No more proselytizing. Just harmony, honor, and joy. Could it be true?

To help us think this through, let's ask ourselves what things might have looked like if Jesus had been a Gentile rather than a Jew. What if His parents were named Guiseppe and Maria rather than Joseph and Miriam (Mary)? And what if they lived on the outskirts of ancient Rome rather than in Nazareth? What if the Savior's name was Gesù (pronounced *jay-zoo*) rather than Yeshua, and what if His followers were named Pietro and Matteo and Luca and Giovanni rather than Peter and Matthew and Luke and John? What if Gesù, an unusual and special child, had been divinely called to tell the nations—not the Jewish people—about the one true God?

139

After all, the Jewish nation already knew about the one and only God, and they had received His message centuries ago. They had the Torah—the divine instructions for life—and they had the words of the prophets like Isaiah and Jeremiah and Ezekiel. They had their sacred history, celebrating the exodus from Egypt, remembering great leaders like King David, and commemorating the miraculous deeds of Elijah and Elisha and others too many to name. They had the holy temple in Jerusalem, the one place on earth that was home to God's presence. They had their priests and wise men and teachers. And they had their unique traditions, carefully passed on from generation to generation.

But the nations of the world lived in darkness, steeped in idolatry and superstition. Who would bring the knowledge of God to them?

It's true that in some cities in the ancient world there were Jewish synagogues where interested Gentiles could go and learn about the God of Israel. But these synagogues were, relatively speaking, few and far between, as were the God-fearing Gentiles who would visit every Sabbath. As for converting to Judaism, which would mean taking on hundreds of laws and thousands of traditions, even fewer Gentiles took that step, while the masses in every country lived and died in spiritual ignorance.

How long would the Creator allow His creation to flounder? Hinduism revealed a multiplicity of gods, none of them equal to the Lord. Buddhism taught a way of life devoid of an encounter with the divine. (Did Buddhism even believe in an eternal God?) Zoroastrianism, found in ancient Persia, spoke of a wise lord, Ahura Mazda. But it also spoke of a competing, lesser lord, Angra Mainyu, the angry spirit, and Ahura Mazda was clearly not the same as Yahweh (or Jehovah), the God of Israel, the one true God. As for the Greco-Roman pantheon, those gods resembled sinful humans more than the transcendent Lord.

Some people prayed to the elements, believing the sun and moon and stars and sea were deities. Others prayed to their ancestors, believing in an unseen realm filled with spirits and demons and departed loved ones yet devoid of the Creator and King. Some even sacrificed their sons and daughters, burning them alive on a fiery altar to appease their angry deities. And virtually all lived and died without spiritual hope, without assurance of eternal life, without the knowledge that their sins could be forgiven, without experiencing the love of God. How long would the heavenly Father allow this to continue?

Let's imagine that it was against this backdrop that Gesù was born two thousand years ago. From his childhood his parents recognized there was something special about him, something unusual that set him apart from his peers. He seemed to know there was more to this world than working and eating and drinking and getting married and having a family. He seemed to have a spiritual hunger that drove him to search for truth, for answers. How did we get here, and what is our purpose on this earth? And why is there so much suffering and pain? If there really is a God (or gods), what does it (or they) want from us? And so Gesù would often sit alone, meditating and reflecting and seeking.

But something else set him apart. He really cared about others, putting them first and feeling their pain as if it was his own. He would weep at the funeral of a stranger. He would skip meals and secretly leave the food for the hungry. He considered every man his brother and every woman his sister. And as he grew into adulthood, he sensed a calling, a kind of mission. Someone was beckoning him from above. Someone was marking him for life. Someone was calling him by name. But who, and why?

Gesù had always been fascinated by the religious Jews of Rome. They ordered their lives by different standards and lived by a different calendar. They worshipped one deity only. They refused to be changed by the world, and they would not conform to the spirit of the age. As a people, they seemed to be marked and called, just as Gesù somehow felt marked and called. Perhaps they could help him discover his own sacred mission.

So it was that Gesù walked into the local synagogue one Sabbath and, for the first time in his life, heard the Scriptures read. What a story they told! The Creator God had chosen Israel as His own sacred treasure, giving them His laws and commandments and making an eternal covenant with them. He would be their Father, and they would be His sons and daughters. "Surely this is the real God," Gesù thought to himself with wonder. "Surely this is the One who has been calling me from my youth."

That much was becoming clear. But still the question lingered: Calling him to do what? What is God's mission for Gesù?

Gesù returned to the synagogue the following Sabbath, intrigued but confused, yet sensing a breakthrough was near. Then it happened, quite unexpectedly and out of the blue. As the holy scrolls were opened, a passage from the prophet Isaiah was read, and in a moment everything became clear. The words seemed to pass right through him, filling his heart with fire and consuming his every thought: *I am the Lord. I have called you to be a light to the nations. You will take My message to the ends of the earth. You have been chosen.*[1]

Staggering under the weight of these words, Gesù made his way out of the building, holding the walls to steady himself, overwhelmed with the light that now flooded his soul. *The God of Israel—the one true God—has appointed me to take His message to the nations. This is my sacred life calling.*

Suddenly the world looked different. That couple walking down the street was wearing shackles. That vendor in the village square was totally blind. Those majestic buildings in the heart of the city were smoldering ruins. The world was lost, lost, lost! People were perishing in darkness and ignorance, and it was his sacred mission to show them the truth. Now he understood!

For the next two years Gesù learned from his Jewish teachers, asking endless questions about this God and His requirements. Perhaps all the nations should convert to Judaism? Perhaps he too should convert, calling fellow Gentiles to follow in his steps?

The teachers explained to him that it was not the Lord's will for everyone to become Jewish. Only Israel was given the holy Torah. Only Israel was called to keep the 613 commandments. Only Israel was entrusted with the sacred traditions. As for the nations, God only required basic morality from them: that they would turn from idols to the Creator, that they would treat each other justly, that they would not murder or steal or commit sexual sins—in short, that they would love God and love their neighbor. This was what God required. It was all becoming clear!

Armed with that sense of divine destiny, Gesù began to share this news with his neighbors, who were strangely drawn to his words and who in turn told their friends about this charismatic young man, this prophet of sorts. Could his message be true?

Soon enough, crowds followed him wherever he taught. And to his utter amazement, as he shared his message with the multitudes, miracles began to happen. Blind eyes were opened and deaf ears unstopped. Cripples jumped up and danced. The one true God was displaying His power. The Creator was shouting, "I am He!"

And something else began to happen. The crowds began to weep in repentance, recognizing how selfish they had been, how wicked, how carnal, how sinful. They went home and smashed the statues of their idols. They confessed their sins to each other, making restitution for fraud and theft. They burned their magic books and severed their adulterous relationships. And with Gesù's guidance, they began to meet together regularly, praying to the one true God and discussing their leader's teaching. "The Creator has sent us a prophet," they said, "who has shown us the path of life."

As for Gesù, he gathered around himself a close-knit group of followers who compiled a written manual of his teachings, and they began to spread his message far and wide. The Gentile communities were thrilled to hear they could worship the God of Israel without having to become Jews, and they were discovering a new and better way to live. This was good news to them!

The local Jewish communities were thrilled with the results too. They were now revered rather than reviled, praised rather than persecuted, honored as elders rather than hated as outsiders. Surely God was with Gesù! He was even given the title "Christ," which meant "anointed one," since the Lord had clearly anointed him for this mission. Within a decade his followers were dubbed "Christians."

By the time of his death, the Christian faith—or Christianity, as it became known—had spread to all the surrounding nations, liberating and enlightening countless thousands. They had a special day of worship and rest (not to be confused with the Jewish Sabbath) and their own special calendar to follow. Two thousand years later, one in three people on the planet identified as a Christian as the movement continued to grow and prosper. As for the Jewish people, they continued to honor the Torah and keep God's commandments, profoundly grateful for the positive world impact of Christianity, a wonderful sister religion.

COULD IT BE?

It sounds like a lovely story, doesn't it? There's only one problem. It's not true. Jesus was not a Gentile named Gesù. He was a Jew named Yeshua, and all His disciples were Jews. And He did not simply sense a calling to teach the nations about the God of Israel. Rather, He declared Himself to be Israel's Messiah. He even claimed to be the only way to God. In fact, He predicted that the holy temple in Jerusalem would be destroyed because His Jewish people rejected Him as Messiah. He even said they would be scattered around the world in judgment for their sins.[2] This is not a popular message!

And this is where we get to the crux of the problem. If Yeshua is who He and His followers claimed Him to be—the Messiah of Israel—then Jewish people around the world should follow Him. All Jews should be Jews for Jesus! And if He *wasn't* who He and His followers claimed Him to be—if He was *not* the Messiah of Israel—then no one should follow Him. There should be no Gentiles for Jesus, no Christians on the planet. It's either all or nothing at all. The words of Jesus and the words of the rest of the New Testament leave us with no other choice.

And yet some scholars argue that although Jesus was Jewish, just as the New Testament records, His mission was to make the God of Israel known to the nations. So, Jews would follow Judaism while Gentiles would follow Christianity, and Jews could express their appreciation for this beautiful faith for the nations. And Christians, for their part, would not try to convince Jews to believe in Jesus, since His message was for the Gentiles, not for His fellow Jews. Everyone could live happily ever after.

But again, that's not what the New Testament says in passage after passage. Instead, from beginning to end it claims that Yeshua came as Israel's Messiah, because of which He was also the Savior of the world. Consequently, if Yeshua was not the Messiah of Israel, then He was not the Savior of the world. He was a deceiver, not a prophet; a fraud, not a messenger sent by God. And if He did not fulfill the ancient prophecies of Moses and Isaiah and others, then His Jewish people were right in rejecting Him and the nations should not listen to Him. If He was not Israel's Messiah, then Christianity is a lie.

To summarize the evidence of the New Covenant Writings:

- Yeshua was called "King of the Jews" at His birth and at His death (Matt. 2:2; 27:37).

- Matthew's Gospel introduced Him as "Jesus Christ, the son of David, the son of Abraham" (Matt. 1:1).

- He was given the title "rabbi," not "reverend" (John 9:2).

- He said He did not come to abolish the Torah or Prophets but to fulfill them (Matt. 5:17–20).

- He wore the fringes on His garments, as prescribed by the Torah (Luke 8:44; see also TLV, RSV, NRSV, and NASB).

- He said His first mission was to the "lost sheep of the house of Israel" (Matt. 10:5–6; 15:24).

- He said His message should be declared to all nations, beginning in Jerusalem (Luke 24:45–47).

- When His first followers discovered Him, they exclaimed, "We've found the One that Moses in the Torah, and also the prophets, wrote about—Yeshua of Natzeret, the son of Joseph!" (John 1:45, TLV).

- According to the writers of the Gospels, Yeshua's birth, life, death, and resurrection were all predicted in the Tanakh. (Read Matthew!)

- After His resurrection Yeshua said to two of His followers (who had doubted that He would rise), "How foolish you are, and how slow to believe all that the prophets have spoken! Did not the Messiah have to suffer these things and then enter his glory?" (Luke 24:25–26, NIV).

- Not long after that, Yeshua spoke to His eleven core disciples, saying, "These are My words which I spoke to you while I was still with you—everything written concerning Me in the Torah of Moses and the Prophets and the Psalms must be fulfilled" (Luke 24:44, TLV).

- Several weeks later, speaking to a large crowd in Jerusalem at Shavuot (Pentecost), Peter said, "And all the prophets who have spoken, from Samuel and those who came after him, also proclaimed these days" (Acts 3:24).

This is just the small tip of a very large (Jewish) iceberg: either Yeshua the Jew is the Messiah of Israel or He is the Savior of no one. You cannot have a Jesus for the Gentiles and another Messiah for the Jews. It simply will not work.

ANOTHER ATTEMPT TO SOLVE IT

But that doesn't mean some well-meaning religious leaders won't try to make this work. And that's why in 2015, twenty-five Orthodox rabbis signed a landmark, seven-paragraph document, in which they stated, "We acknowledge that the emergence of Christianity in human history is neither an accident nor an error, but the willed divine outcome and gift to the nations."[3] Yes, "We Jews and Christians have more in common than what divides us: the ethical monotheism of Abraham; the relationship with the One Creator of Heaven and Earth, Who loves and cares for all of us; Jewish Sacred Scriptures; a belief in a binding tradition; and the values of life, family, compassionate righteousness, justice, inalienable freedom, universal love and ultimate world peace."[4] In short, "In separating Judaism and Christianity, G-d willed a separation between partners with significant theological differences, not a separation between enemies."[5]

These are truly amazing sentiments, especially in light of the ugly history of "Christian" anti-Semitism, because of which Jews were persecuted, tortured, exiled, and killed for their refusal to embrace Christianity.[6] How remarkable, then, that these Orthodox rabbis had something positive to say about the Christian faith, seeing Christians as partners rather than enemies.

But this statement was not made in a vacuum. The rabbis were also responding to changes within the church, specifically within Catholicism. As they explain:

> We recognize that since the Second Vatican Council the official teachings of the Catholic Church about Judaism have changed fundamentally and irrevocably. The promulgation of Nostra Aetate fifty years ago started the process of reconciliation between our two communities. Nostra Aetate and the later official Church documents it inspired unequivocally reject any form of anti-Semitism, affirm the eternal Covenant between G-d and the Jewish people, reject deicide and stress the unique relationship between Christians and Jews, who were called "our elder brothers" by Pope John Paul II and "our fathers in faith" by Pope Benedict XVI.[7]

Again, it is highly significant that these rabbis composed such a positive statement, and they should be commended for their courageous efforts to be peacemakers and bridge builders. Unfortunately what they are saying cannot be entirely true, since either Judaism is correct in its claims or Christianity is correct in its claims (or neither is correct, at least in full). But both cannot be correct at the same time, since they make mutually exclusive claims.

That's why another Orthodox rabbi, Moshe Ben-Chaim, argued that there can be "no religious coexistence." Responding to the statement of these twenty-eight rabbis, he wrote:

> God equates with truth, and no consideration must obscure those truths. For by obscuring truth, we mislead ourselves, other Jews, and gentiles. Jews and Christians share a close relationship today built on honesty and openness. As religions conflict on core tenets, religionists agree that all religions cannot be God's word, for He does not contradict Himself. Only one religion is God's word. Intelligence alone will determine this.[8]

Consequently:

> We cannot suggest that God desired Christianity to arise. God desires no other religion than Judaism. In the Jewish year 2448 upon Mt. Sinai, God revealed Himself to man once. 2.5 million people witnessed this event. God publicly instructed man in only one religion: Judaism. God gave a Bible that includes prohibitions against altering His word. This is perfectly clear. Maimonides does not indicate that God desired Christianity's existence. This directly opposes God's Bible.[9]

The rabbi is being consistent: if his faith is right, Christianity is wrong. Similarly, Joseph Klausner, one of the earliest professors at Hebrew University in Jerusalem, engaged with the New Testament in his writing and yet wrote, "My deepest conviction is this: Judaism will never become reconciled with Christianity... nor will it be assimilated by Christianity; for Judaism and Christianity are not only two different religions but they are also *two different world-views*."[10] About fifty years later the prolific Jewish scholar Jacob Neusner wrote, "Judaism and Christianity are completely different religions."[11] He also said the two faiths "stand for different people talking about different things to different people."[12] He asked:

> Is there no bridge from Christianity "back" to Judaism, and is there
> no connection that links Judaism to Christianity? My argument is
> that there is none, there should be none, and when we recognise that
> the two are utterly distinct and different families of religions, the
> work of attempting a dialogue can begin.[13]

To illustrate the point that Rabbi Ben-Chaim and Professors Klausner
and Neusner were making, imagine for a moment that you're a committed
Christian of Gentile background and you are speaking with a traditional
Jew named Yehudah. When you ask Yehudah why he lives the way he does,
he tells you proudly, "I learned this from my father, who learned it from his
father, who learned it from his father, all the way back to Moses. This is
how we please God—we call Him HaShem. This is what He requires of us,
and this is what I teach my children."

You then ask Yehudah, "Then how come you're not going around the
world like the missionaries do, spreading your faith? Shouldn't you be
telling everyone what you believe?"

He replies, "That's not our job. We teach the world about God by living
as faithful Jews. Plus, HaShem doesn't want everyone to become Jewish.
Each person can find his own way to God. That's why we respect other
religions."

"But have you heard my story?" you ask. "I was a drug addict, and Jesus
set me free. My best friend was addicted to gambling, and Jesus set him
free too. My wife used to be an atheist, and Jesus opened her eyes and now
she believes in God. And that's just the beginning. I can take you around
the world, where you can meet followers of Jesus who used to be prostitutes or thieves or drunkards or even terrorists. They've been dramatically
changed and have become fine, upstanding people today. Without Jesus
we'd all be lost. Surely that must mean something to you."

Without missing a beat, he replies, "I'm glad to hear that—for you and
your wife and your friends and your colleagues. That's great, and more
power to you. But I've never been a drug addict or gambler or atheist or
prostitute or thief or drunkard or terrorist. I'm a God-fearing Jew. Let Jesus
go and save the rest of the world. Good for Him! But Jesus is not for me.
Why would I need Him?"

Then, with a twinkle in his eye, Yehudah says something you weren't
expecting. "You know, I once read some verses in your New Testament, and

I discovered that your Jesus agrees with me too. Do you remember that He said He didn't come to call the righteous but sinners? That it was the sick who needed a doctor, not the people who are well? That's my whole point. I'm well, not sick. With God's help, I keep the commandments, and when I fall short, I repent and ask for forgiveness. Jesus didn't come for people like me. He came for the *goyyim*—the Gentiles—who are lost in sin.

"In fact, I remember that Jesus explained in a famous parable that there's more joy in heaven for one sinner who repents than for ninety-nine righteous people who don't need to repent. I'm one of the ninety-nine! I never did drugs or got drunk or slept around or hurt other people, and I didn't need the help of Jesus to turn me around. You should go and find that one lost sinner and tell him about Jesus. But leave us Jews alone. We already have a fine relationship with God."

"But," you protest, "how can you explain all the miracles? Jesus Himself rose from the dead, and ever since then, miracles have been happening in His name. Your God seems to be backing up His mission! In fact, on a regular basis, Muslims are having visions of Jesus and becoming Christians, Hindus are being healed and becoming Christians—it's happening around the world all the time. If God is not with Jesus, who is performing the miracles?"

Yehudah replies, "That's not my concern. As I said, if Gentiles are turning away from their sins and believing in God, I'm happy."

"But it's not that simple," you persist. "Do you believe that Jesus died for the sins of the world?"

"No, I don't," he answers.

"Do you believe that He rose from the dead?"

"Certainly not," he replies.

"Do you believe that He ascended to heaven and sits at the right hand of God?"

"Of course not," he responds firmly.

"Then it looks like we have a problem," you say, "since if you're right, then everything I believe is a lie. Not only so, but all those former atheists and Buddhists and Hindus and Muslims and drug addicts and prostitutes and terrorists and thieves that I mentioned are also believing a lie. Every single one of them. And that means that all the miracles happening around the world in Jesus' name are based on a lie. How can that be? Would God be backing a lie?

"On the other hand, if Jesus really did die for the sins of the world and God vindicated Him by raising Him from the dead, and if He is seated by God's throne in heaven, then He's not just for the Gentiles. Everyone needs to believe in Him."

Yehudah replies, "Like I said, we Jews have our own covenant with God. If the *goyyim* want to believe in Jesus and they find inspiration and hope, good for them."

"I'm sorry, but that just won't work," you answer. "First, it sounds like spiritual snobbery to me, as if it's not acceptable for Jews to believe a lie but it's fine for Gentiles to believe a lie. Is that what you're saying? Second, either Jesus has risen from the dead or He hasn't. I say that God Himself is backing the message of Jesus, performing miracles in His name and changing lives in His name around the world. So, which is it? Is the whole world being deceived, or are you rejecting the One whom God sent?"

Yehudah replies, "You raise lots of interesting points, but this is what I know. God gave the Torah to Israel, and that's our responsibility—to observe the commandments of the Torah, not to figure out all these other things. That's for you and your friends to figure out."

You respond, "But the Torah speaks of Jesus! If you read the New Testament, then you know that Jesus was a Jew and that He claimed to be the Messiah. He even said that Moses spoke about Him in the Torah, and He claimed that if His Jewish people truly believed Moses, then they would believe Him. And if you read the New Testament, you know Jesus claimed to fulfill the words of Moses and the prophets. So, it's got to be one thing or the other, and as a religious Jew, you've got to accept Him or reject Him.

"If Moses spoke of Jesus and He is the promised Messiah, then He's for you first. If Moses didn't speak of Him and He wasn't the promised Messiah, He's not for any of us. We're not going to follow a lie."

With that, the discussion ends abruptly.

If this dialogue accurately reflects traditional Jewish beliefs, how then did these Orthodox rabbis arrive at such an affirming view of Jesus and Christianity? First, they did not address the claims of the New Testament but rather focused on the positive aspects of the Christian faith, which they found to be largely in harmony with Judaism. Second, they found affirming statements about Jesus in the writings of previous rabbis, most notably Rabbi Jacob Emden, who famously wrote in the 1700s:

Jesus brought a double goodness to the world. On the one hand he strengthened the Torah of Moses majestically...and not one of our Sages spoke out more emphatically concerning the immutability of the Torah. On the other hand he removed idols from the nations and obligated them in the seven commandments of Noah so that they would not behave like animals of the field, and instilled them firmly with moral traits....Christians are congregations that work for the sake of heaven who are destined to endure, whose intent is for the sake of heaven and whose reward will not denied.[14]

Third, the rabbis cited two great medieval Jewish thinkers, Rabbi Yehudah Halevi, author of the Kuzari, and Rabbi Moses Maimonides, author of many influential works, including his fourteen-volume code of law called the *Mishneh Torah*. In one of those volumes Maimonides explained that although Christianity and Islam were false religions, they still advanced the concepts of the Messiah and observing God's commandments, thereby paving the way for the coming of the Messiah. As he wrote:

But the thoughts of the Creator of the world are beyond any man's understanding. For our ways are not His ways, and our thoughts are not His thoughts. And all the doings of Jesus the Nazarene and that of that Ishmaelite [meaning Muhammad] who came after him are nothing but to pave the way for the King Messiah and prepare the entire world to worship G-d together, as it says, "For then I will turn to the peoples a pure language, that they may all call upon the Name of the Lord, to serve Him with one consent" (Zephaniah 3:9).[15]

In that spirit the rabbis stated, "As did Maimonides and Yehudah Halevi, we acknowledge that the emergence of Christianity in human history is neither an accident nor an error, but the willed divine outcome and gift to the nations."[16]

A FULLER PICTURE MAKES IT IMPOSSIBLE

But there's more to the story—something these rabbis did not quote (although, without a doubt, they were fully aware of it and, obviously, chose to emphasize the positive). You see, this very same Maimonides, one of the greatest thinkers in Jewish history, also had this to say about Jesus (in fact, he wrote this immediately before the text just quoted, which is why he began with the word "But," as just cited above). It is hardly a flattering description:

> Even Jesus the Nazarene who imagined he would be the Messiah and was killed by the Court [meaning the Jewish court] was prophesied about by Daniel as it says, "and also the children of the violent among your people will lift themselves up to establish the vision, but they shall stumble" (Daniel 11:14). Was there ever a greater impediment than this one? All the Prophets spoke of the Messiah, Redeemer of Israel and Savior and Gatherer of the Exiles and Strengthener of the Commandments. But this one caused the ruin of Israel by the sword and the dispersal of its remnant and its humiliation and changed the Torah, and caused most of the world to err and worship a god other than the Lord.[17]

What an indictment of the Christian Savior! According to Maimonides, Jesus was an evildoer and deceiver and destroyer and idolater. He was anything but the Messiah of Israel, anyone but the Redeemer who died and rose for our sins, anyone but the Son of God incarnate who will one day return to rule the world. In short, the Jesus of Maimonides (and traditional Judaism), referred to by them as Yeshu,[18] is not the Yeshua of the New Testament. That means that if Maimonides is right, then the New Testament, along with every Christian, is wrong. But if the New Testament is right, then Maimonides, along with every traditional Jew, is wrong—at least when it comes to Jesus. This may not be the language of religious ecumenism, and it certainly sounds harsh. But it is the language of truth, and without truth, there can be no true love.

That doesn't mean Jews and Christians cannot learn from each other, and that doesn't mean we can't work together and respect each other and treat each other with kindness. But it does mean we must not deceive ourselves into thinking that Judaism and Christianity—or more accurately, the traditional Jewish faith and the Messianic Jewish faith—can coexist in a mutually affirming way. *It is the Jewish Jesus that reminds us of this reality*, since a Gentilized Jesus neither intersects with Judaism nor calls Christians to recognize their Jewish roots. A Gentilized Jesus is not a stumbling block for Judaism or Christianity. A Jewish Jesus most certainly is.

In keeping with this either-or dichotomy, Rabbi Moshe Ben-Chaim, whom we noted above rejected the positive statement of the twenty-five rabbis, wrote:

> All peoples must respect one another's lives. We all must abstain from harming anyone, except those who physically attack us. However, today, this respect has grossly overgrown its borders to violate God's words. I refer to the current tide of mutual religious acceptance, and worse; the admiration of religions other than God's Torah, His Bible. Throughout the Bible, God warns against following other religions, altering His Bible, adding to it, subtracting from it, and deifying man. He also warns us not to lie, "From a false matter, distance yourself" (Exod. 23:7). These are perpetrated by all other religions, and today, by many Jewish leaders. God's Prophets discuss the corruptions of other nations and religions, their eventual rejection of their religions as lies, and their ultimate acceptance of the unaltered Bible, the Torah:
>
> > *"Nations will come from the corners of the land and say,*
> > *'In truth, our fathers gave us an inheritance of lies'"*
> > *(Jer. 16:19).*[19]

Yes, according to Maimonides and many traditional Jewish thinkers, including Rabbi Ben-Chaim, when the Messiah comes, many Christians and Muslims will renounce their faiths, using these words from Jeremiah 16:19, as quoted above: "In truth, our fathers gave us an inheritance of lies." If Maimonides is right, this would mean that all Christian missionaries who sacrificed their lives to spread the gospel were only spreading lies and that all Christian martyrs who died rather than deny the Lord died to defend a lie. It would mean that every noble and good and kind act done in the name of Jesus was based on a lie. What do the twenty-eight Orthodox rabbis say about this? Will they look their Christian friends in the eyes and say, "You are believing lies!"?

Rabbi Ben-Chaim added:

> What is more preferable; that Christianity would never had existed, or actual history? God's will is the former, stated quite openly. However, now that Christianity exists, Maimonides indicates it cannot compromise God's plan:
>
> > *"Nevertheless, the thoughts of the Creator of the world are not*

within the power of man to reach them, 'for our ways are not His ways, nor are our thoughts His thoughts.'"

We cannot fathom God's plan. Christianity violates God's words, but can in no way compromise God's ultimate plan, as these events were not thwarted by God. A negative may be utilized for a positive.

To say that Christianity "contributes" to God's plan, is much different than saying it "does not compromise" God's plan. The former suggests it is an inherent good, while the latter retains its true status as violating God's words.[20]

As much as I find the rabbi's opinions about Jesus to be totally wrong, I find his overall argument consistent, and I agree in principle with his point. Judaism and Christianity cannot be mutually affirming faiths for one fundamental, nonnegotiable reason: the New Testament plainly declares Jesus-Yeshua to be the Messiah of Israel, and either He is or He is not. Further, the New Testament plainly teaches that He died for the sins of the world and rose from the dead, and either He did or He did not.

Had Jesus been a Gentile prophet and had the New Testament been written for the Gentile world alone, we would not have this problem. But Jesus said He came first for His Jewish people (Matt. 10:5–6; 15:24), and Paul said the gospel is for the Jew first (Rom. 1:16). That means we have a problem—a large, monumental problem that is not going away anytime soon. Judaism must either accept or reject Jesus the Jew. It cannot be indifferent toward Him, nor can it say Jesus is fine for the Gentiles but not for the Jews. It cannot be both ways. Jesus the Jew makes that impossible, and His resurrection seals the deal.

Through our holy, Jewish Scriptures and through the Messiah's life, death, and resurrection, God is shouting to our Jewish people around the world: *Do not look for the Messiah's coming. Look for His return!*

Jacob Neusner once wrote, "Is Jesus the Christ? If so, then Judaism falls. If not, then Christianity fails."[21] Of course, he was right in saying that both traditional Judaism and traditional Christianity cannot be true at the same time. As we have seen so clearly in this chapter, either Jesus is the Messiah of Israel and therefore the Savior of the world or He is not the Messiah of Israel and therefore not the Savior of anyone.

But the resurrection of Jesus does not mean that "Judaism falls." Instead, it means the ultimate Jewish faith is the Messianic faith, the faith that affirms Yeshua rather than rejects Him. It is the faith of the Hebrew Bible plus the New Covenant Writings. The faith of the Jewish prophets and the Jewish apostles. The faith of the Messiah's death, resurrection, and return, all as predicted in our very own Scriptures, the Tanakh. This is the Jewish faith we must follow, the faith that becomes the light of the world, as we'll see in the next—and last—chapter of this book.

CHAPTER 11

THE EVENT THAT
CHANGED THE WORLD

IN AN IMPORTANT passage in the book *When Prophecy Fails*, the authors lay out a fascinating scenario:

> Suppose an individual believes something with his whole heart; suppose further that he has a commitment to this belief, that he has taken irrevocable actions because of it; finally, suppose that he is presented with evidence, unequivocal and undeniable evidence, that his belief is wrong: what will happen? The individual will frequently emerge, not only unshaken, but even more convinced of the truth of his beliefs than ever before. Indeed, he may even show a new fervor about convincing and converting other people to his view.[1]

Is this what happened to the Lubavitchers who were convinced the Rebbe was the Messiah? Could it also be what happened to the first followers of Jesus, who were likewise convinced that He was the Messiah?

Writing in 1995, sociology professor William Shaffir noted that before the Rebbe's death, he had predicted that once the Rebbe died, his followers would blame other Jews who had doubted his mission. They would say that the generation failed to recognize him and so proved unworthy of him. Other Jews were at fault, and so the Rebbe was never revealed as Messiah. This would be their rationalization.

After the Rebbe died, Shaffir quoted a despairing follower who said, "What happened was not only unexpected, it's much worse. This thing that we didn't believe would happen, happened. We really didn't believe it. I can tell you that I'm a broken man and Lubavitch is broken."[2] Others, however, were convinced the Rebbe would rise. Shaffir even points to an article in the Jewish *Forward* that "reported a few days after the burial that a group asserted that their leader's resurrection was imminent and they were sleeping close to the Rebbe's grave, hoping to be the first to see their Messiah rise from the tomb."[3] Yes, Shaffir notes, "The resurrection theme was to become within days the subject of public sermons within the movement."[4] And that theme continued for months.

As Shaffir wrote:

> In December 1994, the *Forward* printed a front-page story with the headline: "Rabbis Blast Lubavitcher Messianism"; the opening paragraph stated, "The Lubavitcher Chasidim of Crown Heights are alarming Jewish theologians with their growing fervor of their belief in the imminent 'resurrection' of Menachem Mendel Schneerson as the 'Messiah,' and some critics are warning that eerie parallels to Christianity are flickering inside the Lubavitch movement."[5]

But there was no need for the warning about "eerie parallels." They exist only on the surface, not in real substance. The differences between Messianic belief in the Rebbe and Messianic belief in Rabbi Yeshua are great and profound.

A PRONOUNCED DIFFERENCE

You see, while it's true that the Lubavitcher movement has experienced great growth since the Rebbe's death, the movement remains splintered, with the mainstream leaders distancing themselves from any public proclamation that the Rebbe is, in fact, the Messiah. And despite all the talk about his resurrection, he has not yet risen from the dead. Those who camped out at the Rebbe's grave site, waiting to see him after he rose, eventually left disappointed. They never saw what they were waiting to see.

That's why, in keeping with the quote from *When Prophecy Fails* at the beginning of this chapter, the Rebbe's followers have concocted every kind of theory to explain away his death (as we saw earlier in the book), including that he never died; he is spiritually present; he was the potential Messiah; he *will* rise from the dead.

The contrast between the belief in the Rebbe as Messiah and the belief in Yeshua as Messiah could not be more pronounced. To review what we previously learned, when Jesus died a criminal's death at the hands of the Romans, having been rejected by the Jewish leadership and condemned to die, His disciples, each of them a Jew, lost all hope. They were cowering in fear. They were heartbroken and depressed. They were *not* looking for His resurrection; instead, they were overcome with disappointment and confusion. Their world had just come crashing down at their feet, and there it lay, in tatters.

Yeshua's resurrection was a complete shock to them, despite the fact that He told them He would be brutally killed and then rise on the third day. Their ears were hard of hearing and their minds dull of understanding. They simply did not get it.

That's why when some of the women went to visit the tomb in honor of their fallen leader and, to their amazement, found the tomb empty, they could hardly believe their eyes. And when they met the risen Jesus face to face and reported this to the other, male disciples, these Jewish men didn't believe them. Impossible, they thought!

This was not a matter of cognitive dissonance or of failed prophecy syndrome. This was a matter of life from the dead, of literal, physical resurrection, right in front of their eyes. And they met with their Master and King day after day for a period of forty days. The doubts were gone and the questions erased. He is risen, indeed!

That's why they never denied Yeshua's death. Instead they proclaimed it passionately, recognizing Him as the perfect Lamb of God, sacrificing His own life to pay for our sins. And that's why they were totally united in proclaiming Him as the risen Messiah. There was no splintering among them, no question about whether He really resurrected, no doubt about whether He was the promised Redeemer. On these truths they were unanimous.

The contrast, then, between what happened to Yeshua and what happened to the Rebbe is great. Twenty-five years after the Rebbe's death, his devoted followers are divided into two major camps: those who openly proclaim him as Messiah and those who openly deny it (or avoid the subject). Nearly two thousand years after Yeshua's death, however, devoted followers of Yeshua are united in proclaiming Him as Messiah.

Many of the followers of the Rebbe expected him to rise from the dead, but he did not. The followers of Yeshua did not expect Yeshua to rise from the dead, but He did.

To this day many of the followers of the Rebbe deny that he actually died on the third of Tammuz 1994. In stark contrast, the followers of Yeshua fully acknowledge Yeshua's death, preaching it as one of the foundations of their faith. So much for the alleged "eerie parallels" to Christianity!

Again, this is not an attack on the Rebbe, whose profound giftings and sacrificial service as a traditional Jewish leader are undeniable. It is, rather, a reminder of his mortality. Only one Jewish leader conquered death. Only one great Rabbi died for the sins of the world and then resurrected from the grave. That's why we are sure that He will return one day to set up His kingdom here on the earth. He began His mission right on time, just as the prophets predicted. He will return at the end of this age, and when He does, the whole world will see Him.

THE RESURRECTION CHANGED THE WORLD

And what if He didn't rise from the dead? Virtually no one would know His name today, and the world would be a much different, infinitely worse place. Allow me to explain.

In 2005, Orthodox Jewish journalist David Klinghoffer published a fascinating book titled *Why the Jews Rejected Jesus: The Turning Point of Western History.* His thesis was that people today should be thankful that the Jews rejected Jesus, since Christianity has been good for the world. As he wrote, "The Jewish rejection of Christ made possible the sublime culture of Europe in which Felix Mendelssohn flourished, as well as the sublime politics of America whose blessings we enjoy.... For that, thank the Jews."[6]

In Klinghoffer's view, had the Jews embraced Jesus as Messiah and brought Judaism to the nations, the rest of the world would not have embraced the Jewish faith, since it was too demanding. But the Christian message, which, Klinghoffer believes, the Jews rightly rejected, was just what the world needed. And so the world should be glad that the Jews rejected Jesus!

Actually, it is only because many Jews did *not* reject Jesus—I mean Jews like Peter and John and Paul and Matthew and thousands of others—that the world has been blessed by the power of the gospel—the power of the good news of the Messiah's life, death, and resurrection. Jesus is just what this world needed.

Now, many Jews will be surprised to hear this, associating Christianity with the Crusades and Inquisitions and even the Holocaust. The truth is that the Crusades and Inquisitions were completely unrelated to the teachings of Jesus and the New Testament—in fact, they were completely antithetical to those teachings—while the Holocaust was completely and totally anti-Christian.

In stark contrast, where the message of Jesus has been spread—the real message, not a later, counterfeit message—it has brought blessing and transformation and improvement. The world today is massively different because of Jesus. But that is only because He rose from the dead.

According to one Catholic website, "There is no doubt that Christianity had affected the world in almost every single way for the better. There was no such thing as charity in the proper Christian sense that would have possibly existed in the ancient world. Nor would there have been a proper sense of human dignity, the sacredness of marriage, sex, life, and the family all of which came to us through Christian teachings and understandings."[7]

Over at the very liberal Huffington Post website, pastor John Ortberg wrote an article titled "Six Surprising Ways Jesus Changed the World."[8] Specifically, Ortberg listed the positive impact the teachings and example of Jesus had on the following:

1. **Children**. In the ancient world, unwanted babies (especially girls or the handicapped) were left to die by exposure (or at the hands of wild animals). Ortberg says, "Jesus' treatment of and teachings about children led to the forbidding of such practices, as well as orphanages and godparents."

2. **Education**. Christianity spread the love of learning, leading to the founding of universities like Cambridge, Oxford, and Harvard, which were devoted to helping students love God with all their mind.

3. **Compassion**. Jesus cared for sufferers from all backgrounds and walks of life, and "His compassion for the poor and the sick led to institutions for lepers, the beginning of modern-day hospitals."

4. **Humility**. Ortberg says that according to historian John Dickson, "It is unlikely that any of us would aspire to this virtue were it not for the historical impact of his

crucifixion....Our culture remains cruciform long after it
stopped being Christian."

5. **Forgiveness**. Through the cross, Jesus showed the power of
forgiveness in contrast with the power of conquest and vengeance and retaliation.

6. **Humanitarian reform**. Jesus stood up for those marginal-
ized by the society—including women and the poor—often
to the consternation of the religious leaders.

All this and much more has been expanded on by historians and sociolo-
gists and other scholars, as they point to the positive, life-giving, culture-
improving impact that this Jesus-faith, called "Christianity," has had around
the world. As noted by culture commentator Bill Muehlenberg:

> In Kenneth Scott Latourette's massive 7-volume history of the expan-
> sion of the Christian Church, the Yale historian concluded by noting
> just how much good this expansion had contributed to the world.
> More recently D. James Kennedy wrote a brief volume entitled *What
> if Jesus Had Never Been Born?* The world would be much worse off,
> he argued, if it weren't for this man Jesus.[9]

THE RESURRECTION CHANGES LIVES

To illustrate this point, let me give you just two examples from Kennedy's
book that demonstrate the powerful, life-transforming effect of the message of the good news of the Messiah, examples that show how God's love
for us—expressed through Yeshua—in turn produces supernatural love for
others. And remember: these are merely two examples out of tens of millions, and I mean that with no exaggeration.

Consider the stories of Sergeant Jacob DeShazer and Captain Mitsuo
Fuchida, mortal enemies during World War II. DeShazer was downed in
Japan during a bombing raid. Fuchida led the infamous Pearl Harbor attack
in 1941. Both were soldiers at heart, and killing was their business during
the war. But God had other plans.

The story begins in a prison camp and a five-foot-wide cell where
DeShazer was kept after being shot down by the Japanese. Kennedy writes:

He was treated with the most horrible forms of cruelty. He developed an intense hatred for his Japanese guards. All he wanted was to get his hands on one of their throats to squeeze the life out of him. But they continued to torture him. Day by day his hatred grew until it became a veritable mountain. He lived for only one reason, and that was to seek revenge on his torturers.

One day a Bible was brought into the prison. It was passed around and finally came to DeShazer. He read it. He devoured it eagerly! And he came across the words of Jesus, who said [as he was being crucified!], "Father, forgive them, for they do not know what they do" (Luke 23:34a). The love of Christ melted that mountain of hatred inside of Jacob DeShazer and filled him with the joy of Jesus Christ. He said, "My heart was full of joy. I wouldn't have traded places with anyone." Soon after that a guard slammed the cell door on DeShazer's bare foot and began kicking at the foot with hobnailed boots. DeShazer said nothing but thought of Jesus' words, "Love your enemies." That guard's attitude changed substantially.[10]

Upon his release after the war, DeShazer had opportunity to return to Japan, and he did, but not as a solider. Rather, he went as a missionary, sharing the message of Messiah's love with the Japanese people. So wonderful was his story that it was printed as a tract in Japanese. But that was only the beginning:

One day a Japanese man who was disheartened, broken, dejected, and hopeless was given that tract by an American stranger. He read that tract, and his heart was touched. He sought out Christian missionaries and the Bible. He too was converted. His name was Captain Mitsuo Fuchida. He was the Japanese officer who spearheaded the 1941 attack on Pearl Harbor on December 7. The very man who had declared, "Tora! Tora! Tora!" [Japanese for "Tiger! Tiger! Tiger!"] gave his heart and life over to Jesus Christ. He too began to preach the gospel of Jesus Christ to people all over Japan and America. He even came back to Pearl Harbor on the twenty-fifth anniversary of the attack with a gift in hand for the survivors: a Bible with Luke 23:34a inscribed in it ("Father, forgive them, for they do not know what they do"). Fuchida asked for forgiveness, for he had acted a quarter century earlier in moral ignorance.[11]

This is the infectious power of Messiah's love! In fact, because examples such as these can so easily be multiplied, the Jewish objection I hear from those who work with true followers of Jesus around the world is generally the *opposite* objection of the one being raised here, viz., "It's unnatural to turn the other cheek and love your enemies. Christianity doesn't allow for a healthy expression of human emotion!"

To the contrary, there is a wonderful, cleansing, liberating, God-ordained emotional *release* that comes through forgiveness and love. And this divinely empowered, unconditional love helps explain why there is a direct correlation between the spread of true Christianity and dramatic increases in health care, education, and acts of kindness to the suffering and poor. There is no denying the profound humanitarian effect that the gospel message has made around the world!

Muehlenberg also points to Alvin Schmidt's 2004 volume, *How Christianity Changed the World*, highlighting a few of Schmidt's important findings. He writes:

In spite [of] the claims of some today that Christianity oppresses women, the historical record shows just the opposite. Women were oppressed in almost every culture prior to the coming of Christianity. By elevating sexual morality, and by conferring upon women a much higher status, the Christian religion revolutionised the place and prestige of women.

For example, the great importance given to marriage meant that women were spared much of the abuse and mistreatment that they were accustomed to. By rejecting polygyny, prostitution, homosexuality and bestiality—all common during the time—the early Christians not only sheltered women but protected children and family.[12]

Another example is health care. As Muehlenberg notes:

Prior to Christianity, the Greeks and Romans had little or no interest in the poor, the sick and the dying. But the early Christians, following the example of their master, ministered to the needs of the whole person. During the first three centuries of the church they could only care for the sick where they found them, as believers were then a persecuted people. Once the persecutions subsided, however, the institutionalisation of health care began in earnest.

For example, the first ecumenical council at Nicea in 325 directed bishops to establish hospices in every city that had a cathedral. The first hospital was built by St Basil in Caesarea in 369. By the Middle Ages hospitals covered all of Europe and even beyond. In fact, "Christian hospitals were the world's first voluntary charitable institutions."

Care for the mentally ill was also a Christian initiative. Nursing also sprang from Christian concerns for the sick, and many Christians have given their lives to such tasks. One thinks of Florence Nightingale, for example, and the formation of the Red Cross.[13]

You might say, "But Judaism contains many elevating truths as well and has wonderful family values and lofty ethics, while Jews have developed great education networks and other important institutions." That is absolutely true. But, as David Klinghoffer recognized, as noted above, Judaism did not bring these advances to the nations. Rather, they came through the Messianic faith—ultimately called Christianity—which built on Israel's calling to be a light to the nations. And this happened because of Jesus the Messiah.

About ten years ago an Orthodox rabbi gave a lecture to Christian students at a ministry school I was leading, and in his lecture, he referenced the Jewish calling to be a light to the world. During the Q and A session that followed, a student from Ghana asked the rabbi a penetrating question. He said, "Rabbi, could you explain how the Jewish people were a light to my nation? You see, it wasn't a Jewish rabbi who came to my country and turned us away from idols. It was a Christian missionary."

And that is the whole point. To quote Muehlenberg again, with reference to Alvin Schmidt's book:

> The bottom line, as Schmidt notes, is that if Jesus Christ had never been born, to speak of Western civilisation would be incomprehensible. Indeed, there may never have been such a civilisation. The freedoms and benefits we enjoy in many modern cultures are directly due to the influence of this one man. And besides all the institutional, cultural, social, political and artistic benefits, there is one last benefit: the countless millions of changed lives due to a liberating encounter with the risen Christ. It is this benefit, first and foremost, which of course accounts for all the institutional benefits.
>
> One could argue that changed lives alone are a sufficient testimony

to this unique man. But of course changed lives result in changed families, changed neighborhoods, changed societies. The transformation of individuals and nations for the better can all be attributed to this one man, born in a manger but soon to return as ruler of the universe.[14]

One of my closest friends in the world is an Indian named Yesupadam, and he has a remarkable story. (I am an eyewitness to what God does has done through this humble man, having made twenty-seven trips to India since 1993.) Born an untouchable, he almost died of malnutrition while just a boy, being found on the side of the road by a Canadian missionary who brought him to a local hospital and nursed him back to health. But Yesupadam despised all religions, despite the fact that his father had become a Christian and had given him his name, which, in Telugu, means "Jesus foot."

While still young, he watched his mother die, knowing that simple medication would have saved her life. But they were too poor to afford it. Even at school, when other kids were getting a drink at a fountain, he could only try to catch the water that fell through their hands. As a result, he developed a hatred for the caste system, and when a Maoist Communist (called a Naxalite) came to his village and took a personal interest in him when he was just eleven years old, he was sold.

Yesupadam would fight the system, stealing from the rich and even doing violence to the rich. He had found his purpose, signing with his own blood to become a Naxalite. And so it was that Yesupadam's life spiraled out of control. He became an alcoholic. He engaged in acts of terror. And he was a strident atheist. But his wife was a godly Christian who prayed fervently for him, even though others considered him a lost cause.

And then it happened. He was attending a church service when he looked into the sky and saw a vision of Jesus—not perfectly clear, but clear enough to recognize—and Jesus stood there, with the holes in His hands, declaring His love for Yesupadam.

The Lord said to him, "Son, I have done all this for you. What will you do for Me?"

At once Yesupadam melted, receiving God's love with many tears and giving his life unconditionally to the Lord. That was almost forty-five years ago, and since then, Yesupadam has been a literal world changer. He has built thriving schools. Compassionate orphanages. Homes for the elderly. Training centers for the handicapped. He has started a nursing college. Words fail to tell the whole story, and it is breathtaking to see the scope of this work firsthand.[15]

He has planted roughly eight thousand churches in unreached tribal regions, and in each case the standard of living in these villages has greatly improved. In Germany, he has established a ministry to help the homeless and drug addicts. In poverty-stricken Madagascar, one of his protégés (a Korean man, with his Korean wife) has established feeding programs and schools and has even built a church building inside the grounds of a prison, resulting in the transformation of many lives.

And Yesupadam's story is just one among countless millions of others, all of them changed by Yeshua the Messiah. And that is for one reason only. It is because He rose from the dead!

My own life was radically transformed by Him as a sixteen-year-old, LSD-using, heroin-shooting, hippie rock drummer. I was in this state of prideful rebellion despite the fact that I was raised in a Conservative Jewish home, that my dad was the senior lawyer in the New York Supreme Court, and that my mom and dad had a wonderful, happy marriage.

Of course, when I came to faith, while my dad was thrilled to see me off drugs, he wasn't happy that I believed in Jesus, simply stating to me, "Michael, we're Jews. We don't believe this." And so it was that he brought me to meet the local rabbi, who in turn introduced me to other rabbis, until he brought me into Brooklyn in 1973 to spend the day with Lubavitch rabbis.

They graciously challenged me to learn Hebrew. They questioned the accuracy of the Christian Bible translation that I quoted. And they told me stories about the Rebbe, whose picture was everywhere.

On subsequent trips I spent hours with their rabbis, even staying with one family for Yom Kippur (the Day of Atonement) and meeting religious Jews who had stories similar to mine. They too had been getting high and living in rebellion, and now they were ultra-Orthodox Jews.

Yet the more I talked with these sincere, devoted men, the more I saw the differences between us. They could not relate to the intimacy I enjoyed with God, nor could they relate to the depth of forgiveness of sins I had experienced. And the more I studied the Hebrew Bible, looking at it from every angle, considering the best arguments of the rabbis and counter-missionaries and even skeptical university professors with whom I also studied, the clearer the picture became: Jesus-Yeshua is the Messiah of Israel and the Savior of the world. And as great a leader as the Rebbe was, he did not rise from the dead. He did not ascend bodily to heaven. He does not sit at the right hand of God. And he will not return in the clouds of heaven for the whole world to see.

But Jesus died. And rose. And ascended. And He sits at the Father's right hand, awaiting the day when He will return to be with His followers and to rescue Israel from her enemies and to establish God's kingdom on earth. As surely as He rose, He will return!

But will you be ready for that day? When He returns, will it bring you terror or relief, sorrow or joy? It is written in Revelation, with references to the words of the Hebrew prophets:

> "Look, he is coming with the clouds," and "every eye will see him, even those who pierced him"; and all peoples on earth "will mourn because of him." So shall it be! Amen.
>
> —REVELATION 1:7, NIV

Will you also mourn on that day? If so, will it be the mourning of grief and agony, recognizing that your judgment is at hand? Or will it be the mourning of repentance, as you recognize your error in rejecting Yeshua the Messiah and call out to God for mercy? What will it be?

May I urge you now, in the words of Psalm 95, that if you hear His voice *today*, you do not harden your heart? The risen Messiah is present right now, working by His Spirit, calling you by name. To resist Him means spiritual death. To receive Him means life everlasting. Which will it be?

The resurrection of Jesus changed everything, and today, if you don't know Him as Messiah and Lord, it's time for the risen Jesus to change you, right here, right now. What do you say?

Of this you can be sure: Yeshua "is able to save completely those who come to God through him, because he always lives to intercede for them" (Heb. 7:25, NIV).

Call to Him today!

NOTES

INTRODUCTION: FROM GALILEE TO BROOKLYN: IN SEARCH OF THE REAL MESSIAH

1. This is the title for the Grand Rabbi of a Hasidic movement, explained in greater detail in chapter 1.
2. Scholars debate the exact year of Jesus' death, placing it somewhere between AD 30–33.

CHAPTER 1: COULD A RABBI FROM BROOKLYN BE THE MESSIAH?

1. This is a paraphrase of many such documented statements uttered at that time.
2. Yossi Newfield, "The Night We Lost the Messiah Rabbi Menachem Mendel Schneerson," *Forward*, June 11, 2018, https://forward.com /culture/402046/the-night-we-lost-the-messiah-rabbi-menachem-mendel-schneerson/.
3. Newfield, "The Night We Lost the Messiah Rabbi Menachem Mendel Schneerson." For an explanation of the term *Hasidic*, see the section later in chapter 1, "Who Was the Rebbi?"
4. Newfield, "The Night We Lost the Messiah Rabbi Menachem Mendel Schneerson."
5. Laurie Goodstein, "Death of Lubavitcher Leader, Rabbi Schneerson, Stuns Followers," *Washington Post*, June 13, 1994, https://www. washingtonpost.com/archive/politics/1994/06/13/death-of-lubavitcher-leader-rabbi-schneerson-stuns-followers/d22c9af8-7510-4adc-b12e-52bac6946977/.
6. Goodstein, "Death of Lubavitcher Leader, Rabbi Schneerson, Stuns Followers."
7. These are representative quotes rather than exact quotes.
8. "The Rebbe as Moshiach," Chabad of Central New Jersey, accessed November 5, 2019, http://www.chabadnj.org/

page.asp?pageID=21B2CAF6-8CBC-4843-8085-
C1EA5D80CB85&moshHdr=1.

9. Heshy Fried, "How to Tell if Your Local Chabad Rabbi Believes That the Rebbe Is Moshiach," Frum Satire, March 12, 2013, http://www.frumsatire.net/2013/03/12/how-to-tell-if-your-local-chabad-rabbi-believes-that-the-rebbe-is-moshiach/.

10. Lucette Lagnado, "Rabbis Blast Lubavitcher Messianism, Warn Resurrection Talk Echoes Christian Themes," *Forward*, December 2, 1994, archived at http://israel613.com/books/LUBAVITCH_FORWARD_REPUGNANT.pdf.

11. Lagnado, "Rabbis Blast Lubavitcher Messianism, Warn Resurrection Talk Echoes Christian Themes." See also "Rabbi Ahron Soloveichik on the Rebbe as Moshiach," Can the Rebbe Be Moshiach?, accessed November 5, 2019, http://moshiachtalk.tripod.com/ras.html; but note his subsequent statement, cited in chapter 2.

12. "Statement Regarding Chabad Messianism," Rabbinical Council of America, June 1, 1996, https://rabbis.org/statement-regarding-chabad-messianism/.

13. As translated by J. Immanuel Schochet, "Laws Concerning Kings and the Messiah," in *Mashiach: The Messianic Era in Jewish Law*, Chabad.org, accessed November 5, 2019, https://www.chabad.org/library/moshiach/article_cdo/aid/101744/jewish/Laws-Concerning-Kings-and-the-Messiah.htm.

14. Joel Greenberg, "Rabbi Eliezer Schach, 103; Leader of Orthodox in Israel," *New York Times*, November 3, 2001, https://www.nytimes.com/2001/11/03/world/rabbi-eliezer-schach-103-leader-of-orthodox-in-israel.html.

15. Glenn Frankel, "Brooklyn Rabbi a Power in Israel," *Washington Post*, November 23, 1988, https://www.washingtonpost.com/archive/politics/1988/11/23/brooklyn-rabbi-a-power-in-israel/a3a6c0fe-1523-4abe-8bc5-4679eb3978bc/. Schach was famous for statements such as this, also denouncing other respected Jewish leaders of his day. See also M. Avrum Ehrlich, *The Messiah of Brooklyn: Understanding Lubavitch Hasidism Past and Present* (Brooklyn, NY: Ktav, 2005), 110, n. 15; for some of his relevant comments in Hebrew, see chabad-mafia1, "Rav Shach Attacks Chabad Lubavitch Rebbe," YouTube, December 22, 2010, https://www.youtube.com/watch?v=x2Lud8KGA8Y.

16. The Satmar Rebbe, as quoted in Simon Dein, *Lubavitcher Messianism: What Really Happens When Prophecy Fails?* (London: Continuum International Publishing Group, 2011), 50.

17. Aryeh A. Gotfryd, as quoted by Chaim Dov Keller in "G-d-Centered or Rebbe/Messiah-Centered: What Is Normative Judaism?," posted by the Center for Torah Demographics, "Identifying Chabad," accessed November 5, 2019, https://identifyingchabad.org/rabbikeller.html.

18. "Hasidic Movement: A History," My Jewish Learning, accessed November 5, 2019, https://www.myjewishlearning.com/article/hasidic-movement-a-history/. For a full study, see David Biale et al., *Hasidism: A New History* (Princeton, NJ: Princeton University Press, 2018).

19. Louis Jacobs, "The Tzaddik, or Rebbe," My Jewish Learning, accessed November 5, 2019, https://www.myjewishlearning.com/article/zaddik/3/.

20. See, for example, *Wonders and Miracles: Stories of the Lubavitcher Rebbe* (n.p.: Maareches Ufaratzta, 1993).

21. Herman Branover, *The Ultimate Jew: A Biography of the Lubavitcher Rebbe* (n.p.: Shamir Books, 2015).

22. Wikipedia, s.v. "Herman Branover," last modified September 22, 2019, https://en.wikipedia.org/wiki/Herman_Branover.

23. See also Herman Branover and Joseph Ginsburg, *Mind Over Matter: The Lubavitcher Rebbe on Science, Technology and Medicine*, rev. ed., trans. Arnie Gotfryd (New York: FREE Publishing House, 2003).

24. David Berger, "Did the Rebbe Identify Himself as the Messiah—and What Do His Hasidim Believe Today?," Tablet, July 21, 2014, https://www.tabletmag.com/jewish-news-and-politics/179435/berger-rebbe-messiah.

25. The older spelling of Schneersohn was modified to Schneerson over time.

26. Notice the emphasis on a seventh righteous leader in his last public discourse, translated into English: Yosef Yitzchak Schneerson of Lubavitch, "Basi Legani - 5710: Chapter 1," trans. Eli Touger, Chabad.org, accessed November 7, 2019, https://www.chabad.org/therebbe/article_cdo/aid/115102/jewish/Basi-Legani-5710-Chapter-1.htm.

27. Chabad is an acronym for *chokhmah* (wisdom), *binah* (understanding), and *daat* (knowledge); see further David Eliezrie, *The Secret of Chabad: Inside the World's Most Successful Jewish Movement* (New Milford, CT: The Toby Press, 2015).

28. See Chaim Miller, *Turning Judaism Outwards: A Biography of the Rebbe, Menachem Mendel Schneerson* (New York: Kol Menachem, 2014), 303–304.

29. Stories like these, and countless others, are shared in Branover, *Ultimate Jew*; Miller, *Turning Judaism Outwards*; and Joseph Telushkin, *Rebbe: The Life and Teachings of Menachem M. Schneerson, the Most Influential Rabbi in Modern History* (New York: Harper Wave, 2016).

30. Miller, *Turning Judaism Outwards*, 194.

31. Shmully Hecht, "The Power of a Deed," *New York Times*, June 28, 2014, https://www.nytimes.com/2014/06/29/opinion/sunday /remembering-rabbi-menachem-mendel-schneerson.html?_r=0.

32. Shmuley Boteach, "The Incorruptible: My Thoughts on the Lubavitcher Rebbe," HuffPost, April 22, 2011, https://www.huffpost.com/entry/the-incorruptible-my-thou_b_852771.

33. David Singer, "The Rebbe, the Messiah, and the Heresy Hunter," OrthodoxyToday.org, reprinting a May 2003 *First Things* article, https://www .orthodoxytoday.org/articles2/SingerHeresyHunter.php.

34. Singer, "The Rebbe, the Messiah, and the Heresy Hunter."

35. Wikipedia, s.v. "Shmuel Butman," last modified May 9, 2019, https:// en.wikipedia.org/wiki/Shmuel_Butman.

36. Shmuel Butman, *Countdown to Moshiach: Can the Rebbe Still Be Moshiach?* (New York: International Campaign to Bring Moshiach, 1995), http://www.moshiach.net/blind/count.htm, emphasis in the original.

37. As quoted in Dein, *Lubavitcher Messianism*, 47–48.

38. As quoted in Dein, *Lubavitcher Messianism*, 48.

39. Dein, *Lubavitcher Messianism*, 48.

40. Miller, *Turning Judaism Outwards*, 406.

41. Miller, *Turning Judaism Outwards*, 406.

42. See "The Rebbe as Moshiach—Based on Torah Sources," Living With Moshiach, accessed November 5, 2019, http://www.torah4blind.org/ itmotrw.htm.

43. See Telushkin, *Rebbe*, 431; for other perspectives, see Dein, *Lubavitcher Messianism*, 53–55.

44. For the claim that the Rebbe said he was Messiah, see, for example, GeulaNovelties, "The Rebbe Says That He Is Moshiach, the Geula

Is HERE!!!," YouTube, June 15, 2010, https://www.youtube.com/watch?v=887vWdyWXFg.

45. Bruce Warshal, "Is the Lubavitcher Rebbe the Messiah?," Crown-Heights.info, March 20, 2007, http://crownheights.info/general/5611/is-the-lubavitcher-rebbe-the-messiah/.

46. Eli Soble, "Our Rebbe Is the Messiah," *Jerusalem Post*, January 30, 2008, https://www.jpost.com/Opinion/Op-Ed-Contributors/Our-Rebbe-is-the-messiah.

47. Soble, "Our Rebbe Is the Messiah."

48. Soble, "Our Rebbe Is the Messiah."

49. Soble, "Our Rebbe Is the Messiah."

50. See, for example, Online videos from Israel, Middle East, & Jewish World, "The Lubavitcher Rebbe as a God," YouTube, December 1, 2012, https://www.youtube.com/watch?v=yxXGthzcpR0.

51. Saul Sadka, "The Lubavitcher Rebbe as a God," Haaretz.com, February 11, 2007, https://www.haaretz.com/1.4804959.

CHAPTER 2: THE MESSIAH CONCEALED AND THEN REVEALED

1. Professor David Berger, who claimed that Lubavitchers who believed the Rebbe was Messiah even after his death should not be considered as part of Judaism, admitted that Soloveichik's letter hit like a "thunderbolt," but he sought to discredit its impact by claiming that it was written under duress when the rabbi was infirm; see David Berger, *The Rebbe, the Messiah, and the Scandal of Orthodox Indifference* (Oxford, UK: Littman Library of Jewish Civilization, 2001), 70. Rabbi J. Immanuel Schochet, who has extensively critiqued Berger's book, wrote that he contacted Rabbi Soloveichik's family about the matter. They told him that Soloveichik "regarded the attribution of messiahship to the deceased Rebbe as a *shtut* (folly) but definitely not heretical"; as quoted in Jim Melnick, "The Struggle Within Chabad Lubavitch and Orthodox Judaism: A Resurrected King Messiah," *Mishkan* 43 (2005), 12. For a response to the most common arguments from Lubavitchers who believe the Rebbe is Moshiach, see Gil Student, *Can the Rebbe Be Moshiach?: Proofs From Gemara, Midrash, and Rambam That the Rebbe Zt"l Cannot Be Moshiach* (Irvine, CA: Universal Publishers, 2002). See further Berger, *The Rebbe, the Messiah, and the Scandal of Orthodox Indifference*.

2. Aaron Soloveichik, as quoted (as Aharon Soloveichik) in "A Preface to Moshiach: Setting the Record Straight," Beis Moshiach Online Edition, accessed November 5, 2019, http://www.beismoshiach.org/Moshiach/moshiach354.htm.

3. Chaim Dalfin, *Attack on Lubavitch: A Response* (New York: Jewish Enrichment Press, 2002).

4. Melnick, "The Struggle Within Chabad Lubavitch and Orthodox Judaism: A Resurrected King Messiah," 58.

5. "The Rebbe as Moshiach," Chabad of Flatbush, accessed November 5, 2019, http://chabadflatbush.org/mobile/page.asp?pageID=21B2CAF6-8CBC-4843-8085-C1EA5D80CB85&moshHdr=1.

6. "The Rebbe as Moshiach." Note that Luria is referenced by his acronym "the Arizal."

7. Branover, *The Ultimate Jew*, 256.

8. Efraim Palvanov, "Is the Lubavitcher Rebbe Mashiach?," *Mayim Achronim* (blog), June 27, 2017, https://www.mayimachronim.com/is-the-lubavitcher-rebbe-mashiach/.

9. Palvanov, "Is the Lubavitcher Rebbe Mashiach?"

10. Palvanov, "Is the Lubavitcher Rebbe Mashiach?"

11. Telushkin, *Rebbe*, 426–428.

12. As recorded in Miller, *Turning Judaism Outwards*, 185.

13. Shloma Majeski (Stump the Rabbi), "If the Rebbe Discouraged Saying Yechi and He Is Moshiach, Why Do People Say It Anyways?," YouTube, December 25, 2017, https://www.youtube.com/watch?v=8CZps41B3r4.

14. Sue Fishkoff, *The Rebbe's Army: Inside the World of Chabad-Lubavitch* (New York: Schocken, 2003), 263.

15. Described by Fishkoff, *The Rebbe's Army*, 267.

16. Fishkoff, *The Rebbe's Army*, 263.

17. Ari Feldman, "Is Rebbe Schneerson the Jewish Messiah? Faith Survives in Chabad," *Forward*, December 10, 2017, https://forward.com/news/388439/is-rebbe-schneerson-the-jewish-messiah-faith-survives-in-chabad/.

18. Fishkoff, *The Rebbe's Army*, 263.

19. Fishkoff, *The Rebbe's Army*, 268. Note that Rabbi Shmotkin is explaining this position; it is not his own.

20. Melech Jaffe, "Critique to a Response," MoshiachListen.com, accessed November 5, 2019, http://web.archive.org/web/20160305164824/http://www.moshiachlisten.com/critique.html.

21. Jaffe, "Critique to a Response."

22. Jaffe, "Critique to a Response."

23. See 1 Corinthians 15:20, 23.

24. "A Preface to Moshiach," Beis Moshiach Online Edition.

25. "A Preface to Moshiach," Beis Moshiach Online Edition.

26. Majeski, "If the Rebbe Discouraged Saying Yechi and He Is Moshiach, Why Do People Say It Anyways?"

27. Shloma Majeski (Stump the Rabbi), "Why Identify One Person as Moshiach Instead of Waiting to See Who He Is When He Comes?," YouTube, October 24, 2018, https://www.youtube.com/watch?v=GdTDmzhcmMI.

28. Shloma Majeski (Stump the Rabbi), "What Are We Waiting For if We Are Told That Moshiach Is Already Here?," YouTube, January 16, 2019, https://www.youtube.com/watch?v=cU392U4Gufk&t=1s.

29. "A Preface to Moshiach," Beis Moshiach Online Edition.

30. "A Preface to Moshiach," Beis Moshiach Online Edition.

31. Elliot R. Wolfson, *Open Secret: Postmessianic Messianism and the Mystical Revision of Menaḥem Mendel Schneerson* (New York: Columbia University Press, 2009), 5.

32. Wolfson, *Open Secret*, 6.

33. Wolfson, *Open Secret*, 6–7.

34. Wolfson, *Open Secret*, 6–7.

35. "In Its Time I Will Hasten Him," *Law of Messiah* (blog), July 18, 2013, https://lawofmessiah.wordpress.com/2013/07/18/in-its-time-i-will-hasten-him/.

36. "In Its Time I Will Hasten Him," *Law of Messiah*.

37. "In Its Time I Will Hasten Him," *Law of Messiah*.

38. See Student, *Can the Rebbe Be Moshiach?*

39. Heschel Greenberg, Moshiach Time, accessed November 6, 2019, http://moshiachtime.com/the-purpose-of-our-site/.

40. Michael L. Brown, *Answering Jewish Objections to Jesus, Volume 3: Messianic Prophecy Objections* (Grand Rapids, MI: Baker Books, 2003), 5–6. For more on the concept of a rejected-hidden-revealed Messiah, see also Raphael Patai, *The Messiah Texts: Jewish Legends of*

Three Thousand Years (Detroit: Wayne State Univ., 1979), xxx–xxxv.
For additional thoughts on the parallels between Joseph and Jesus, see
Michael L. Brown, *Answering Jewish Objections to Jesus, Volume 2:
Theological Objections* (Grand Rapids, MI: Baker Books, 2000), 232–
235.

41. Corey Gil-Shuster, "If the Lubavitch Rebbe Can Be the Messiah,
    Why Can't Jesus?," YouTube, May 9, 2018, https://www.youtube.com/
    watch?v=w6HicyaLf6I.

42. Micah 4:8, as rendered in *The Aramaic Bible: The Targum of the
    Minor Prophets*, trans. Kevin J. Cathcart and Robert P. Gordon, vol. 14
    (Collegeville, MN: The Liturgical Press, 1990), iii.

43. Chayalei Beis Dovid, comp., *And He Will Redeem Us: Moshiach in
    Our Time* (New York: Mendelsohn Press, 1994), 10, emphasis in the
    original.

CHAPTER 3: THE GILGUL, REINCARNATION, AND A POTENTIAL MESSIAH IN EACH GENERATION

1. See "The Messiah Is Living Among Us!," TORCH, accessed November
   6, 2019, https://www.torchweb.org/torah_detail.php?id=448.

2. According to Rabbi Chaim Kanievsky, "one of the greatest Torah
   scholars of our generation," it could be the case that "on the day that
   the Temple was destroyed, the messiah was born and his soul inhabited
   the body of a live person. When that person died, the messiah's soul
   entered the body of another live person, and so it continues throughout
   the centuries and millennia until the time comes for him to reveal himself and to come and redeem us." As cited in "The Messiah Is Living
   Among Us!"

3. See Pesachim 54a, Sefaria, accessed November 5, 2019, https://www
   .sefaria.org/Pesachim.54a?lang=en.

4. For Messianic Jewish reflections on this, see John J. Parsons, "The
   Leper Messiah: Further Thoughts on Parashat Metzora," Hebrew4Chris-
   tians.com, accessed November 5, 2019, https://hebrew4christians.com/
   Scripture/Parashah/Summaries/Metzora/Leper_Messiah/leper_messiah.
   html.

5. See b. Sanhedrin 98a.

6. See b. Sanhedrin 98a.

7. See Pesikta Rabbati 37. For English translation, see William G. Braude, trans., *Pesikta Rabbati: Homiletical Discourses for Festal Days and Special Sabbaths* (New Haven, CT: Yale University Press, 1968).

8. Dovid, *And He Will Redeem Us*, 145–146.

9. Moshiach Time, accessed November 5, 2019, https://moshiachtime.com/the-purpose-of-our-site/.

10. Yossi Schneerson, *Jerusalem Post*, international ed., March 14, 1992, as quoted in Susan Perlman, "What the Press Wrote About Schneerson," in Kai Kjær-Hansen, ed., *The Death of Messiah* (Baltimore: Lederer Publications, 1994), 12. Used with permission of Messianic Jewish Publishers, Clarksville, MD 21029. www.messianicjewish.net.

11. See b. Sanhedrin 94a.

12. Berel Wein, "Hezekiah: The Messiah Who Was Not," JewishHistory .com & The Destiny Foundation, accessed November 5, 2019, https://www.jewishhistory.org/the-messiah-who-was-not/.

13. Wein, "Hezekiah."

14. Gershom Scholem, *Sabbatai Ṣevi: The Mystical Messiah* (Princeton, NJ: Princeton University Press, 1973), 56.

15. See b. Sanhedrin 99a.

16. Ovadia Yosef, as quoted in Lazar Berman, "Five of Ovadia Yosef's Most Controversial Quotations," *Times of Israel*, October 9, 2013, https://www.timesofisrael.com/5-of-ovadia-yosefs-most-controversial-quotations/.

17. See "Before Retiring at Night—10th Step," Chabad.org, accessed November 5, 2019, https://www.chabad.org/library/article_cdo/aid/732811/jewish/Before-Retiring-at-Night-10th-Step.htm, emphasis added.

18. See, for example, Shmuly Yanklowitz, "Sinai and the Social Contract," *New York Jewish Week*, October 8, 2013, https://jewishweek.times ofisrael.com/sinai-and-the-social-contract/.

19. "Transmigration of Souls (Terms Also Metempsychosis)," JewishEncyclopedia.com, accessed November 5, 2019, http://www.jewish encyclopedia.com/articles/6676-gilgul-neshamoth.

20. "Gilgul," Jewish Virtual Library, accessed November 6, 2019, https://www.jewishvirtuallibrary.org/gilgul.

21. Louis Jacobs, "What Judaism Says About Reincarnation," accessed November 6, 2019, https://www.myjewishlearning.com/article/reincarnation-the-transmigration-of-a-jewish-idea/.

22. Yanklowitz, "Sinai and the Social Contract."

23. Yanklowitz, "Sinai and the Social Contract."

24. Rashi, commentary on Deuteronomy 29:14, Sefaria, accessed November 5, 2019, https://www.sefaria.org/Deuteronomy.29.14?lang=en&with=Rashi&lang2=en. See also Ramban.

25. Sforno, commentary on Deuteronomy 29:14, Sefaria, accessed November 5, 2019, https://www.sefaria.org/Deuteronomy.29.14?lang=en&with=Sforno&lang2=en.

26. Jeffrey H. Tigay, *Deuteronomy: The JPS Torah Commentary* (Philadelphia: Jewish Publication Society, 1996), 278. According to Midrash Tanchuma, "You should know that every soul, from Adam to the end of the world, was formed during the six days of creation, and that all of them were present in the Garden of Eden and at the time of the giving of the Torah, as it is said: *With him that standeth here with us this day, and also with him that is not here with us this day* (Deut. 29:14)"; Midrash Tanchuma, Pekudei 3:4, Sefaria, accessed November 6, 2019, https://www.sefaria.org/Deuteronomy.29.14?lang=en&with=Midrash%20Tanchuma&lang2=en.

27. Saadia Gaon, as quoted by Mesora.org, accessed November 6, 2019, http://www.mesora.org/SaadiaGaon-Reincarnation.htm.

28. Naftali Silberberg, "Is It True the Messiah Will Be Born (or Was Born) on Tishah b'Av?," AskMoses.com, accessed November 6, 2019, http://www.askmoses.com/en/article/110,43879/Is-it-true-that-the-Messiah-will-be-born-or-was-born-on-Tishah-bAv.html. See also footnote 2 in this article, with reference to R. Ovadiah of Bartenura's commentary on Ruth.

29. Harris Lenowitz, *The Jewish Messiahs: From the Galilee to Crown Heights* (Oxford, UK: Oxford University Press, 1998), 216.

30. As quoted in Eliyahu Touger, *Sound the Great Shofar: Essays on The Imminence of the Redemption Adapted from Addresses of the Lubavitcher Rebbe* (n.p.: n.p., 1992), loc. 473–480, Kindle.

31. Touger, *Sound the Great Shofar*, loc. 473–480, Kindle.

32. Touger, *Sound the Great Shofar*, loc. 271–276, Kindle.

33. Touger, *Sound the Great Shofar*, loc. 278–286, Kindle.

34. Touger, *Sound the Great Shofar*, loc. 189–193, Kindle. See also Sholem Lougov, "Do Everything You Can to Bring Moshiach, Here and Now, Immediately," Moshiach Time, January 24, 2018, http://moshiachtime.

com/do-everything-you-can-to-bring-moshiach-here-and-now
-immediately/.

35. Perlman, "What the Press Wrote About Schneerson," 16.

36. Perlman, "What the Press Wrote About Schneerson," 16.

37. Perlman, "What the Press Wrote About Schneerson," 13–14.

38. See b. Sanhedrin 98a.

39. J. Immanuel Schochet, "Appendix II," Chabad.org, accessed November 6, 2019, https://www.chabad.org/library/article_cdo/aid/101747/jewish/Appendix-II.htm.

40. See Michael L. Brown, *Answering Jewish Objections to Jesus, Volume 1: General and Historical Objections* (Grand Rapids, MI: Baker Books, 2000), 75–80.

41. See b. Sanhedrin 97a, discussed in Brown, *Answering Jewish Objections to Jesus, Volume 1*, 70–71.

CHAPTER 4: THE MYSTICAL MESSIAH WHO CONVERTED TO ISLAM

1. For other possible events that took place on this same day, see m. Taanit 4:6; as well as "What Is Tisha B'Av?," Chabad.org, accessed November 6, 2019, https://www.chabad.org/library/article_cdo/aid/144575/jewish/What-Is-Tisha-BAv.htm.

2. Silberberg, "Is It True That the Messiah Will Be Born (or Was Born) on Tishah b'Av?"; see further chapter 3 about a potential Messiah in each generation.

3. For the argument that he did not suffer from a psychosis but rather reflected the practices of Sufi mystics, see the discussion in Robert Sepehr, *1666: Redemption Through Sin* (Encino, CA: Atlantean Gardens, 2015), 6.

4. Matt Plen, "Who Was Shabbetai Zevi?," My Jewish Learning, accessed November 6, 2019, https://www.myjewishlearning.com/article/shabbetai-zevi/.

5. Matt Goldish, *The Sabbatean Prophets* (Cambridge, MA: Harvard University Press, 2004), 2.

6. This theory is found throughout Scholem, *Sabbetai Sevi*.

7. Plen, "Who Was Shabbetai Zevi?"

8. Plen, "Who Was Shabbetai Zevi?"

9. Plen, "Who Was Shabbetai Zevi?"

10. Goldish, *The Sabbatean Prophets*, 1.

11. Goldish, *The Sabbatean Prophets*, 65.

12. Goldish, *The Sabbatean Prophets*, 1.

13. Juan Marcos Bejarano Gutierrez, *Conversos and the Sabbatean Movement: The Unlikely Supporters of Sabbatai Zevi* (Grand Prairie, TX: Yaron, 2019), 23.

14. Gutierrez, *Conversos and the Sabbatean Movement*, 23–24.

15. Gutierrez, *Conversos and the Sabbatean Movement*, 43–44.

16. Sepehr, *1666*, 5.

17. Sepehr, *1666*, 5.

18. Sepehr, *1666*, 5.

19. "Shabbetai Zvi (1626–1676)," Jewish Virtual Library, accessed November 6, 2019, https://www.jewishvirtuallibrary.org/shabbetai-zvi.

20. Plen, "Who Was Shabbetai Zevi?"

21. See, for example, Marc David Baer, *The Dönme: Jewish Converts, Muslim Revolutionaries, and Secular Turks* (Stanford, CA: Stanford University Press, 2010); and Cenzig Sisman, *The Burden of Silence: Sabbatai Sevi and the Evolution of the Ottoman-Turkish Dönmes* (New York: Oxford University Press, 2015).

22. "Redemption Through Sin," in Gershom Scholem, *The Messianic Idea in Judaism and Other Essays on Jewish Spirituality* (New York: Schocken Books, 1971), 78–141. See also Sepehr, *1666*.

23. Sepehr, *1666*, 9.

24. See, again, Sanhedrin 98a.

25. Also in Sanhedrin 98a.

26. See Sanhedrin 97a.

27. Scholem, *Sabbatai Ṣevi*, 227.

28. Baer, *The Dönme*, 4.

29. Lenowitz, *The Jewish Messiahs*, 149.

30. Gad Nassi, "Secret Muslim Jews Await Their Messiah: Shabbetai Tzvi," Los Muestros, accessed November 6, 2019, http://sefarad.org/lm/009/nassi.html. He writes, "Jewish messianic fervor is not a relic from past centuries: Witness the happenings this spring around the 90th birthday of the Lubavitcher rebbe, Menachem Mendel Schneerson, who, according to some of his followers, will soon reveal himself as the messiah. One week before the birthday, 800 sympathizers from the intellectual, political and religious community of Washington, D.C., gathered

for dinner to praise and honor the man who is known simply as the Rebbe. On the day itself—April 14 (11 Nisan)—10,000 followers filled Yad Eliyahu Stadium in Tel Aviv; in Crown Heights, where the revered sage lives surrounded by 15,000 followers, emotional pandemonium swept through the community as children took the streets and sang—'We want Moshiach now!'"

31. Jerry Rabow, *50 Jewish Messiahs: The Untold Life Stories of 50 Jewish Messiahs Since Jesus and How They Changed the Jewish, Christian, and Muslim Worlds* (Jerusalem: Gefen, 2002), 123, 127.

32. Sepehr, *1666*, 19–20.

33. Sepehr, *1666*, 20.

34. Sepehr, *1666*, 20.

35. Sepehr, *1666*, 21.

36. Sepehr, *1666*, 21.

37. As quoted in Gershom Scholem, *The Messianic Idea in Judaism and Other Essays on Jewish Spirituality* (New York: Schocken Books, 1971), 130.

38. As quoted in Scholem, *The Messianic Idea in Judaism and Other Essays on Jewish Spirituality*, 130.

39. As quoted in Scholem, *The Messianic Idea in Judaism and Other Essays on Jewish Spirituality*, 130.

40. "An Interview With Larry G. Corey," Empty Sink Publishing, December 7, 2014, http://emptysinkpublishing.com/archives/issue-10/interview-larry-g-corey/.

41. "Yakov Leib haKohain," Kheper.net, accessed November 6, 2019, http://www.kheper.net/topics/Kabbalah/Yakov.htm.

42. "Yakov Leib haKohain."

CHAPTER 5: THE REBBE DIDN'T RISE

1. Kendra Cherry, "What Is Cognitive Dissonance?," July 8, 2019, https://www.verywellmind.com/what-is-cognitive-dissonance-2795012.

2. Kris Komarnitsky, "Cognitive Dissonance and the Resurrection of Jesus," *The Fourth R*, September/October 2014, https://www.westarinstitute.org/resources/the-fourth-r/cognitive-dissonance-resurrection-jesus/.

3. Komarnitsky, "Cognitive Dissonance and the Resurrection of Jesus."

4. Komarnitsky, "Cognitive Dissonance and the Resurrection of Jesus."

5. According to Komarnitsky, "Of course, the Lubavitchers' rationalization is not quite the same as that of Jesus' followers, who claimed that Jesus had already been resurrected from the dead, but there is a good reason for this difference. In Lubavitcher theology, a 'prince,' in this case Rebbe Schneerson (who did not designate a successor), must be present in this world in some physical capacity in order to mediate the world's divine force or the world would cease to exist. Since the world still existed, Rebbe Schneerson had to still be physically present in the grave; he could not have been resurrected from the dead and transported up to heaven as Jesus' followers believed about him"; Komarnitsky, "Cognitive Dissonance and the Resurrection of Jesus." In my view, that is too sophisticated an answer, since many of the Rebbe's followers *were* expecting his literal resurrection from the dead. In fact, as the resurrected Messiah, he would then have stepped into his full Messianic role, leading the world into the Messianic era. In my view, Komarnitsky's explanation is based on later Lubavitcher speculation and rationalization in light of the Rebbe's failure to resurrect.

6. Simon Dein, "What Really Happens When Prophecy Fails: The Case of Lubavitch," *Sociology of Religion* 62, no. 3 (2001): 399.

7. Branover, *The Ultimate Jew.*

8. *Wonders and Miracles*, 7.

9. *Wonders and Miracles*, 11.

10. Berger, *The Rebbe, the Messiah, and the Scandal of Orthodox Indifference*, 11.

11. Dein, *Lubavitcher Messianism*, 78.

12. Dein, *Lubavitcher Messianism*, 78–79.

13. Berger, *The Rebbe, the Messiah, and the Scandal of Orthodox Indifference*, 86. He also wrote, "Because all of this seems so strange to outsiders, many observers cannot bring themselves to see the truth: the dominant elements among hasidim in the major Lubavitch population centres of Crown Heights in Brooklyn and Kfar Chabad in Israel— perfectly normal people representing a highly successful, very important Jewish movement—believe that Rabbi Menachem Mendel Schneerson will return from the dead (or from his place of concealment) and lead the world to redemption"; Berger, *The Rebbe, the Messiah, and the Scandal of Orthodox Indifference*, 26.

14. Shaul Magid, "The Divine/Human Messiah and Religious Deviance: Rethinking Chabad Messianism," *Rethinking the Messianic Idea in Judaism*, Michael L. Morgan and Steven Weitzman, eds., (Bloomington, IN: Indiana University Press, 2015), 324.

15. Christopher Rowland, *Christian Origins: An Account of the Setting and Character of the Most Important Messianic Sect of Judaism*, 2nd ed. (London: Society for Promoting Christian Knowledge, 2002), 186.

16. Jim Yardley, "Messiah Fervor for Late Rabbi Divides Many Lubavitchers," *New York Times*, June 29, 1998, https://www.nytimes .com/1998/06/29/nyregion/messiah-fervor-for-late-rabbi-divides-many-lubavitchers.html.

17. Jonathan Mark, "Messiah Fervor for Rebbe Denounced," *New York Jewish Week*, March 6, 1997, https://jewishweek.timesofisrael.com /messiah-fervor-for-rebbe-denounced/.

18. Mark, "Messiah Fervor for Rebbe Denounced."

19. Yardley, "Messiah Fervor for Late Rabbi Divides Many Lubavitchers."

20. Perlman, "What the Press Wrote About Schneerson," 10.

21. Dein, *Lubavitcher Messianism*, 139.

22. Michael R. Licona, *The Resurrection of Jesus: A New Historiographical Approach* (Downers Grove, IL: InterVarsity Press, 2010), 484.

23. Gary Sibcy, as quoted in Licona, *The Resurrection of Jesus*, 484.

24. Licona, *The Resurrection of Jesus*, 485–486.

25. Note 271 in Craig S. Keener, *Miracles: The Credibility of the New Testament Accounts* (Grand Rapids, MI: Baker Academic, 2011), 540.

26. Published in *Tyndale Bulletin* 60, no. 1 (2009): 69–105.

27. Note 272 in Keener, *Miracles*, 541.

28. N. T. Wright, *The Resurrection of the Son of God*, Christian Origins and the Son of God Series, vol. 3 (Minneapolis: Fortress Press, 2003), 690.

29. Pinchas Lapide, *The Resurrection of Jesus: A Jewish Perspective* (Eugene, OR: Wipf & Stock, 2002), 125.

30. Rabbi J. Immanuel Schochet, "The Professor, Messiah, and Scandal of Calumnies," Shmais News Service, accessed November 6, 2019, https://web.archive.org/web/20091101025345/http:/shmais.com/chabad_Detail.cfm?ID=279.

31. Michael Freund, "The Emergence of Turkey's Hidden Jews," *Jerusalem Post*, March 23, 2011, https://www.jpost.com/Opinion/Columnists/The-emergence-of-Turkeys-hidden-Jews.

CHAPTER 6: THE RABBI WHO REALLY ROSE

1. Joel Marcus, "The Once and Future Messiah in Early Christianity and Chabad," *New Testament Studies* 47, no. 3 (July 2001): 381–401, citing the official abstract of the article.

2. I am not downplaying other quite major theological differences or, of course, major differences in praxis.

3. Matthew V. Novenson. *The Grammar of Messianism: An Ancient Political Idiom and Its Users* (Oxford, UK: Oxford University Press, 2017), 191.

4. See, for example, J. Warner Wallace, "Good Reasons to Believe Peter Is the Source of Mark's Gospel," Cold-Case Christianity, August 24, 2018, https://coldcasechristianity.com/writings/good-reasons-to-believe-peter-is-the-source-of-marks-gospel.

5. See Michael Brown, "Recovering the Lost Letter of Jacob," Ask Dr. Brown, March 11, 2013, https://askdrbrown.org/library/recovering-lost-letter-jacob.

6. For the term "Son of Man" in the New Testament, see Don Stewart, "Why Did Jesus Call Himself the Son of Man?," accessed November 6, 2019, https://www.blueletterbible.org/faq/don_stewart/don_stewart_793.cfm; for academic insights, see Ben Witherington III. *The Jesus Quest: The Third Search for the Jew of Nazareth* (Downers Grove, IL: Inter-Varsity Press, 1995).

7. See Licona, *The Resurrection of Jesus*, section 4.2.3, especially 4.2.3.2.

8. The twelfth disciple, Judas Iscariot, was the one who betrayed Jesus and then went out and killed himself, riddled with guilt.

9. Note also the discussion in Licona, *The Resurrection of Jesus*, section 4.3.2.6, of Matthew 28:17–18, where it states that some of the disciples still doubted even after seeing the resurrected Jesus.

10. See further Sean McDowell, *The Fate of the Apostles: Examining the Martyrdom Accounts of the Closest Followers of Jesus* (New York: Routledge, 2015).

11. Wright, *The Resurrection of the Son of God*, 699–700.

12. Israel Knohl, *The Messiah Before Jesus: The Suffering Servant of the Dead Sea Scrolls* (Berkeley, CA: University of California Press, 2000), 2–3, as quoted in Novenson, *The Grammar of Messianism*, 170.

13. Paula Fredriksen, *When Christians Were Jews: The First Generation* (New Haven, CT: Yale University Press, 2018), 74–75.

14. Randy Clark, *Eyewitness to Miracles: Watching the Gospel Come to Life* (Nashville: Thomas Nelson, 2018), 20.

15. Clark, *Eyewitness to Miracles*, 20–21.

16. Clark, *Eyewitness to Miracles*, 21.

17. For a nuanced, anthropological study by a professor of religious studies with a PhD from Harvard, see Candy Gunther Brown, *Global Pentecostal and Charismatic Healing* (New York: Oxford University Press, 2011).

18. See the references in Clark, *Eyewitness to Miracles*; see also Candy Gunther Brown, *Testing Prayer: Science and Healing* (Cambridge, MA: Harvard University Press, 2012).

19. Clarissa Romez, David Zaritzky, and Joshua W. Brown, "Case Report of Gastroparesis Healing: Sixteen Years of a Chronic Syndrome Resolved After Proximal Intercessory Prayer," *Complementary Therapies in Medicine* 43 (April 2019): 289–294, https://doi.org/10.1016/j.ctim.2019.03.004; see also Sean McDowell, "A Remarkable Case of a Peer-Reviewed Modern Miracle," SeanMcDowell.com, June 25, 2019, https://seanmcdowell.org/blog/a-remarkable-case-of-a-peer-reviewed-modern-miracle.

20. Clark, *Eyewitness to Miracles*, 7.

21. Clark, *Eyewitness to Miracles*, 8.

22. "Reinhard Bonnke Tells of Nigerian Man Raised From the Dead," CBN.com, accessed November 6, 2019, https://www1.cbn.com/features/reinhard-bonnke-tells-of-nigerian-man-raised-from-the-dead; for the full account in incredible detail, see Reinhard Bonnke, *Raised from the Dead: The Miracle That Brings Promise to America* (New Kensington, PA: Whitaker House, 2014).

23. "Florida Man Raised From the Dead by Praying Cardiologist," The Rising Light, November 27, 2010, http://therisinglight.com/2010/11/27/florida-man-raised-from-the-dead-by-praying-cardiologist/.

24. "Florida Man Raised From the Dead by Praying Cardiologist," The Rising Light.

25. "Florida Man Raised From the Dead by Praying Cardiologist," The Rising Light.

26. See Keener, *Miracles*, 220.

27. See, for example, Tom Doyle with Greg Webster, *Dreams and Visions: Is Jesus Awakening the Muslim World?* (Nashville: Thomas Nelson, 2012); for a collection of anecdotes online, see Darren Carlson, "When Muslims Dream of Jesus," The Gospel Coalition, May 31, 2018, https://www.thegospelcoalition.org/article/muslims-dream-jesus/.

28. Reza Safa, *The Coming Fall of Islam in Iran: Thousands of Muslims Find Christ in the Midst of Persecution* (Lake Mary, FL: FrontLine, 2006), 185.

CHAPTER 7: REDISCOVERING ISRAEL'S SUFFERING AND RISING MESSIAH

1. "Statement Regarding Chabad Messianism."

2. "RCA Bans 'Messianic Rabbis,'" COLlive.com, November 21, 2009, https://collive.com/rca-bans-messianic-rabbis/.

3. For background to the statement and further discussion, see Berger, *The Rebbe, the Messiah, and the Scandal of Orthodox Indifference.*

4. See, conveniently, Stuart Dauermann, "Daniel Boyarin Answers My Aunt, and Maybe Yours: Is Jesus a Goyishe Fraud?," Interfaithfulness, January 2, 2014, https://www.interfaithfulness.org/2014/01/02/daniel-boyarin-answers-my-aunt-and-maybe-yours-is-jesus-a-goyishe-fraud/, citing from Daniel Boyarin, *The Jewish Gospels: The Story of the Jewish Christ* (New York: The New Press, 2012).

5. Dauermann, "Daniel Boyarin Answers My Aunt, and Maybe Yours."

6. See Brown, *Answering Jewish Objections to Jesus, Volume 2*, section 3.15; see also Michael L. Brown, *The Real Kosher Jesus: Revealing the Mysteries of the Hidden Messiah* (Lake Mary, FL: FrontLine, 2012), 149–158.

7. See b. Shabbat 33b.

8. Abraham Cohen, *Everyman's Talmud: The Major Teachings of the Rabbinic Sages* (New York: Schocken Books, 1995), 118.

9. See b. Sanhedrin 43b.

10. Cited in S. R. Driver and Adolph Neubauer, eds. and trans., *The Fifty-Third Chapter of Isaiah According to the Jewish Interpreters*, 2 vols. (Oxford, UK: Hall and Stacy, 1877), 15. The Zohar states that this explains Ecclesiastes 7:15 (NIV): "In this meaningless life of mine I

have seen both of these: the righteous perishing in their righteousness, and the wicked living long in their wickedness." Cf. also b. Shabbat 33b, "The righteous are taken by the iniquity of the generation."

11. Daniel Travis, ed., *Living On: Messages, Memories, and Miracles from the Har Nof Massacre* (New York: Philipp Feldheim, 2014), 104.

12. One traditional website cites Shabbos 33b; Mo'ed Katan 25a; 28a; Yerushalmi Yoma 1:1 (2a); Shemos Rabbah 35:4; Vayikra Rabbah 27:7; and Pesikta 27 (174b); see "RaMChaL Zt"l on Suffering of a Tzaddik, Atonement, and Perfection," 13 Petals, December 3, 2015, https://www.13petals.org/ramchal-ztl-on-suffering-of-a-tzaddik-atonement-and-perfection/. Also cited are Nega'im 2:1; Bertinoro ad loc. s.v. Beis; Bava Metzia 84b; Yerushalmis Berachos 2:8 (20a), Bereshis Rabbah 33:1; 44:6; Vayikra Rabbah 2:5; Shir ha-Shirim Rabbah 6:6; Koheles Rabbah 5:14; Pesikta 30 (191a); Zohar 165a; 167b; 1:180a; 2:10b; 2:36b; 2:53a; 2:195a; 2:212a; 2:269a; 2:257a; 3:17b; 3:38a; 3:46b; 3:118a; and Sefer Chasidim § 528. Additionally cross-referenced are Shabbos 139b; Sanhedrin 39a; Zohar 3:20b; 3:115a; Ramban on Shemos 32:32; and Ikkarim 4:13.

13. Moshe Chaim Luzzatto, *Derech Hashem [The Way of God]*, trans. Aryeh Kaplan (Nanuet, NY: Feldheim Publishers, 1997), 121–123.

14. This is the rendering of Jacob Neusner in his American translation; the words in the brackets reflect the universal understanding of the passage. See Jacob Neusner, *The Babylonian Talmud: A Translation and Commentary* (Peabody, MA: Hendrickson Publishers, 2011). Rashi explains Shimon bar Yochai's statement as follows: "Through my merit, I bear all your iniquities and cancel them from the judgment." Note also the comments of R. Hananel, another of the major Talmudic commentators. See also b. Eruvin 64b–65a.

15. Sukkah 45b, The William Davidson Talmud, Sefaria, accessed November 6, 2019, https://www.sefaria.org/Sukkah.45b.4?lang=bi.

16. Daf Shevui, commentary on Sukkah 45b:5, Sefaria, accessed November 6, 2019, https://www.sefaria.org/Sukkah.45b.4?lang=bi&with=Daf%20Shevui&lang2=en.

17. Luzzatto, *Derekh Hashem*, 125.

18. See Bartenura, Mishnah Negaim 2:1, Sefaria, accessed November 6, 2019, https://www.sefaria.org/Mishnah_Negaim.2.1?lang=en&with=Bartenura&lang2=en. This is restated in the commentary of Kehati.

Pinchas Kehati, *Mishnayot Kehati* (Eng. Translation, Edward I. Levin, Brooklyn, NY: Philip Feldheim, 2005).

19. English explanation of Mishnah Negaim 2:1:3, Mishnah Negaim 2:1, Sefaria, accessed November 6, 2019, https://www.sefaria.org/Mishnah_Negaim.2.1?lang=en&with=English%20Explanation%20of%20Mishnah&lang2=en, accessed November 6, 2019.

20. Shalom M. Paul, *Isaiah 40–66: Translation and Commentary* (Grand Rapids, MI; William B. Eerdmans, 2012), 404, 406, to 53:4 and 53:6. Note that the author does not understand Isaiah 53 to be referring to the Messiah, but I quote him in terms of explaining the straightforward meaning of the text.

21. *And He Will Redeem Us*, 147, referring to the sixth Rebbe; see also Lubavitcher Rebbe, "Basi Legani–5711: Chapter 9," trans. Eli Touger, Chabad.org, accessed November 6, 2019, https://www.chabad.org/therebbe/article_cdo/aid/115150/jewish/Basi-Legani-5711-Chapter-9.htm.

22. Wolfson, *Open Secret*, 5; see further the discussion in chapter 2.

23. Carol Calise, "The Habad Movement and Its Messiah," in Kjær-Hansen, *The Death of Messiah*, 73.

24. Schochet, "The Professor, Messiah, and Scandal of Calumnies."

25. Patai, *The Messiah Texts*, 2.

26. For responses to the arguments that Isaiah 53 does not describe vicarious suffering and does not speak of the servant's resurrection because it does not actually describe his death, see John D. Barry, *The Resurrected Servant in Isaiah* (Bellingham, WA: Lexham Press, 2010).

27. Midrash Tanchuma Buber, Toldot 20:1, commentary on Isaiah 52:13, Sefaria, accessed November 5, 2019, https://www.sefaria.org/Isaiah.52.13?lang=bi&with=Midrash%20Tanchuma%20Buber&lang2=en.

28. See b. Sukkah 52a, Sefaria, accessed November 5, 2019, https://www.sefaria.org/Sukkah.52a?lang=en.

29. Patai, *The Messiah Texts*, 166.

30. As cited in David Baron, *The Visions and Prophecies of Zechariah, "The Prophet of Hope and Glory": An Exposition* (London: Morgan and Scott, 1918), 442, emphasis added.

31. *Machzor Korban Ha'aron* (Warsaw: n.p., 1867), 61, as translated by Yitzchaq Shapira.

CHAPTER 8: THE MYSTERY OF THE DIVINE ANGEL AND THE MESSIAH

1. Dan Cohn-Sherbok, *The Jewish Messiah* (Edinburgh: T&T Clark, 1997), xvi.

2. David Berger, "Rabbi Boteach, You're Wrong About Chabad," *Jerusalem Post*, January 23, 2008, https://www.jpost.com/Opinion/Op-Ed-Contributors/Rabbi-Boteach-youre-wrong-about-Chabad.

3. Berger, "Rabbi Boteach, You're Wrong About Chabad."

4. Berger, "Rabbi Boteach, You're Wrong About Chabad."

5. Berger, "Rabbi Boteach, You're Wrong About Chabad."

6. Wolfson, *Open Secret*, 6.

7. Wolfson, *Open Secret*, 7.

8. "Rabbi Yitz Greenberg Debates Chabad Messianist Rabbi on Talkline," FailedMessiah.com, January 13, 2008, https://failedmessiah.typepad.com/failed_messiahcom/2008/01/rabbi-yitz-gree.html.

9. "Rabbi Yitz Greenberg Debates Chabad Messianist Rabbi on Talkline," FailedMessiah.com.

10. Adam Kirsch, *The People and the Books: Eighteen Classics of Jewish Literature* (New York: W. W. Norton & Company, 2016), 204.

11. Kirsch, *The People and the Books*, 204–205.

12. "Kabbalah's Best Kept Secret?," Jews for Jesus, accessed November 6, 2019, https://jewsforjesus.org/publications/issues/issues-v18-n02/kabbalahs-best-kept-secret/.

13. Kirsch, *The People and the Books*, 207.

14. "The Ten Sefirot: Shekhinah, Malkhut," Jewish Virtual Library, accessed November 6, 2019, https://www.jewishvirtuallibrary.org/ten-sefirot-shekhinah-malkhut.

15. Kirsch, *The People and the Books*, 210–211.

16. According to the website editor at Sefaria.org, where this commentary is posted, this refers to "a divine voice much closer to G'd's Essence than 'mere' angels."

17. Rabbeinu Bahya, commentary on Genesis 22:13, Sefaria, accessed November 6, 2019, https://www.sefaria.org/Genesis.22.13?lang=bi&with=Rabbeinu%20Bahya&lang2=en.

18. Rabbeinu Bahya, commentary on Genesis 22:13.

19. Rabbeinu Bahya, commentary on Genesis 22:13.

20. See b. Pesachim 118a.

21. Sforno, commentary on Genesis 48:16, Sefaria, accessed November 6, 2019, https://www.sefaria.org/Genesis.48.16?lang=bi&aliyot=0&p2=Sf orno_on_Genesis.48.16&lang2=bi. To quote him literally, he wrote that Jacob was asking God to "to bless the lads" through his guardian angel "if they do not deserve to be blessed directly by You, without an intermediary"; see Raphael Pelcovitz, *Sforno: Commentary on the Torah* (New York: Mesorah Publications, 1997), 260.

22. Chizkuni, commentary on Genesis 48:18, Sefaria, accessed November 6, 2019, https://www.sefaria.org/Genesis.48.16?lang=bi&aliyot=0&p2=Chi zkuni%2C_Genesis.48.16.1&lang2=bi.

23. Derek Kidner, *Genesis: An Introduction and Commentary* (Downers Grove, IL: InterVarsity Press, 1967), 225.

24. Ernst Jenni and Claus Westermann, eds., *Theological Lexicon of the Old Testament* (Peabody, MA: Hendrickson Publishers, 1997), 669.

25. According to Jenni and Westermann, "The expression *mal'āk yhwh* (always sg.) occurs 58x: Gen 16:7, 9–11; 22:11, 15; Exod 3:2; Num 22:22–35, 10x; Judg 2:1, 4; 5:23; 13:3–21, 10x; 2 Sam 24:16; 1 Kgs 19:7; 2 Kgs 1:3, 15; 19:35 = Isa 37:36; Hag 1:13; Zech 1:11f.; 3:1, 5f.; 12:8; Mal 2:7; Psa 34:8; 35:5f.; 1 Chron 21:12, 15f., 18, 30. The combination *mal'ak (ha)'elōhîm* is attested 11x: Gen 21:17; 31:11; 32:2; Exod 14:19; Judg 6:20; 13:6, 9; 1 Sam 29:9; 2 Sam 14:17, 20; 19:28; also in pl. Gen 28:12; 32:2"; *Theological Lexicon of the Old Testament*, 667.

26. Note that the JPS Tanakh renders *'elohim* in Judges 13:22 as "divine being" rather than God, which is possible. The Targum, the ancient synagogue translation into Aramaic, renders with "angel of the LORD," which is more interpretive.

27. Notice how many times *'elohim* (God) occurs in Exodus 3:1–6: "mountain of God" in 3:1; "God called" in 3:4; then five times in verse 6: God of your father, God of Abraham, God of Isaac, God of Jacob, and "he was afraid to look at God." It could not be clearer!

28. Elliot R. Wolfson, *Through a Speculum That Shines: Vision and Imagination in Medieval Jewish Mysticism* (Princeton, NJ: Princeton University Press, 1994), 256, emphasis added.

29. A. Bowling, in R. L. Harris, G. L. Archer Jr., and B. K. Waltke, eds., *Theological Wordbook of the Old Testament* (Chicago: Moody Press, 1999), 465.

30. Jenni and Westermann, *Theological Lexicon of the Old Testament*, 671.

31. Nahum M. Sarna, *Genesis*, The JPS Torah Commentary (Philadelphia: Jewish Publication Society, 1989), 328. He added, "Nevertheless, this verse may reflect some tradition associated with Bethel, not preserved in Genesis, concerning an angelic guardian of Jacob (cf. 31:13; 35:3). An echo of this may be found in Hosea 12:5."

32. Y. Moshe Immanueli, *The Book of Genesis: Explanations and Notes* (Hebrew; Tel Aviv, Israel: The Society for the Study of Scripture, 1978), 602.

33. C. F. Keil, and F. Delitzsch, *Commentary on the Old Testament*, vol. 1, trans. James Martin (Edinburgh: T & T Clark, 1866), 383–384. See also the rabbinic commentary Haamek Davar.

34. Franz Delitzsch, *Biblical Commentary on the Prophecies of Isaiah*, vol. 2, trans. James Martin (Edinburgh: T & T Clark, 1868), 454–455.

35. Jacob Neusner and William Scott Green, eds., *Dictionary of Judaism in the Biblical Period: 450 BCE to 600 CE* (New York: MacMillan Library Reference, 1996), 427–428.

36. "Kabbalah's Best Kept Secret?"

37. "Kabbalah's Best Kept Secret?"

38. "Kabbalah's Best Kept Secret?," citing Yehudah Liebes, "Who Makes the Horn of Jesus to Flourish," *Immanuel* 21 (Summer 1987): footnote 28, p. 67; see more fully (in Hebrew), Yehuda Liebes, "The Angels of the Shofar and Yeshua Sar Ha-Panim / קול השופר וישוע שר הפנים מלאכי." *Jerusalem Studies in Jewish Thought / במחשבת ישראל ו* מחקרי ירושלים, no. א/ב (1987), 171–195 (available at http://www.jstor.org/stable/23363659). And see Daniel Abrams, "The Boundaries of Divine Ontology: The Inclusion and Exclusion of Metatron in the Godhead," *Harvard Theological Review* 87, no. 3 (1994): 317. For further background to the provenance of these traditions, see Moshe Idel, "Some Forlorn Writings of a Forgotten Ashkenazi Prophet: R. Nehemiah Ben Shlomo Ha-Navi'," *The Jewish Quarterly Review* 95, no. 1 (2005): 183–196.

39. On this point, see the debate between Messianic rabbi Itzhak Shapira, *The Return of the Kosher Pig* (Clarksville, MD: Lederer Messianic Publications, 2013); and counter-missionary rabbi Yisroel C. Blumenthal, "Innocent Trust," 1000 Verses—A Project of Judaism Resources, February 17, 2014, https://judaismresources.net/2014/02/17/innocent-trust/ (with links to videos by Shapira). Shapira sees this text as pointing to Yeshua as divine, a point which Blumenthal strongly

rejects. Rabbi Blumenthal also rejects the idea that Yeshua here is related to Jesus. See also Yehuda Liebes, "Untying the Jewish-Christian Knot," Haaretz.com, November 16, 2001, https://www.haaretz.com/life/books/1.5453419.

CHAPTER 9: WAS THE RESURRECTION A TEST?

1. In Christian translations, these are verses 1–5.
2. Rabbi Yisroel C. Blumenthal, "Resurrection," Jews for Judaism, accessed November 4, 2019, https://jewsforjudaism.org/knowledge/articles/resurrection/.
3. For more on this, see Brown, *Answering Jewish Objections to Jesus, Volume 2*, sections 3.1–4; see also Brown, *The Real Kosher Jesus*.
4. Kirsch, *The People and the Books*, 203.
5. This a paraphrase of their comments. See "If the Lubavitch Rebbe Can Be the Messiah, Why Can't Jesus?"
6. Wikipedia, s.v. "Talk: Chabad Lubavitch/Sources 1," last modified December 4, 2005, https://en.wikipedia.org/wiki/Talk%3AChabad_Lubavitch/Sources_1.
7. "Iggerot HaRambam, Iggeret Teiman," Sefaria, accessed November 6, 2019, https://www.sefaria.org/Iggerot_HaRambam%2C_Iggeret_Teiman?lang=en.
8. "A Preface to Moshiach."
9. For an interesting perspective, see John Kampen, *Matthew Within Sectarian Judaism* (New Haven, CT: Yale University Press, 2019).
10. Foreword to H. Chaim Schimmel, *The Oral Law: A Study of the Rabbinic Contribution to Torah She-be-al-Peh, 2nd rev. ed.* (Jerusalem: Feldheim, 1996).
11. Schimmel, *Oral Law*, 19, emphasis added.
12. My appreciation to Jonathan Mann, a young Messianic Jewish leader, for sharing this argument with me; for his detailed line of reasoning, see his forthcoming article, "The Resurrection of Jesus: Another Jewish Perspective." Part of the inspiration for this book came from a conversation I had in my radio studio on August 7, 2018, with Jonathan and his colleague Erik Mattson, another young Messianic Jewish leader. Both Jonathan and Erik are on the front lines of Messianic Jewish apologetics.
13. Brown, *Answering Jewish Objections to Jesus, Volume 1*, 156.

14. See Gil Student, "Jesus in the Talmud: Introduction," The Real Truth About the Talmud, accessed November 6, 2019, http://talmud.faithweb .com/; more fully, and with different conclusions, see Peter Schäfer, *Jesus in the Talmud* (Princeton, NJ: Princeton University Press, 2007).

15. Brown, *Answering Jewish Objections to Jesus, Volume 1*, 156, citing Touger, *Maimonides Mishneh Torah*, 235–236.

16. "Iggerot HaRambam, Iggeret Teiman," paragraph 111.

17. Yehezkel Kaufmann, *Christianity and Judaism: Two Covenants*, trans. C. W. Efroymson (Jerusalem: The Magnes Press, 1996), 133.

18. Ellis Rivkin, "The Meaning of the Messiah in Jewish Thought," in *Evangelicals and Jews in Conversation, on Scripture, Theology, and History*, ed. M. H. Tanenbaum, M. R. Wilson, and J. A. Rudin (Grand Rapids, MI: Baker, 1978), 62, as quoted in David Mishkin, *Jewish Scholarship on the Resurrection of Jesus* (Eugene, OR: Pickwick Publications, 2017), 188. My appreciation to Jonathan Mann for the quotes from Kaufmann and Rivkin.

19. Blumenthal, "Resurrection."

20. See b. Yoma 9b.

CHAPTER 10: WHY NOT JUDAISM FOR JEWS AND CHRISTIANITY FOR GENTILES?

1. See, for example, Isaiah 42:1–8; 49:1–8.

2. See John 4:24–25; 14:6; Luke 19:41–44.

3. "Orthodox Rabbinic Statement on Christianity," The Center for Jewish-Christian Understanding and Cooperation, December 3, 2015, http:// cjcuc.org/2015/12/03/orthodox-rabbinic-statement-on-christianity/. See further Lauren Markoe, "Rabbis Term Church a Divine 'Partner,'" *Christian Century*, December 9, 2015, https://www.christiancentury.org/ article/2015-12/orthodox-rabbis-say-christianity-willed-god.

4. "Orthodox Rabbinic Statement on Christianity."

5. "Orthodox Rabbinic Statement on Christianity."

6. See further Michael L. Brown, *Our Hands Are Stained With Blood: The Tragic Story of the Church and the Jewish People*, rev. and exp. ed. (Shippensburg, PA: Destiny Image, 2019).

7. "Orthodox Rabbinic Statement on Christianity."

8. Moshe Ben-Chaim, "No Religious Coexistence," as quoted by Mesora .org, accessed November 6, 2019, https://www.mesora.org/coexist5776. html.

9. Ben-Chaim, "No Religious Coexistence."

10. Joseph Klausner, *From Jesus to Paul*, trans. William F. Stinespring (London: George Allen & Unwin, n.d.), 609, as quoted in Shirley Lucass, *The Concept of the Messiah in the Scriptures of Judaism and Christianity* (London: Bloomsbury T & T Clark, 2013), 36, emphasis in original.

11. Jacob Neusner, *Jews and Christians: The Myth of a Common Tradition* (London: SPCK, 1991), 1, as quoted in Lucass, *The Concept of the Messiah in the Scriptures of Judaism and Christianity*, 36.

12. Neusner, *Jews and Christians*, 1, as quoted in Lucass, *The Concept of the Messiah in the Scriptures of Judaism and Christianity*, 36.

13. Neusner, *Jews and Christians*, 120, as quoted in Lucass, *The Concept of the Messiah in the Scriptures of Judaism and Christianity*, 36.

14. Jacob Emden, as quoted in "Orthodox Rabbinic Statement on Christianity." For further discussion of Rabbi Emden's words, along with related quotes from other traditional Jewish leaders, see Michael L. Brown, *The Real Kosher Jesus*, 17.

15. Hilkhot Melakhim.

16. "Orthodox Rabbinic Statement on Christianity."

17. Hilkhot Melakhim.

18. See Brown, *The Real Kosher Jesus*, 1–11.

19. Ben-Chaim, "No Religious Coexistence."

20. Ben-Chaim, "No Religious Coexistence," emphasis in the original.

21. Neusner, *Jews and Christians*, 49, as quoted in Lucass, *The Concept of the Messiah in the Scriptures of Judaism and Christianity*, 4.

CHAPTER 11: THE EVENT THAT CHANGED THE WORLD

1. Leon Festinger, Henry W. Riecken, and Stanley Schachter, *When Prophecy Fails* (Minneapolis: University of Minnesota Press, 1956), 3, cited in Jon R. Stone, ed., *Expecting Armageddon: Essential Readings in Failed Prophecy* (New York: Routledge, 2000), 1.

2. William Shaffir, "When Prophecy Is Not Validated," in Stone, *Expecting Armageddon*, 253.

3. Shaffir, "When Prophecy Is Not Validated," 254.

4. Shaffir, "When Prophecy Is Not Validated," 254.

5. Shaffir, "When Prophecy Is Not Validated," 257.

6. David Klinghoffer, *Why the Jews Rejected Jesus: The Turning Point in Western History* (New York: Doubleday, 2005), 220.

7. Arturo Ortiz, "Seven Ways Christianity Changed the World," Walking in the Desert, June 26, 2015, http://walkinginthedesert .com/2015/06/26/7-ways-christianity-changed-the-world/.

8. John Ortberg, "Six Surprising Ways Jesus Changed the World," Huff-Post, August 13, 2012, https://www.huffpost.com/entry/six-surprising-ways-jesus_b_1773225.

9. Bill Muehlenberg, "A Review of *How Christianity Changed the World.* By Alvin Schmidt," CultureWatch (blog), September 7, 2005, https:// billmuehlenberg.com/2005/09/07/a-review-of-how-christianity-changed-the-world-by-alvin-schmidt/. See also Ralph Smith, "What Jeffrey Epstein Got Right," Theopolis, August 14, 2019, https://theopolis institute.com/leithart_post/what-jeffrey-epstein-got-right/.

10. D. James Kennedy and Jerry Newcombe, *What If Jesus Had Never Been Born? The Positive Impact of Christianity in History* (Nashville: Thomas Nelson, 1994), 196–197.

11. Kennedy and Newcombe, *What If Jesus Had Never Been Born?*, 197.

12. Muehlenberg, "A Review of *How Christianity Changed the World.* By Alvin Schmidt."

13. Muehlenberg, "A Review of *How Christianity Changed the World.* By Alvin Schmidt."

14. Muehlenberg, "A Review of *How Christianity Changed the World.* By Alvin Schmidt."

15. For more information, see http://lncministries.org.